"This is an inspiring book, filled with excellent examples, valuable advice, and warnings not to be overlooked. Every executive would be well-served to read this book cover-to-cover."

— *Robert Porter Lynch, chairman emeritus, Association of Strategic Alliance Professionals*

"Paul Lawrence tracks leadership qualities into the deepest recesses of the human brain. Listen up, business! Tapping into this scientific understanding of leadership is key to your company's success or failure."

— *William C. Frederick, professor emeritus, Katz Graduate School of Business, University of Pittsburgh*

"Paul Lawrence proposes that nature has provided us with individuals of conscience who are capable of good leadership, but also with a small number of individuals whose lack of conscience typically makes them bad leaders. He refers to such individuals as free riders, psychopaths, or 'people without conscience,' and discusses in detail the devastating impact they have when placed in a leadership role, particularly in business, politics, the military, and religion. His thesis is brilliant and compelling, and in line with current research on the neuroscience of psychopathy. *Driven to Lead* is essential reading for anyone who hopes to gain some understanding of the scandals and disasters that result from bad leadership."

— *Robert D. Hare, professor emeritus of psychology, University of British Columbia*

Praise for *Driven: How Human Nature Shapes Our Choices*

"In this pathbreaking book, Paul R. Lawrence and Nitin Nohria show [that] ... the deep study of human nature does not justify Social Darwinism and gladiatorial commercial combat of the kind often portrayed in popular media. On the contrary, it offers formulas for a more harmonious and efficient conduct of human affairs. The approach ... is naturalistic, based on self-understanding and the cultivation of the strong cooperative instincts that have favored group survival for countless millennia."

— *Excerpt from the Foreword by Edward O. Wilson*

DRIVEN TO LEAD

Good, Bad, and Misguided Leadership

Paul R. Lawrence

Foreword by Warren Bennis

JOSSEY-BASS
A Wiley Imprint
www.josseybass.com

Published by Jossey-Bass
A Wiley Imprint
989 Market Street, San Francisco, CA 94103-1741—www.josseybass.com

Library of Congress Cataloging-in-Publication Data

Lawrence, Paul R.
  Driven to lead: good, bad, and misguided leadership / Paul R. Lawrence; foreword by Warren
Bennis. —1st ed.
    p. cm. — (Warren Bennis series)
  Includes bibliographical references and index.
  ISBN 978-0-470-62384-8 (hardback)
  1. Leadership. 2. Executive ability. I. Title.
  HD57.7.L379 2010
  658.4'092—dc22

                                                          2010016270

Printed in the United States of America
FIRST EDITION
HB Printing 10 9 8 7 6 5 4 3 2 1

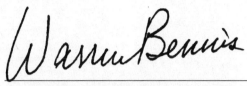

A WARREN BENNIS BOOK

This collection of books is devoted exclusively to new and exemplary contributions to management thought and practice. The books in this series are addressed to thoughtful leaders, executives, and managers of all organizations who are struggling with and committed to responsible change. My hope and goal is to spark new intellectual capital by sharing ideas positioned at an angle to conventional thought—in short, to publish books that disturb the present in the service of a better future.

Books in the Warren Bennis Signature Series

Contents

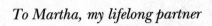

To Martha, my lifelong partner

FOREWORD
by Warren Bennis

This book is truly amazing—actually, a masterpiece. It tells the story of the human condition. It tells this story across human history, *deep* human history. Lawrence realizes that our under-standing of leadership can be no better than our understanding of what makes humans, all humans, tick—what are the ultimate motivators of our behavior. This is true because leadership is *all* about relationships with others. So that is where he starts—with the basic few motives, the innate drives that have been essential to our survival and development into the dominant species on earth.

To do this, Lawrence had to rediscover Darwin's insights about humans in Darwin's second epic book, *The Descent of Man*, which evolutionary biologists have, strangely, ignored. This reveals a new Darwin that turns the public's assumptions about Darwin upside down. The key is Darwin's revolutionary observation that the *most important* difference between humans and lower species is our innate moral sense, our conscience. What an observation—and now we have evidence that it is a valid observation—except for the very few people who are missing the key mutation in their brain.

But this is enough of the story for me to tell here. Read on and you will find explanations of key turning points in human history, explanations of good, bad, and misguided leaders, and even evil leaders like Hitler, Stalin, and Mao. Lawrence provides an explanation of the greatness of America's governmental form as well as the nature of its current crisis, and the same is true of the greatness and the current crisis of our vast corporations.

And, finally, *Driven to Lead* offers a path toward a better future for all.

ACKNOWLEDGMENTS

Over the years that I have worked on this research project I have benefited greatly from the many scholars and friends who have studied various drafts of this work and helped me develop its strengths and avoid its pitfalls. The following people have read and provided insightful comments on one or more drafts of the work: Louise Ames, Oakes Ames, Max Bazerman, Michael Beer, Robin Ely, William Frederick, Benjamin Freidman, William George, Joshua Greene, Boris Groysberg, Ranjay Gulati, Marc Hauser, Linda Hill, Rakesh Khurana, John Kotter, Anne Lawrence, William Lawrence, Hans Loeser, Jay Lorsch, Robert Porter Lynch, Joshua Margolis, Kenneth Miller, Lynn Paine, Steven Pinker, Joseph Platt, Jo Procter, Robert Simon, Scott Snook, Renato Taguiri, David Thomas, Andrew Towl, Michael Tushman, Andrew Van de Ven, Charalambos Vlachoutsicos, and Richard Wrangham.

In addition, I wish especially to recognize the help of the following:

- Nitin Nohria, my coauthor of *Driven*, who throughout the work on this follow-on book has been a steady and wise advisor to me every step of the way.
- Warren Bennis, the general editor of the Jossey-Bass series on leadership, for his unwavering support of the merit of this work.
- Kathe Sweeney, our senior editor, and Rob Brandt, our associate editor at Jossey-Bass, for their wise guidance and hard work throughout the publication process.
- Fred Dalzell, who provided valuable historical consultation, especially on the U.S. Constitution.
- Janice Simmons, who provided secretarial assistance and good humor with printing and copying numerous drafts of the book.

- John Elder, for all his splendid editing and his insightful comments on the several rewrites.
- Ed Wilson and Ernst Mayr, the deans of evolutionary biology who have generously guided my biological education.
- Martha, my wife, for her constant support and her amazing patience with my many years of preoccupation with this project.

Especially because this book is pushing on the edges of knowledge in a diverse set of fields, it is by no means perfunctory for me to add that I take full responsibility for any errors and other shortcomings of the text.

Bedford, Massachusetts   PAUL R. LAWRENCE
May 2010

THE AUTHOR

Paul R. Lawrence is Wallace Brett Donham Professor of Organizational Behavior at Harvard Business School. He grew up in Michigan, where he did his undergraduate work in sociology and economics at Albion College. After serving in the Navy in World War II he finished his masters and doctoral training in organizational behavior at the Harvard Business School. He was the cofounder of the Society for the Advancement of Socio-Economics. His research, published in twenty-five books and numerous articles, has dealt with the human aspects of management, organizational change, organization design, human nature, and leadership. His best-known titles (with coauthors) are *Organization and Environment, The Changing of Organizational Behavior Patterns, Renewing American Industry,* and *Driven: How Human Nature Shapes Our Choices.*

INTRODUCTION

Humans have studied human behavior and leadership behavior for as long as we've had written records. In the past four centuries or so, the methods of systematic science have been applied to this study, at both the individual and collective levels. But it has been a somewhat messy pursuit.

As this book will show, the truly scientific understanding of human behavior began with the work of Darwin, published some 150 years ago. Since that time, however, the study of human behavior has become a story of fragmentation. Each of the disciplines shown in Figure I.1 was launched and carried forward primarily by the intellectual leadership of the persons named beneath each discipline. The prominent newer fields are also named. Figure I.1 illustrates not only the fragmentation of the effort to understand human behavior scientifically but also the nature of the task of integrating these various fields in order to develop a unified theory of human behavior and leadership. The repetition of the question "only?" at the bottom of the figure indicates the limitations, as I see it, of each discipline's approach to human behavior.

Specialization, as illustrated, is an essential phase in the advancement of knowledge, but it needs to be balanced with continual efforts to integrate and unify our ever-growing understanding. This integration process has been badly neglected in the human sciences, largely, I believe, for institutional and organizational reasons. University departments compete for funding, personnel, and attention. A scholar who hopes to advance within a discipline is expected to make noteworthy specialized contributions for his or her "team." Who can afford to collaborate with the competitive teams? Perhaps a senior professor, such as myself, whose career struggles are over but whose intellectual life is not.

FIGURE I.I. SCHEMATIC OF THEORY FLOW REGARDING HUMAN BEHAVIOR SINCE DARWIN.

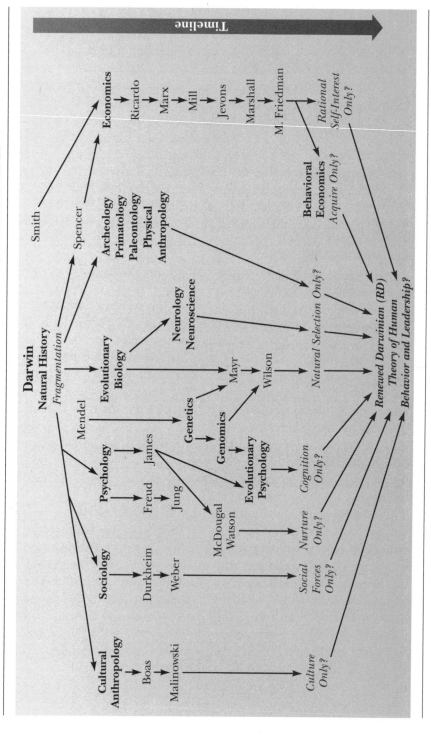

In 1991, when I moved to emeritus status at Harvard Business School, I started working full time (on a half-time salary) on the challenge of finding a more accurate model of human behavior and leadership. Although I had been a student of the full spectrum of the disciplines of human behavior since I was a young man, my primary motivation in 1991 was the rapid rise of agency theory, not only at Harvard Business School but also at many other business schools. Agency theory, as proposed by Michael Jensen and others, started with the axiom of economics that rational self-interest motivated all human behavior and built further on Milton Friedman's argument that the sole purpose of business was to maximize shareholder (owner) returns. I deeply believed that this doctrine was seriously flawed and that it was generating many disturbing consequences. But such was the enormous appeal of agency theory that I felt it could only be displaced by a better theory of human behavior and leadership, one which took into account the (to me, obvious) fact that there is much more to human behavior than simply rational self-interest.

But there was more on my mind than the need to move on from agency theory. I and others had long been frustrated by the fragmentation and dissonance of the various human sciences. It seemed to be an outrageous case of the blind men describing the elephant. For these reasons, I felt strongly that the time to try for a better synthesis had arrived.

We continue to be mystified by much of our own behavior, both as individuals and as nations, races, and faiths. The historian Norman Davies, summing up the period of the two world wars, wrote,

> At a time when the instruments of constructive change had outstripped anything previously known, Europeans acquiesced in a string of conflicts, which destroyed more human beings than all past convulsions put together.... What is more, in the course of those two war-bloodied generations, the two most populous countries of Europe fell into the hands of murderous political regimes whose internal hatred killed even more tens of millions than their wars did.... Future historians, therefore, must surely look back on the three decades between August 1914 and May 1945 as the era when Europe took leave of its senses.... In the course of the horrors, Europeans threw away their position of world leadership.[1]

We can ill afford to remain such a deadly mystery to ourselves. The human race now faces more than one danger that (1) could end civilization as we know it and (2) is of our own making. Nuclear war, environmental collapse, and the spread of pandemics such as AIDS readily come to mind. And how can we account for the fact that people such as Hitler can cause so much damage to so many other people? A more adequate theory of human behavior and leadership would generate practical applications and would distinguish the possible from the impossible. Such a theory would surely be worth a mighty effort.

And although the fragmentation of the human sciences was discouraging, the sheer variety of findings was most encouraging. Amongst so many pieces, there might be enough to put together a unified picture. Particularly exciting were recently developed techniques such as brain imaging, which is giving us fantastic new insights into what happens in the brain during various kinds of normal human behavior, such as remembering and deciding. Gene analysis has also made tremendous advances recently and can throw a bright light not only on what makes us uniquely human but also on how we became uniquely human through the processes of evolution. Hard data on the wellsprings of human behavior were starting to accumulate and, to my mind, demanding to be brought together.

But most of all (and most surprising of all), the time was right because a scientific theory which could account for the new findings and provide understanding of the big questions we want to answer—about consciousness, ultimate motives, conscience, morality, the sense of self, emotions, and complex decision making—*had been available for many years.* As we will see in Part One, Darwin's theory of evolution, formulated in 1842 and published in 1859 (*Origin of the Species*) and 1871 (*Descent of Man*), is quite up to the task. For the most part, all I had to do was (1) pay close attention to certain aspects of Darwin's theories about *humans* that had largely been ignored since his time and (2) give Darwin's insights the benefit of contemporary research.

This fortunate discovery came about when I collaborated with my Harvard Business School colleague Nitin Nohria on *Driven: How Human Nature Shapes Our Choices,* published in 2002.[2] In that book, we proposed a foundation for a new model of human behavior, based on four innate drives and a mechanism for keeping them in balance as a choice is made amongst possible actions. That is the one element of this book's theories which is original work. The rest is pure synthesis of the work of others.

When *Driven* was published, our four-drive model of man was highly controversial. It bucked the prevailing paradigms of the major disciplines concerned with human behavior. Economics explained all behavior with the axiom of rational self-interest; sociology explained it all with social forces; psychology with the learning that filled the "blank slate" of the mind; anthropology with the teachings of the local culture; and evolutionary biology with natural selection and our "selfish" genes, as Richard Dawkins memorably called them. Since then, these oversimplified (in my opinion) positions have been rapidly changing. While the struggles over these fundamental assumptions about human nature are by no means over, the tide has turned. There can be no going back.

But neither could I stand still. *Driven* was a success as far as it went, but it was still not an adequate theory of human behavior and certainly not of leadership, my central focus. What was missing was the process by which the prefrontal cortex not only came up with all the options for action but also, by working back and forth with the four drives, made the final action decision that was reasonably balanced as regards to all four drives. This was the impulse/check/balance mechanism that was not addressed in *Driven*. More important, the theory in *Driven* was not yet applied to leadership.

I believe that the Renewed Darwinian theories presented in this book are stronger theories of human behavior and of leadership than any of the current alternatives. They are theories that are universal, testable, and actionable. Now it is up to you, the reader, to decide whether or not this outrageously bold claim is justified.

CHAPTER ONE

HOW MUCH CAN WE HOPE FOR?

It is not the strongest of the species that survive, nor the most intelligent. It is the one most adaptable to change.
— CHARLES DARWIN[1]

Helen's boss, Peter, has just informed her that her unit is going to be eliminated and that, while she and some of her employees will be offered jobs elsewhere in the company (and possibly elsewhere in the country), she will have to lay off the rest of her team. What's more, Peter doesn't want her to let anyone know yet because the company needs her team to finish its current project ahead of schedule. Peter has always looked out for Helen, and now he says he is counting on her to manage this with as little damage to the company as possible. "We're in enough trouble as it is," he confides, "or I wouldn't be asking you to do this." He doesn't say what the trouble is.

We can imagine that Helen has many conflicting motives. She wants to do her best for the company, or at least to live up to Peter's expectations and to repay his past generosity. She wants to come out of this looking good, to protect her own career. There are a few of her people she could afford to be rid of, but she is anxious to be fair. She'd very much like to know what has made this layoff necessary, but she is reluctant to ask Peter for more information than he chose to give. She doesn't feel right keeping the impending layoff secret from her team, yet she thinks that if

1

she lets the cat out of the bag now, it would be very difficult to finish the current project, never mind speeding it up. Not that her team would deliberately sabotage the project, but keeping them extra motivated while waiting to be laid off would take some very skillful management on her part, and she's not sure she's up to that.

Clearly, some of her impulses are contradictory. She can't let people know *and* keep it a secret at the same time—but there are good reasons for both. She can't lay off a long-time-but-not-very-useful employee *and* keep a new-but-harder-working employee while appearing completely fair—but there are good reasons for both. It ought to be a mental train wreck, and yet somehow she will come to a decision of an acceptable course of action. She will not go crazy. Her head will not explode.

GOOD LEADERSHIP IS A NATURAL HUMAN BEHAVIOR

The poet John Donne noted that many everyday occurrences would seem miraculous if they happened only once.[2] I think we can look at Helen's eventual decision as just such an occurrence. Forming a decision out of such a tangle of motivations would seem miraculous if it weren't something we all do regularly. In this book we will examine what makes human beings capable of this everyday miracle of leadership and how we can all make better and more consistent use of it.

If we saw a cow flying through the air, we would wonder how the cow did it. We don't usually wonder how a bird does it; we know a bird is designed to fly. What I want to show you in this book is that human beings are designed to feel simultaneous conflicting motivations and to arrive at an acceptable decision—not *in spite of* the conflicting motivations but *because of* them. It is the very tangle of Helen's motivations, we might say, that will enable her to solve them satisfactorily.

How can that be? All living things react to certain aspects of their environments, but no living thing can react in as many different ways to as many things as a human being can. There are several reasons for this, but the most important is the fact that more things strike us as *significant* or worth reacting to. You might say that more things can push our buttons because we have more buttons to push. Four, to be precise—the four basic drives that I will discuss fully in Chapter Two. Other animals have a basic drive to get what they need—food, shelter, a mate, and so on—and a basic drive to defend themselves against whatever threats they can recognize. Humans of course have these two drives, but we have two others equally important to us—a basic drive to bond, to trust and care for others and to be trusted and cared for by others, and a basic drive to make some sense of our lives. While these two drives sound "fuzzier" than the other two, we will see in the next chapter that they are just as real. It is because we have four drives—four buttons to be pushed—rather than two that we are so much more responsive to our environment. As far as we know, no other creature could have so many different and conflicting things on its mind as Helen has on her mind in the story after hearing Peter's request.

But how does this responsiveness result in decisions and leadership rather than confusion and stalemate? It happens because our brains have evolved a way to let all four drives "have their say" and then to use our knowledge and experience to arrive at a solution that is acceptable to all four. This is not a metaphor; this is really what happens in the brain, as we will see in Chapter Two. And it is the need to accommodate such a variety of motivations—Helen's predicament—that brings forth such a variety of responses. To put it crudely, for most creatures, the only problems are to feed and mate and to fight or flee enemies. There are only so many ways they can do those few things, amazing as some of those ways may seem to us. (We are amazed that a spider can make a web, but that's about the only thing a spider can make.) Helen, though, has so many different impulses to take into account—so many more things that matter to her—that her solution cannot be the same thing that has already been done a million times.

She cannot just spin another web. She has to come up with a unique solution to an immediate situation. That is what humans are uniquely able to do, and that is a pretty good description of leadership. It is obvious from everyday life and from history that this decision-making process is not perfect, but it is also obvious from everyday life and from history that it does work pretty well much of the time.

Often our motivations are conflicting because various people are involved who have different—even conflicting—needs and desires. (This is what Helen faces—the needs and desires of her team differ from the needs and desires of Peter and his superiors; her own needs and desires are yet another variable.) But human beings are designed to take other people's differing and conflicting needs and desires into account.

In short, we are designed to accomplish things in groups—to lead and follow (which, we will see, are not simple opposites), to learn from each other, to trust and protect and care for each other, to acquire what we need collectively even if we then enjoy it individually. We have evolved this way because it turned out to be a very successful means of survival.

And it still is. In the 1990s and early 2000s, a surprising transformation took place on two offshore oil rigs. Thanks to a deliberate management effort, an extremely macho culture that rewarded intimidation, recklessness, and a cocksure attitude, even when this resulted in injuries and deaths (not to mention inefficient oil drilling), changed into a culture in which these same tough men took their own and each other's safety seriously, asked for and accepted help from each other, and would even admit out loud in front of visiting women professors that they were afraid or unsure. As one worker put it, "We went from living in one world to living in a good world."[3] Meanwhile, the drilling was accomplished more efficiently and more profitably.

Here, leadership took the role formerly played by evolution. In fact, leadership has become our primary means of *adapting* to changing circumstances, which Darwin cited earlier as the key to our survival. Since circumstances are always changing, we all have to lead ourselves. In addition, many of us lead others or would like to. This is not a glib comparison; we will see in Part One that the leadership most fit for a group is an extension of the self-leadership that is built into a normal individual's brain. And as we will see in detail in Chapter Four, this was exactly the kind of leadership that altered the crews of the oil rigs.

Is Bad Leadership Part of the Human Condition?

This book about good leadership will have a lot to say about bad leadership. Because humans survive and accomplish things in groups, and because groups always have leaders (often multiple leaders), a bad leader is a serious problem. Although bad leadership has always plagued mankind, we seem particularly aware now of political, business, and organizational failures all over the world—the financial meltdown on Wall Street, Bernie Madoff, the tolerance of child abuse in religious institutions, Osama bin Laden, the awful governments of Zimbabwe, North Korea, Sudan, Burma (Myanmar), and so on. Not only do we know much more about what leaders do and how they fail than would have been possible in previous times, we also expect better of them—a legacy of the Enlightenment. That is why it is so frustrating to see these bad leaders causing so much pain and suffering in so many people's lives.

Many people are understandably skeptical that leadership as a whole can be improved. Although it has been studied and written about for centuries, has there been any improvement in leadership comparable to the improvements in our material well-being brought about by science, engineering, and medicine? You may expect me to say "no," but actually my answer is, "Yes, but the advancements are too easily reversed." The U.S. Constitution, for example, can be seen as a social technology that has been as beneficial since its invention as inoculation or the electric light. (This is discussed at length in Chapter Five.) But we have not been able to nail down our advancements in leadership so that they stay put, the way the advances made by Jenner or Edison seem irreversible. There are always big steps backward.

Is bad leadership an inescapable part of the human condition? My response is that once we understand what makes for good leadership, we can see that the *potential* for bad leadership is indeed part of the human condition, but not the necessity of enduring it. Consider pneumonia: it used to be a deadly disease, but today it is rare for anyone in the developed world to die of pneumonia unless he or she is already weakened by age or chronic illness. Our "human condition" has not changed; we have the same potential to die of pneumonia as ever. But it is no longer necessary for us to die of pneumonia because we finally understand it and know what do about it. I think we are now on the verge of understanding bad leadership and what to do about it.

LEADERSHIP IS DECISION MAKING, AND WE ARE DECISION MAKERS

Leadership is always associated with action. But to understand leadership and to practice better leadership, we will need to take a closer look at inaction. Think of all the things we don't do—all the things we want but don't buy (or steal), all the things we think but don't say, all the people we don't like but don't attack, all the choices we consider but don't take.

One way of looking at this is that, more than any other species, human beings are decision makers. Other animals make choices, but they do not choose from the infinite possibilities from which humans must choose. (At least, we don't see the variety in animal activity that we see in human activity.) How is it that, in any particular circumstance, we are capable of so many different responses and yet manage to choose one—usually a workable one? It is possible because we make our decisions in a unique way. We are certainly not the machines of "rational self-interest" that leading economic theories imagine we are (which should be obvious by the frequency with which we undermine ourselves). But there is a logic at work. While in some ways it is non-negotiable, it is fantastically flexible. As I said earlier, it is designed to arrive at good decisions because of—not in spite of—conflicting motivations. The process is certainly not foolproof, but it is well-designed for self-correction and improvement.

This decision-making process—so familiar yet so surprising when we really examine it—is the basis of good self-leadership and good leadership of groups. We will learn about it in Part One; that will be the first step in learning to lead with your whole brain.

This book is organized into three parts:
Part One, "The Leadership Brain," presents the biological underpinnings of leadership behavior.

Part Two discusses the history of leadership, examining critical turning points in the leadership of political institutions; the rise of corporations as the leading economic institution; and the leadership of religious, artistic, and scientific institutions.

Part Three focuses on modern (mostly twentieth-century) political and economic leadership. Chapter Eight is concerned with contemporary corporate leadership, including the contrasting leadership styles of firms such as Enron and Medtronic. Chapter Nine extends that discussion to the crisis of the 2007–2009 subprime mortgage financial meltdown. Chapter Ten moves to contemporary issues of multinational corporations and world-level political institutions. Chapter Eleven discusses the practice of good/moral leadership and ends with ideas for action on the high-priority issues of our time. Chapter Twelve provides a fresh look at the age-old question of the meaning of human life and the question of human progress.

PART ONE

THE LEADERSHIP BRAIN

CHAPTER TWO

A BRAIN DESIGNED FOR LEADERSHIP?

Man is a social animal endowed with reason.
— PARAPHRASED FROM ARISTOTLE

The small strength and speed of man, his want of natural weapons, etc., are more than counterbalanced by his intellectual powers through which he has formed himself weapons, tools, etc., and secondly by his social qualities which lead him to give and receive aid from his fellow-men.
— CHARLES DARWIN[1]

What is leadership? It is a particular kind of decision making—decisions a leader makes in guiding and motivating a group of people in responding to a particular set of circumstances. The circumstances may be immediate or they may be something the leader foresees in the future, but in either case, there are choices to be made.

This is unique to human beings. For example, bees do what seem to be very complex things, but they do not have leaders who decide among competing courses of action. A queen bee is not a leader; she does not devise solutions to problems and convince other bees to do what needs to be done.

The human brain is also unique in many ways, some of which are directly related to this uniquely human type of decision making. We will see that the human brain is specifically designed to solve problems that must be figured out rather than handled by instinct, to solve problems facing a group, to solve problems through the efforts of a group, to consider multiple—even conflicting—impulses and options, and to arrive at pretty effective decisions. In the past two decades, new methods of neurological research have been showing us more and more (though we still need more) of what is actually going on in the brain when we react to our surroundings, consider choices, remember experiences, and make decisions. We are able to see certain parts of the brain "lighting up" while making certain kinds of decisions, and we are able to see people unable to make certain kinds of decisions when certain parts of the brain have been damaged. Many of these observations and results can be seen to build off of the basic insights of Darwin's about human nature as reflected in his quotation at the beginning of this chapter. They indicate that leadership is an expression of the survival mechanism, which human beings have evolved. In plain terms, leadership is what we as a species do well.

I am emphasizing the brain because that's literally where our capacity for leadership is lodged. When I speak of "leading with the brain," I don't just mean "using your head" or "being smart" in the ordinary sense; I mean, making full use of the structures in the brain that are specifically involved in—and have evolved for—leadership.

Every species on earth has, obviously, evolved to survive. Most species have evolved to survive by possessing and passing on to their offspring physical characteristics and instinctive behaviors, which give them a particular advantage in a particular environment. Within a limited range of circumstances, they can do exactly what it takes to survive. In most cases, each individual can do exactly what it takes *by itself* to survive. Humans have evolved to survive in a completely different way—by working together and by relying more on problem-solving skills than on instincts. This is a pretty good working definition of leadership. This unique way of surviving involves solving new problems as they arise and solving a wide variety of problems in a wide variety of ways. These are normally considered characteristic of good leadership.

Helen's response to her situation, for example, would differ if any of a number of circumstances differed; if she did not feel loyal to her boss, if her team were not halfway through a key project, if she had a great job offer somewhere else, or if she herself had ever been laid off unexpectedly. No set of instincts could cover such a variety of circumstances. What Helen has instead is a brain designed to weigh her need to make a living, her need to avoid the anger and hostility of others, her need to trust others and be trusted by them, her desire not to hurt others, and her need to figure out what to do rather than letting events overwhelm her—and to come up with a solution to this particular set of circumstances.

People do have instincts, but they account directly for only a fraction of our actions. What is built into us is not *what* we will do in a particular situation, but *how* we will decide what to do. It is because we generally rely on a decision-making process rather than on instincts that we have both the need and the capacity for leadership. It could even be said that, for humans, decision making and leadership have replaced the earlier, simpler processes of biological survival.

Description of the Decision-Making Process in Action

People don't necessarily see, hear, smell, taste, and feel more than other creatures, but we do react to much more of what our senses tell us than any other species. We make use of this flood of information by filtering it, so to speak, through a set of four priorities, which I call our "drives."[2] We have these particular four drives because, taken together, they constitute a very successful survival mechanism. (How this evolved will be explained in Chapter Three.) These criteria are not learned, they are innate—we are born with them. They are unconscious, although, as I will explain further on, we are conscious of the emotions that they generate.

A drive is not simply an imperative. We do not have a constant signal in our brain telling us to "eat, eat, eat." What we have are criteria by which we judge our circumstances. For example, in order to survive, I need enough food. Will this particular circumstance help me get enough food, or might it prevent me from getting enough food, or does it have no bearing at all on my getting enough food?

Two of these drives, or criteria, are the obvious drives any animal species must have in order to survive as a species:

- The drive to *acquire* what one needs for one's survival and the conception and survival of one's offspring;
- The drive to *defend* oneself and, as needed, one's offspring from threats.

The other two drives, or criteria, are unique to human beings (note Darwin's quote earlier):

- The drive to *bond;* that is, to form long-term, mutually caring and trusting relationships with other people;
- The drive to *comprehend;* that is, to learn, to create, to innovate, and to make sense of the world and of oneself.

To say that we have these four drives means that these are the criteria by which our brain's decision-making mechanism evaluates the circumstances it faces and, as we will see further on in this chapter, by which it evaluates possible responses in order to choose the "best available." Put another way, these are the criteria by which well-adjusted people lead themselves and by which good leaders lead others. This means that good leadership is rooted in the inherent workings of a very successful survival mechanism, which makes me very hopeful.[3]

Now, of course, we'd like to turn back to Helen and see if the four drives tell us anything useful about her situation and what she's going to do about it. But first, I need to say a little more about the drives themselves. The addition to the first two of the drive to bond and the drive to comprehend makes all the difference between human and nonhuman, between leadership and mere dominance of a pack:

- These two drives are not frosting on the cake. They are as much a part of our way of surviving as the other two. While other species survive by feeding, mating, fighting, and fleeing, our species survives by feeding, mating, fighting, fleeing, *befriending,* and *figuring out.* This means that, in any situation, we have many more factors to take into account. We could see that in Chapter

One with the list of things Helen would have on her mind as she tries to decide what to do. But the fact that everything is so much more complicated for humans than it is for bees or horses is what makes us so versatile and why we can do so much more than just survive. Being a leader is much more complicated than being a queen bee, but (as far as I can tell) much more rewarding.

- These two drives make us able to work in cooperative groups according to the needs of a particular situation rather than relying on instinct as social insects and schools of fish must do. These are the drives that make leadership, as opposed to sheer dominance, possible and necessary. As Darwin noted, we were never the strongest or fastest species, but we work together more effectively under more different circumstances than any other species, as many a harpooned whale could attest.

- These two drives make us able to survive mostly by figuring out what to do rather than relying entirely on instinct. But whereas any member of a particular species has the same instincts, humans do not all have the same problem-solving capabilities. There are innumerable different kinds of knowledge and ability, not to mention inherent differences in intelligence. We cannot instinctively take on the roles of drones and worker bees; at all levels we need to lead and be led.

- These two drives enormously expand the meaning of the first two drives. (Which is why the brief descriptions earlier may not have seemed very applicable to actual leadership.) Because we have a drive to bond and a drive to comprehend, the human drive to acquire goes far beyond the drive to acquire food, water, warmth, and a mate. For example, we have a drive to acquire things which interest us or which give us a sense of who we are or which would please other people whom we care about—even future generations. The drive to defend goes far beyond the drive to remain alive and well. We have a drive to defend groups to which we belong, even when there is no direct threat to ourselves. We have a drive to defend ideas and beliefs. We have a drive to defend our pride and hope and self-image as well as our physical well-being. We have a drive to protect strangers and future generations from danger and harm—that's why we fill in potholes and build hospitals.

Having four drives, or four criteria for evaluating our circumstances, opens up enormous possibilities. It's like judging a
figure skating routine as opposed to judging a shot-put event.
For the latter, there is only one criterion—distance. There can
be little doubt about who won. For the former, there are multiple criteria, such as form, difficulty, errors, and beauty. This
creates a problem for the judges, but it creates opportunity for the
skaters.

It is obvious that the drives can conflict with each other.
Indeed, the observant among us have always known that humans
are a mysterious bundle of drives which often conflict with each
other inside our heads. As the poet Stevie Smith wrote:

> Only human beings feel like this,
> It is because they are so mixed.[4]

Helen's desire to further her career by carrying out her boss's
wishes, an expression of her drive to acquire, conflicts with her
desire to be honest and compassionate with her subordinates, an
expression of her drive to bond. Her desire to know what trouble
the company is in, an expression of her drive to comprehend,
conflicts with her fear of aggravating Peter by pushing him for an
answer, an expression of her drive to defend.

How is it, then, that these four drives—these four different
criteria for judging the same situation—can constitute a successful
survival mechanism? How can they produce anything but discord
and stalemate? How can they add up to leadership? If an Olympic
figure skating event were judged by one Form Judge, one Difficulty
Judge, one Error Judge, and one Beauty Judge, there would be
many a standoff. Instead, each judge has to weigh all the criteria,
and as we will see, that's what the brain does, too.

The drives are something like four lobbyists meeting with
a senator, each alert to a certain category of what matters and
making sure the senator takes that priority into account. Imagine
a meeting in the senator's office before a vote on a climate
change bill. One lobbyist is insisting that reducing greenhouse
gas emissions as quickly as possible is the single goal. One is
insisting that economic growth matters. One is insisting that

good relations with China matter. One is insisting that scientific certainty matters.

The senator profits from hearing all four of these points of view. For one thing, all these concerns really do matter. A country that poisons the air can't survive. A country that lets its economy stagnate will be weak. A country that can't get along with China is vulnerable. A country that embraces scientific fallacies will be in error. On the other hand, each point of view would bring disaster if it were the only one taken into account. A country whose only priority was clean air would revert to the Stone Age. A country whose only priority was economic growth would create environmental havoc. A country whose only priority was appeasing China would become a vassal state. A country whose only priority was scientific certainty would be unable to act on most of the issues it faced. Only when all four priorities are evenly matched can they provide the basis for a sound decision.

But that is all they can do—provide the criteria for choice. It is the senator who must weigh these conflicting demands and make a decision that does as much good and as little harm as possible. In the same way, our drives are alert for what matters according to their particular criteria. They provide a foundation for a sound decision, but a different part of the brain has to come up with multiple options and propose the "best" decision. As we will see, there is a part of the brain (the prefrontal cortex) that does exactly that. (Which, of course, is why a senator or an Olympic judge or Helen can do it.)

I pointed out in Chapter One that we can make good decisions not *in spite of* conflicting impulses but *because of* them. Our four drives give our brain a picture of the world that is much more complete—multifaceted rather than one-sided—than it could be with only the two animal drives to acquire and defend. This four-drive picture can be complex and perhaps conflicted and confusing, but it has also been underlined and highlighted, so to speak, in terms of what we human beings need to survive (sustenance, safety, community, and understanding). Put another way, it is not only a snapshot of what's going on, it is also a blueprint for deciding what to do—a blueprint for leadership.

Evidence of the Decision-Making Process

Many descriptions of human behavior have an imaginary "as if" quality. No one has ever been able to hold up an X-ray or an MRI scan and point to guilt, pride, patriotism, or a soul, but we often behave *as if* we had what is meant by those words. I believe that this book's description of leadership is different. In the following description, I will point out research findings which indicate that the four drives I have described and the decision-making process that they set in motion are not imaginary "as if" concepts; they are what is actually happening in the brain.

This is why I think we are finally on the verge of putting leadership on a scientific basis, as we have already done with healing. Science has not yet given us the cure for everything, nor can it yet explain the observed healing powers of acupuncture or love or true grit. But I hope there is no argument that science has made the overall human effort to heal the sick and injured much more successful, and I believe science can now begin to have the same beneficial effect on leadership.

The Drive to Acquire (dA)

Humans, in common with all animals, have a fundamental drive to get what they need to stay alive and have progeny: food, water, warmth, sex, and so on. This is the easiest drive to understand and, needless to say, it lies behind something almost everyone has to do—work to make a living. While there are other animal species that "make their living" by group efforts, each has evolved a particular way of doing so which suits its particular environment. Humans, on the other hand, have evolved the capacity to make their collective living in a fantastic variety of ways and environments. Put another way, bees have evolved to make honey together but humans have evolved to "make do" together. Making honey together can be done by instinct; "making do" together requires leadership.

Modern neuroscience provides evidence to support the biological basis of the drive to acquire. Brain imaging studies conducted by Becerra have identified a module called the nucleus acumbens—in the limbic area, close to the front of the middle brain—which lights up with increased blood flow when people and animals experience pleasurable sensations from objects they acquire, ranging from tasty food to the sight of a beautiful face.[5] We will see that the limbic area of the brain seems to be the home of the unconscious part of the mind, including all four drives.

Because tangible goods tend to be "scarce"—that is, there is only so much available—the drive to acquire often provokes competition. The obviousness of this effect and the fact that it can be expressed in mathematical models such as supply-and-demand curves has led to the dominance in the academic and policymaking worlds of the neoclassical economic model, which takes man to be exclusively motivated to acquire scarce goods in order to maximize his own rational self-interest.[6]

THE DRIVE TO DEFEND (dD)

For most species, the drive to defend is a sort of mirror image of the drive to acquire. What needs defending is what needed acquiring—food, water, warmth, mates, and so on, along with life itself (which, strictly speaking, was never "acquired"). For humans, with their four drives, the drive to defend covers much more ground—not only the physical necessities of life and procreation but also our relationships, our cooperative efforts, and our understanding of the world—the necessities required by our drives to bond and to comprehend. As with the drive to acquire, humans satisfy their drive to defend in a huge variety of ways and generally in cooperation with others.

The drive to defend seems, like the other drives, to be housed in the limbic area of the brain, specifically in a module called the amygdala. Depending on what part of the amygdala is stimulated, the response will be appeasement, flight, or aggression.[7]

THE DRIVE TO BOND (dB) AND THE INDEPENDENCE OF THE DRIVES

There is no reason why [man] should not have retained from an extremely remote period some degree of instinctive love and sympathy for his fellows.... It is almost certain that he would inherit a tendency to be faithful to his comrades... be willing to defend his fellow-men; and would be ready to aid them in any way which did not too greatly interfere with his own welfare or his own strong desires.

Charles Darwin[8]

The existence of the drive to acquire and the drive to defend seems incontrovertible—how could any species survive without them? But the existence of a drive to bond—to seek social bonds, ties, attachments, and commitments—on equal footing with the others is more controversial, and I will devote more space to providing evidence for it.

Of course, there is nothing new in the observation that people tend to form bonds with other people. We see it in the bond between a couple (married or not), the bond between parents and children, the strength of family ties, the power of patriotism and other kinds of group loyalty, the power of social structures and cultural symbols, and the universal presence in humans of some kind of moral sense regarding social relations. Without this fundamental human behavior, there could be no such thing as companies or any other kinds of organization. Even the most inhumane dictator or business tycoon depends on a certain amount of unforced human cooperation amongst underlings; after all, he or she cannot hold a gun to everyone's head.

But we need now to look at this utterly familiar phenomenon in a new way, not simply as "the way people are" or as "the innate goodness in people," but as one of four survival-oriented criteria by which the brain evaluates what is going on and what should be done about it.

The drive to bond forces us to address an important characteristic of the four drives: they are *independent*. A drive cannot be satisfied by the satisfaction of one or even all three of the other drives. This is a subtle point to which we will return throughout the book because it determines how the brain's decision-making process finally decides and is therefore a key to good leadership. The independence of the drives can be disguised by the fact that they can assist each other. There is no doubt that the drive to have friendly relations with one's fellows can be helpful in acquiring the necessities of life and in keeping safe. What is characteristic of humans is that the drive to have friendly relations persists even when one's needs are fully met and even when the drive works contrary to one's own material interests. For example, a simple thought experiment suggests that the drive to bond is an independent drive, not a tool for satisfying the drives to acquire and defend. Imagine being in solitary confinement, yet provided with every physical need and physical comfort you could want. Even sex, but with someone who simply appears and has sex with you whenever you want it but never speaks or stays. Would that really do? Wouldn't you still be lonely?

Closer to home, we can see that all Helen needs to "survive"—to keep making a living—is to carry out her boss's request. As far as her drive to acquire and her drive to defend are concerned, she doesn't *need* to worry about being fair to her employees, about hurting anyone's feelings, about finding out what's really going on with the company, or about facing herself in the mirror. And yet, she does need to worry about these things, and so would most of us. And I use the word *need* deliberately. It's not just that she does worry about them; she *needs* to worry about them because the drive to bond (and the drive to comprehend, which we will get to shortly) are equal components of her four-drive survival mechanism. Her brain is not simply bent on survival; it is bent on survival by figuring out her situation and coming up with a solution for the group of which she is a part.

The key indicator that the drives are independent is that all four seem to have their own biochemical reward systems in the brain. Becerra's finding dealing with the nucleus acumbens deals with the drive to acquire. We can also observe that we are rewarded with pleasure for having sex, even though the part that would seem most pertinent to species survival—childbirth—comes much later. But since sexual intercourse is the only part of the process that is voluntary—the rest takes care of itself—evolution would favor the genes of individuals most likely to do it. Individuals whose nervous systems rewarded them for sex with a rush of pleasure (that is, for whom the drive to acquire came with its own built-in biochemical reward) had a survival advantage, which became a characteristic of our species.[9]

The drive to defend also has its own biochemical reward system. For example, most of us would take a real risk to save the life of a lifelong friend. Their overwhelming gratitude would be immediately rewarding; it would feel wonderful. This is a survival mechanism; the fact that I feel good having saved a friend's life encourages me to continue to behave that way which, in turn, increases the chances that someone might someday save my life.

This also seems to be the case for the drive to bond. Researchers at the National Institutes of Health scanned the brains of volunteers who had been asked to think about either donating a sum of money to charity or keeping it for themselves. When a volunteer thought about donating the money, a section of the limbic area of his or her brain lit up. This also, surprisingly, was the nucleus accumbens, which usually lights up in response to food or sex. The experiment indicates that acts of generous bonding are neither a superior moral faculty that suppresses the more fundamental urge for self-preservation nor a useful "tool" of the drive to acquire, but a full-fledged drive in its own right, hard-wired into the brain And the brain is even wired to provide the reward of a pleasurable feeling in much the same way that it does for food and sex.[10] As ancient wisdom would have it, "virtue is its own reward." As science would now put it, humans have a drive to bond which is independent, not simply a means to the ends of acquiring and defending our needs.

A number of experiments have offered evidence that there is a drive to bond in the brain:

- When certain parts of the limbic area—the hypothalamus and anterior thalamus—are impaired, individuals have a difficult time forming any meaningful or stable social relationships.[11]
- "Minimal group" experiments—in which a group of strangers is divided into arbitrary subgroups—have shown how easily individuals form surprisingly strong attachments to members of the same group, even if the group is completely meaningless and has no prior history together.[12]
- Human infants between eighteen and twenty-four months old show a spontaneous—that is, unrewarded—impulse to help others when they are far too young to have learned this behavior from adults.[13] Experimenters, who were strangers to the toddlers, did things such as accidentally dropping a clothespin on the floor and unsuccessfully reaching for it. The children

retrieved the clothespin for the experimenter 89 percent of the time.[14]

- As far as we know, all humans, except the rare psychopath, experience pain at the loss of an important long-term relationship, whether by death, divorce, emigration, downsizing, or many other causes. In many cases, this pain cannot be explained by reference only to the drives to acquire and defend. Emigration to the United States from a mother country in which one is not only doomed to poverty but also subject to violent persecution is, rationally speaking, a net gain in terms of maximizing self-interest, yet it will still cause deep and lasting grief.

- A particularly interesting piece of physical evidence for the human drive to bond is the whites of our eyes. The only three primates known to have whites of the eyes that can be easily seen are humans and two rare species of South American monkeys, marmosets and mariqui monkeys. Michael Tomasello, a neuro-scientist, has noted that the whites of the human eyes make it easier to tell what a human is thinking. That would be advantageous only if one can safely assume that one's fellows are driven to be helpful and friendly. This is generally true of humans, but not of chimps. But why do marmosets and mariqui monkeys also have whites to their eyes? It also turns out that, along with humans, they are among the very few primates that are monogamous. The fathers seem to do roughly half the work of raising their progeny. Do these South American monkeys have exactly the same drive to bond that humans have? Probably not, but we can speculate that monogamy and communicative eyes with whites have evolved together. Bonded couples of any primate species must find such eyes helpful for close collaborative work.

I will bring up one more very revealing experiment with chimpanzees. This provides only indirect—but to me, strong—evidence of the existence of the drive to bond in humans through its sharp contrast with the lack of such a drive in chimpanzees.

Researchers hid food in one of two containers, then let a chimpanzee pick one, but only after giving the chimp what to us would have been an obvious hint, such as looking at one of the containers or tapping it or placing a marker on it. The chimps consistently picked the *other* container. A few chimps eventually caught on, but it took dozens of tries. Because these chimpanzees had performed very well on other tests, the researchers wondered why they were "so dumb" on this one.[15]

I would say that it was because chimps simply do not have a drive to bond. While adult chimps have many social interactions, these appear to be entirely opportunistic—more like a means to fulfilling the drive to acquire. (The exception being the mutual love between mother chimps and their infants.) It simply wouldn't occur to a chimp that someone else—chimp or human—was trying to be helpful just to be helpful. Instead, the chimp would understand that this experiment was a competitive two-person game. "If I don't guess the right container, that experimenter will get the food. The smart thing to do, then, is the opposite of what that tricky experimenter is signaling."

On the other hand, the human experimenters do have the drive to bond and this, I believe, is what blinded them to the chimpanzees' motives. While we have all, at one time or another, been deceived or betrayed, most of us find it almost impossible to imagine someone who is consistently distrustful and deceitful. Because the drive to survive jointly is built into our brains, it doesn't occur to us that something as human-seeming as a chimpanzee has no such drive to survive jointly. (We will return to this point later in regard to the behavior of human beings, particularly leaders, who actually do lack the drive to bond and whose behavior the rest of us tend to find incomprehensible and even unimaginable.)

THE DRIVE TO COMPREHEND (DC)

As soon as the important faculties of the imagination, wonder, and curiosity, together with some power of reasoning, had become partially developed, man would naturally crave to understand what was passing around him, and could have vaguely speculated on his own existence.

Charles Darwin[16]

Humans have a fundamental drive to understand themselves and their environment. It can also be thought of as a need to understand how things work. Like the drive to bond, this drive is often clearly in the service of the drives to acquire and defend. For that matter, the drive to comprehend is often in the service of the drive to bond because cooperating—or just getting along—with others can be quite complicated. Nevertheless, it is an independent drive, not simply a tool used by the other drives, as can be seen clearly in the curiosity of children, who ask questions without knowing whether the answers will ever be of any use to them in fulfilling the other drives. Children can also be seen testing our answers to see if they are consistent with what else they know. Even newborns, when they are well fed and securely loved, can be seen exploring their environment with their eyes and their hands. Another strong indicator is the fact that anthropologists seem not to have found a single culture that does not have a creation story and few that do not have an afterlife story. People seem to need these theories to give meaning to their lives, regardless of whether or not the stories confer any advantage in acquiring, bonding, and defending. I argue that religions arose in all societies primarily to help fulfill this drive.

The need for dignity, mastery, self-esteem, or self-actualization[17] is a manifestation of the drive to comprehend—we need to make sense of ourselves as well as make sense of the world. Business leaders sometimes look askance at these "needs," as if they were being told that their employees need to be given milk and cookies and told a story or the company will not be competitive. In fact, the need for mastery or self-actualization is one form of an innate biological drive which, though not as immediately urgent as the need for oxygen, is in the long run just as much a determinant of how people will act.

A remarkable new finding provides empirical evidence of the physical existence of the drive to comprehend. It demonstrates the independence of this drive, and even locates it in the brain. Irving Biederman, of the University of Southern California, found that a part of the brain that helps you recognize what you see seems to be equipped with its own reward system of opiate receptors, which give a pleasurable "high" when they are stimulated by "catching on" to some novel event. He also found that this pleasure response diminished when the same image was recognized repeatedly. As Biederman sees it, these opiate receptors get bored by repetition and thus are freed up to be stimulated again by something new and unrecognized. In short, we are rewarded directly with pleasure for learning something new. Comprehending is independently rewarding, time and again, and only secondarily does this make us more competitive than a species that does not keep learning.[18]

The independence of the drive to comprehend is also seen in the fact that humans tend to think about and figure out all kinds of things that only later, if ever, prove useful for survival. This might seem wasteful, but it has proven to be a valuable key to survival. Humans generally survive by figuring things out rather than by instinct, and the drive to gather up and store information and insights whenever possible makes it much likelier that one will have the knowledge needed for some future situation. Put another way, intellectual scavenging and hoarding is a good survival technique, essential for adaptive leadership.

The drive to comprehend is a cornerstone of leadership in a second way. To lead a group, the leader must impart or maintain some kind of shared understanding. "Our job is to give the customers a good first impression." "We're all in this together." "We're screwed if we don't get the error rate down." "This is the most efficient way to do the job." Shared understandings, along with bonded relationships, are what hold groups together. Groups must therefore learn (that is, improve their understanding) together or suffer the consequences.[19] The auto industry is, currently, one of many facing precisely this challenge. Both management and unions have formed understandings of themselves and each other which no longer correspond well enough to reality to help them succeed.

Before moving on, I would point out that the definition from Aristotle at the beginning of this chapter would translate into four-drive terms as follows: Humans are social (dB) animals (dA and dD) endowed with reason (dC). What an amazingly compact definition of an exceedingly complex subject.

THE ROLE OF EMOTIONS

I have been speaking of the drives as parts of the survival mechanism which our species has evolved—as every species, obviously, must, in some way, if it is not to become extinct. Yet we all sense that our decisions and our leadership are often founded at least partly on something other than our own personal survival or our own best interests. This often puzzles us as individuals pondering our own or other people's behavior. And it certainly poses a challenge for leaders. Why don't workers always follow safety procedures designed to save them from injury? Why won't voters support regulation that would benefit most of them? Why aren't more people buying the product that's easier to use? Why are people willing to be led by a convicted embezzler?

The usual answer is "emotions," which are typically seen as rogue forces, separate from—and sometimes even in opposition to—rational self-interest. They are proving to be something much stronger and more useful. This discovery began when Antonio Damasio, a neurologist who has specialized in patients with significant brain damage, was working with a patient, a portion of whose brain had been "ravaged" by neurological disease. The man had what one would consider all the prerequisites of rational decision making—knowledge, attention, memory, language skill, ability to perform calculations and follow abstract logic—yet his daily life was "a succession of mistakes, a perpetual violation of what would be considered socially appropriate and personally advantageous." Damasio noted one other change: "a marked alteration of the ability to experience feelings." Somehow, this specific brain lesion had caused both a lack of emotions and an inability to reason properly in everyday life. "This correlation suggested to me that feeling was an integral component of the machinery of reason."[20] Damasio followed up this clue with two decades of clinical and experimental work with a large number of neurological patients. The following account of the role of emotions in the human decision-making process is largely based on his work.

The emotions seem to be the way our four unconscious drives—that is, basic components of our well-established survival mechanism—do their lobbying. It is how they make their priorities known to the part of the brain that will generate multiple options. They then make a contribution to the eventual decision. Presented with a particular set of circumstances, the four drives each evaluate, *according to their own criteria*, whether this situation—or some aspect of it—poses a threat, offers an opportunity, or simply doesn't matter. If the situation is either a threat or an opportunity *in terms of a particular drive,* that drive attaches an emotional marker (some kind of a neurotransmitter) to the signal (the sensory input) as it passes through the limbic area of the brain and moves on to the prefrontal cortex, the conscious part of the brain. This means, of course, that a signal may emerge with more than one emotional marker.

Now think again of Helen. All four of her drives will attach emotional markers to the sensory input of her boss's request. Her drive to acquire sees that this is a chance for her to enhance her career, or at least to preserve her job. At the same time, her drive to defend is alert to the threat of losing her job, either through failure on her current assignment or in further layoffs. Her drive to bond is going berserk with the opportunities to enhance or poison her relationship with her boss and also her relationships with her subordinates. Her drive to comprehend is worried that she doesn't know the whole story. We, like Helen, are almost always awash in these emotional markers that give certain sensory impressions *meaning;* that is, which mark them off as something we *might* need to do something about. (I say "might" because the final decision making is still to come.)

This portrayal may sound a bit absurd, as if the brain were plastered with Post-it^R notes. Nevertheless, there is experimental evidence that something like this is actually happening in the brain. Research on this phenomenon has been pioneered by Damasio. As is often the case with brain research, the importance of some part or function of the brain can be revealed—or at least suggested—by the unhappy consequences of its absence. Damasio reports the case of a man who had had a tumor removed from the ventromedial module of his prefrontal cortex. All seemed to have gone well at first, but then the man began to exhibit very strange and utterly debilitating behavior. He couldn't make up his mind about the simplest things, such as which pen to use to sign a paper. Damasio found that the man had no response at all to a set of photographs that would elicit physiological responses from any normal person—a naked woman, a bloody corpse, and so on. Something—presumably either the tumor or the surgery to remove it—had cut off both this man's ability to attach feelings to what he saw with his eyes and his ability to come to a decision. He could mull over the information perfectly logically—this pen versus that pen—but it seems that no piece of information had enough "meaning" attached to it to force a decision.

I said earlier that the drives present our decision-making mechanism with a rich and complex picture of what's going on—sometimes so rich and complex as to be confusing and contradictory—but that this picture has also been helpfully underlined and highlighted. It appears that our emotions are the underlining and highlighting that say, "Here is what you really need to pay attention to. This is what's going to be on the exam." Or in Damasio's terms, our everyday reasoning cannot operate on pure facts. It needs to be powered by a purpose; the unconscious drives are our purposes.

Figure 2.1 arranges a number of emotions with respect to the underlying drive they represent. Obviously this arrangement is both crude and arbitrary. Words are somewhat clumsy symbols for the variety of human emotions. The important point is the variety of emotional information that is available to us about the leadership process going on in our heads, if only we know how to recognize and interpret it. And I would emphasize, emotions are apt to lead us astray *only* if we respond impulsively to just one emotion. Wise judgments are built out of taking account of all the emotional markers triggered by the situation at hand. Can Helen afford to ignore any of the emotions triggered by her situation?

Damasio's findings contradict the commonly held view that emotions are carryovers from early evolutionary history, useful long ago but now more likely to be an impediment than an aid to survival and success. I, too, strongly disagree with this view. I believe the emotions are essential information. For leaders, they can be appreciated as the visible tips of mostly hidden icebergs (the drives), enabling a skillful navigator to steer a safe and productive course. The fact that emotional promptings are not always logical is beside the point. We have evolved to survive by a combination of four independent drives, only one of which—the drive to comprehend—motivates us to be logical for logic's own sake. Pascal's famous statement—"The heart has reasons which reason does not know"[21]—was more scientifically accurate than he could have imagined.

FIGURE 2.1. EMOTIONS ARRAYED ON A FOUR-DRIVE QUADRANGLE.

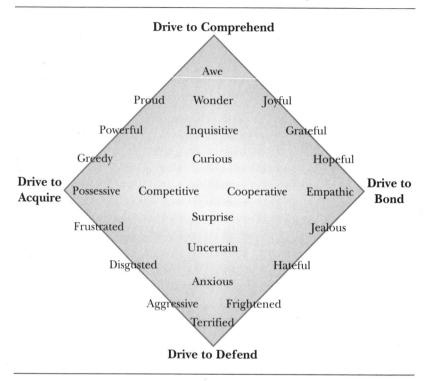

HELEN MAKES HER DECISION

We left Helen with Peter's request passing through her limbic area, the four drives each signaling their concern (or concerns) by means of emotional markers. In some cases, the chance to satisfy one drive is clearly an obstacle to satisfying another drive. At first, she considers doing what Peter has asked her to do—leading her team to finish its project but not telling them that the axe is about to fall, so as not to destroy their motivation. Of course, she doesn't like the idea of pulling a trick on her team, with most of whom she has had very friendly relationships, but she knows that keeping quiet about imminent layoffs is a pretty standard business practice. She's known people who've been on both ends of it and, of course, she has read about it in the papers. Whenever she heard or read about such events, she always hoped she would never have to do such a thing herself, and now here she was.

She wondered how she might be able to work behind the scenes to save her employees' jobs, or at least secure jobs for them elsewhere in the company, so that when the project was done, she could have something more honorable to tell them. But it seemed pretty likely that any such effort on her part would get back to Peter and he would feel she was scheming behind his back. *Then, for Heaven's sake, why not just ask him outright?* she wondered. *Why didn't I think of that in the first place?*

She began to imagine what she would say to him: "I'm going to do what you've asked me to do, but I have to tell you that these are great people. Of course I don't want to lay any of them off, but I also would hate to see the company lose them. Finishing this project ahead of schedule—which I know they can do—will have made them that much more valuable a team, something the company shouldn't lose." She liked the touch of emphasizing that *they* could do it rather than that *she* could do it; she was pretty safe and the point was to save them.

Uh oh. What if the company is about to drop that whole line of work? Her heart sank when she thought of that. Was it possible? She needed to know more about what trouble the company was in and what strategy it was hoping would keep it alive. Peter had done so much over the years to support her, but he had never been one to spill the beans about what top management was up to. *I guess I should admire that, but right now it seems more unfair than admirable.* How could she find out more? Get in touch with an industry analyst? Contact a headhunter and pretend she was looking for a new position? No, too dangerous. She had no gift for deception and subterfuge. One reason she was so loyal to Peter was that, early in her career, he had caught her out at a rather naive attempt and simply advised her not to take that route in life, even if she saw others succeeding at it.

No, anything behind Peter's back was out of the question. Better to ask him something outright and trust that, if he didn't approve, he would impart a lesson without holding a grudge.

She realized she was thinking more about her long relationship with Peter and not about her own people who needed her help, even if they didn't know it yet. A little to her surprise, she felt a wave of tenderness for them. For the most part, they'd had a great time working together and had a lot to be proud of. Even the least efficient of them were likeable teammates. She would hate to lose this bond; even if most of the team survived a layoff, the feeling might never be the same.

Helen decided what to do. First she had a heart-to-heart with her group. Then she told Peter what she had done. "I talked to my group about the urgent need to get our project finished ahead of time in good form. They are all fired up to do it. I am confident we can. But I did this in a way you might not approve. I told them, in confidence, simply that the company was going through a rough patch and that there might be some layoffs coming our way. I told them our best bet for avoiding layoffs is our performing fast and great on our project. While I can't guarantee we will avoid layoffs, if they come our way, I promise to do my very best in helping anybody involved to find a good job elsewhere in the company or, if needed, outside. Now the group is really digging in and working hard. They are good people. You should know I intend to keep my promise to these people."

Helen could not tell for sure how Peter took her story but he didn't explode.

She could still feel anxiety in her body, but she did feel good about what she had done.

THE PREFRONTAL CORTEX

Now let's follow Helen's decision-making process from the inside.

The emotionally marked signals—the collection of concerns registered by the four drives—move from the limbic area, the home of the drives, into another region of the brain: the prefrontal cortex.[22] Neuropsychologist Elkhonon Goldberg gives us this dramatic assessment of the role of the prefrontal cortex (which he refers to as the frontal lobes):

> The frontal lobes perform the most advanced and complex functions in all of the brain, the so-called executive functions. They are linked to intentionality, purposefulness, and complex decision-making. They reach significant development only in man; arguably, they make us human.... The frontal lobes are the brain's command post.... Motivation, drive, foresight, and

clear vision of one's goals are central to success in any walk of life.... [A]ll these prerequisites of success are controlled by the frontal lobes.... Damage to the frontal lobes produces debilitating blindness in judgment.[23]

A gross indication (not a proof in itself) that our humanity is significantly defined by the unique decision-making process carried out by the prefrontal cortex is the following trio of facts:

- The prefrontal cortex has been clearly identified as the place where decision making happens, at least the sort of complex conscious decision making characteristic of humans.[24]
- The prefrontal cortex is the most recently evolved portion of the human brain.
- The prefrontal cortex accounts for 29 percent of the total cortex in humans, as opposed to 17 percent in chimpanzees, 11 percent in gibbons, 8 percent in lemurs, 7 percent in dogs, and 3.5 percent in cats.

These three facts certainly suggest that the evolution of the prefrontal cortex has something to do with our unique ability to absorb such a wide range of information and take such a wide range of actions in response to it. It enables our unique form of leadership.

Many factors come into play simultaneously during this decision-making process, so I will begin with a quick overview of what happens, which can be summarized by the formula *impulse/check/balance.* When conflicting *impulses* arrive in the prefrontal cortex, they can *check* or block one another. At this point, there is a stalemate, but it is a most productive one. The prefrontal cortex calls on a storehouse of knowledge and know-how, located in a different region of the brain, the neocortex, to help it devise a solution—that is, a course of action—which integrates and *balances* the impulses. The prefrontal cortex feeds its integrated and balanced proposal back down to the drives in the limbic area for testing. They react, by means of emotional markers, much as they did to the original sensory input. This feedback loop continues, with proposed solutions passing up and down between the prefrontal cortex and the limbic area until the prefrontal cortex devises a solution which *satisfices* all four of the drives.[25] This choice is sent on to the motor cortex, which sends instructions to the body for speech and action.

In one sense, we all know this is what happens in our heads when we have to make a decision and find ourselves "of two minds" (or more). What is new here is that I am proposing the physical mechanism by which it happens. Of course, I cannot offer a precise blueprint—too much about the workings of the brain is still unknown and I am not even an expert on what is known. But I think enough is known to map out the basic process and to enhance our ability to lead ourselves, our businesses, and our countries.

CONFLICT DETECTOR

The prefrontal cortex itself consists of a number of modules. The first stop for the incoming signals, laden with their emotional markers from the drives in the limbic area, is the ventromedial module, which responds to incoming signals that have conflicting emotional markers. This is where conflicting drives have a chance to check each other. For the moment, there is a stalemate, but it is that very stalemate that allows the prefrontal cortex to work out a mutually satisfactory solution, like a negotiator calling a ceasefire so that one side doesn't just overwhelm the other.

Without this ability to keep a number of impulses in abeyance until a final evaluation is made, we would not be capable of such varied responses to our circumstances. A shark coming upon a helpless victim can only make one decision. The manager of a failing employee can make many decisions. He can fire the employee, chew him out privately, chew him out publicly, give him another warning, try to help him improve, try to arrange training for him, try to transfer him, try to convince him to quit. The manager can even plan a sequence of responses: "I'll have a talk and give him one more month. *If* he shows some improvement..."

Helen, of course, does not just rush off and obey whatever her first powerful emotional impulse happens to be. We take that to be the natural behavior of a mature adult. It is, but it is thanks to her prefrontal cortex.

In order to consider alternatives, however, our brains have to be able to think them up in the first place and then keep a number of them "in mind" simultaneously. We are still far from knowing how the human brain thinks things up. But we do have some idea what resources it uses and where it stores the ideas it does think up.

Treasures of the Neocortex

One reason Helen can have as much on her mind as she does is that she has so much *in* her mind. She is able to summon up and hold in her mind her knowledge of all twelve people on her team—their personalities, their accomplishments and failings, their relationships with her and with each other, what Peter thinks about some of them, which one just put the down payment on a house, which one is just about to send his son off to college; her knowledge of the project, where it stands, what remains to be done, who will be doing what; her knowledge of Peter, all the support and advice he has given her over the years, her feelings about him at different times. She doesn't know much about his family or his relations with his own superiors, but what she does know stands out vividly in her mind. In the background of her mind, as it seems, are articles she has read about how layoffs were conducted in other companies, horror stories of callous treatment, what other people have told her about what happened to them or to people they knew. Also in the background, more "felt" than remembered, it seems, are the moral lessons she has been taught all her life, her own experiences of having been cheated or lied to, her vivid memories of having treated other people badly, whether inadvertently or out of anger.

Where is all this information and how does the prefrontal cortex get the information it needs? A region of the brain called the anterior cingulate cortex seems to be the prefrontal cortex's research librarian. It swings into full operation as soon as the ventromedial module receives the emotionally marked signals from the drives. It then makes contact with a large and powerful region of the brain called the neocortex.

The modern human brain is approximately three times larger than that of our nearest animal cousin, the chimpanzee. Much of this extra capacity is committed to the neocortex, the brain's storehouse of knowledge and know-how which can be retrieved and put to use to make decisions about whatever situation is at hand. The difference this makes is not only quantitative but also qualitative. We use these mental resources to make the kinds of decisions that only human beings can make or need to make. Some of these resources are only recently being properly understood, and the implications for leadership are very important.

An obvious implication, but one that needs to be pointed out from time to time, is that we are designed to make our decisions deliberatively. There is a certain charisma attached to people who can make split-second decisions, and of course sometimes this is necessary. But most important leadership decisions need not and should not be made this way. The previous discussion of the true nature of emotions suggests that emotions should be taken seriously, and indeed effective leadership has always included an element of what is figuratively called "instinctive" reactions. What we can see as we study the leadership brain is that it is not usually necessary to make some sort of choice or trade-off between these two contributions. If we understand the emotions as genuine information, they can take their rightful place with other, seemingly more "objective" information.

MEMORY

I don't think I need to say a lot about memory. We remember a huge variety of things—people, objects, scenes, actions, feelings, meanings, words, images, music, even memory itself (as when we remember that there was something we used to remember)—and although we can't always remember exactly what we want to remember, nevertheless we rely constantly on a vast storehouse of remembered information and know-how. For example, the average English speaker has a vocabulary of between ten and twenty thousand words.

CULTURE

A lot of information comes to us pre-packaged, so to speak, in the form of whatever culture we grow up in or are living in. This includes social norms of behavior, rituals, specific beliefs (from the belief that stealing and burying an egg will cure warts to the belief that democracy is the best form of government), use of various tools and crafts (kids in some cultures learn to use buttons and switches; others learn to live with goats), all forms of art, all forms and styles of buildings, clothing, cooking, dancing, courtship, storytelling, warfare, sports, and, more recently, science, and the list goes on and on.

This greatly reduces the number of things an individual has to figure out; these things have already been figured out at least satisfactorily, if not optimally. And for a species that survives by figuring things out to know how to react to situations, it is a crucial advantage not to have to figure out every piece of every response. Helen, for example, has to figure out how to handle her situation. But if she decides to talk with Peter, she doesn't have to figure out how to approach and carry on a conversation with a higher-status, more powerful person, including how a woman should do so with a man; that's something she has already absorbed from her culture and stored in her neocortex. (Naturally, a Japanese or Austrian or Brazilian woman in Helen's position would have absorbed a different way of taking up a difficult subject with her male boss, or would have learned not to do it at all.) On the other hand, if she decides she has no choice but to keep the layoffs secret and lead her team to the slaughter, she doesn't have to figure out how this will be seen by her team; the ethics of concealing the truth, of "following orders," of saving yourself even if others will not be saved, are a part of her culture which she has already absorbed and stored in her neocortex.

Note, though, how different this kind of cultural know-how is from instinct. For one thing, it does have to be learned, however informally or even unconsciously. For another, cultural knowledge can be deliberately revised over time. How we relate to people of higher status, for example, has changed drastically over the past several decades. Our society and our organizations are still organized into hierarchies of power and status, but the specific techniques for navigating these hierarchies change.

Leadership sometimes means changing the culture in which your followers live and work. One way to look at that is that you are changing the content of other people's neocortexes so that those people's prefrontal cortexes are better equipped to resolve the competing claims of the four drives originating in their limbic areas. That's a lot more personal than "changing the corporate culture," and it's no small thing.

In 1945, George Murdock, a leading anthropologist, produced a list of the cultural traits that were practiced in every single one of the several hundred human societies that were documented in the Human Relations Area Files at Yale University. Exhibit 2.1 presents his whole list. It's a fascinating list and, by now, you should be able to see how some of these cultural traits serve one or more of the four drives.

All this stored treasure of individual and cultural information is amazing enough, but we have something more: built-in capabilities for learning certain particularly important things. This is a subtle concept, somewhere between having an instinct and ordinary learning.

MENTAL SKILL SETS

Many animals have "skills" which amaze us—the ability to spin webs or migrate long distances—but no animal is capable of such a variety of skills as we are, nor of improving and adding to them all through life. Why are we like this? One of the newest developments in our understanding of how the mind works is the avalanche of information about genetically encoded skill sets. For example, scientists now understand that our brains have evolved into a mechanism that can genetically carry some specialized elements of language from one generation to the next. This is what enables children to learn a language (or several) so quickly without any formal instruction. For example, Gary Marcus and his team of psychologists at New York University have found that seven-month-old infants pay more attention to sentences with unfamiliar structures than to sentences with familiar structures.[26] This means that the babies could recognize formal rules of grammar—and when they were being broken—well before they could speak or understand the actual words.

But it appears that language is only one of our built-in skills. Evolutionary psychologist Steven Pinker[27] has suggested a more complete inventory:

- *Intuitive mechanics:* seeing how objects can be manipulated
- *Intuitive biology:* understanding how plants and animals work

EXHIBIT 2.1.   MURDOCK'S LIST OF UNIVERSAL ELEMENTS OF CULTURE.

Age grading	Faith healing	Luck superstitions
Athletic sports	Family feasting	Magic
Bodily adornment	Fire making	Marriage
Calendar	Folklore	Mealtimes
Cleanliness training	Food taboos	Medicine
Community	Funeral rites	Obstetrics
organization	Games	Penal sanctions
Cooking	Gestures	Personal propitiation of
Cooperative labor	Gift-giving	supernatural beings
Cosmology	Government	Puberty customs
Courtship	Greetings	Residence rules
Dancing	Hair styles	Sexual restrictions
Decorative arts	Hospitality	Soul concepts
Divination	Housing	Status differentiation
Division of labor	Incest taboos	Surgery
Dream interpretation	Joking	Tool making
Education	Kin-groups	Trade
Eschatology	Kinship	Visiting
Ethics	nomenclature	Weather control
Ethnobotany	Language	Weaving
Etiquette	Law	

- *Numbers:* recognizing how some numbers are larger or smaller, how numbers can be added and subtracted
- *Mental maps:* picturing large territories
- *Habitat selections:* recognizing how some regions are more conducive to life than others
- *Danger:* understanding major hazards such as snakes and heights
- *Food:* knowing what is good to eat
- *Contamination:* having intuitions about contagion and disease
- *Monitoring:* being aware of current bodily well-being

- *Intuitive psychology:* predicting other people's behavior
- A *mental Rolodex:* keeping a database on important individuals
- *Self-concept:* having a notion of one's own identity
- *Justice:* having sense of rights, obligations, and so on
- *Kinship:* recognizing family structures
- *Mating:* having an intuition about the choice of a mate[28]

Is Pinker serious about all these skills? Is he serious, for example, about our having a genetically available Rolodex of important people in our lives? He is very serious, and we have reason to take him seriously. Consider how many voices you can recognize almost immediately on the phone; within about five words—any words—you know who it is and get right down to business (whether it's dealing or dishing). Helen, of course, knows dozens, perhaps hundreds, of people throughout her organization and can instantly relate them to each other in terms of function, hierarchy, and in some cases office politics—including many people she barely knows or has never met. While the specific information about each of these people has, of course, been learned through experience, the mental mechanism that enables you to access it so quickly is, Pinker argues, an innate skill. Such built-in skills are evidence that we have evolved to work well together in groups. Good leadership and followership are in our natures.[29]

Note that Helen is also aware of the tensions in her body. It is an important survival skill to know how the various parts of one's body are feeling in order to know when one is injured, when one is too tired to do something safely, when one is getting wet, and so on. For inhabitants of an ever-shifting social environment such as ourselves, tensions such as Helen's convey important information with survival value.

THE DORSOLATERAL MODULE AND WORKING MEMORY

Eavesdropping on Helen's interior consultation with herself, we can hear her bouncing back and forth between alternative plans. Maybe she should do what Peter asked her to do. Maybe she should try to circumvent him. No, better not to try that. To pull off this juggling act, Helen's prefrontal cortex needs to keep all these different proposals "in mind," along with the knowledge and know-how relevant to them, such as what she knows about Peter, what she knows about navigating company politics, and so on. And indeed, this "keeping in mind" doesn't happen by magic. Just above the orbitofrontal module lies the dorsolateral module, where, as psychologist Rita Carter puts it, "things are held 'in mind' and manipulated to form plans and concepts."[30]

We know, of course, that this is what we all do all through the day. Leaders need to appreciate this ability for the neurological miracle it is. Without it, the impulse/check/balance process would be impossible. A leading neuroscientist, Joseph LeDoux, writes, "Working memory is one of the brain's most sophisticated capacities and is involved in all aspects of thinking and problem solving."[31] As Elkhonon Goldberg says: "At every point of the [decision-making] process we need to access a particular type of information which represents but a tiny fraction of our total knowledge. Our ability to access it is like an instantaneous finding of a needle in a haystack, and it is nothing short of astounding."[32]

When the prefrontal cortex, aided by the resources of the neocortex, arrives at a tentative decision, this proposal is sent to the orbitofrontal module, which feeds it back downward, through a dense mass of neural connections, to the limbic area to test whether it is at least tolerable to all the four drives.

If the drives are still not satisfied—if the signal reemerges from the limbic area with still another set of conflicting emotional markers—the whole feedback loop will be repeated until a proposal is found which does satisfice all four drives.

The Rostromedial and Rostrolateral Cortexes: What I Am

As we reach the last stages of the work of the prefrontal cortex in decision making, I have to mention some recent research that is powerfully suggestive, although it is too soon to draw any definitive conclusions from it. Kalina Christoff, of the University of British Columbia, has focused her work on the abstract reasoning process, self-reflection, and self-value judgments.[33] It seems that decisions that are so complex that they require self-referential evaluation (such as "Would I do that?") engage the rostromedial cortex of the prefrontal cortex, which seems to function as the emotional self, and the adjacent rostrolateral cortex, which seems to function as a memory of the cognitive self.

These could be the prefrontal cortex modules that process the testing feedback from the drives that are evaluating action options before they are acted on. These may be the prefrontal cortex modules that "will" the final action on the most difficult problems—what Christoff calls the "tip of the consciousness pyramid." It may well be the place where we keep our memories of who we are, what we stand for, what we aspire to be—the seat of our integrity and character.

The final proposal that does satisfice all four drives is then relayed to motor centers that control movement and speech; deliberation—some conscious, some unconscious—will now become action (or restraint).

To fully appreciate the impulse/check/balance mechanism, let's look at two experiments in which it *doesn't* happen. In one experiment, Damasio and other researchers used a game to compare a group of people with normal brains and a group of people who had suffered brain damage in the ventromedial module. Each player was given $2,000 of play money and began picking cards from four decks labeled A, B, C, and D. Depending on the cards chosen, money was lost, gained, borrowed, or repaid. The goal was to end up with as much money as possible. What the participants didn't know was that the decks were rigged; compared to C and D, A and B yielded larger wins but the losses were larger still. Most players favored A and B at first, but players with undamaged brains eventually figured out that C and D were the real winners. Players with ventromedial damage, on the other hand, never did. They stuck with A and B until they went "bankrupt."[34] And this was very much the behavior they had shown in real life since their brain injuries—an inability to steer clear of risks that would seem obvious to the rest of us.

For these unfortunate people, the impulse/check/balance system had been short-circuited by the damage to the module that sent proposed solutions back through the limbic system to be "reviewed" by the four drives. In an undamaged brain, the drive to acquire and the memory of early wins with decks A and B would naturally favor choosing A or B *again*. But then a string of heavy losses would cause the drive to comprehend to object: "It doesn't make sense that the 'winning' decks have been losing so much." The prefrontal cortex, aware of the conflict, would work to come up with a solution that satisficed the drive to acquire by winning money and satisficed the drive to comprehend by making sense, or at least by not obviously failing to make sense. It might suggest favoring C or D simply to try something that hadn't failed. It might go back and forth a few times until it was convinced that the two pairs of decks were consistently different. And then it would stick with C and D. But all of this would depend on the prefrontal cortex being able to send new questions to the drive to comprehend. Is drawing from the A and B decks really winning? Does it make sense? If the prefrontal cortex were unable to do that, the whole process would remain stuck on its first successful strategy.

Psychologist Sarah Boysen and her team at Ohio State conducted a revealing experiment in which chimpanzees chose between two tempting dishes of candy.[35] The chimps had already learned to point at the dish they wanted, but this time there was a catch: when a chimp pointed at dish A, with more candy, he was given dish B and dish A went to another chimp. Although these chimpanzees had shown significant cognitive abilities in other tests, they couldn't seem to learn to pick the smaller dish of candy so they would get the larger one, even though they hated seeing the other chimp get the prize. By contrast, children given this test quickly got the hang of it (although children under two years of age did have some problems).

Human children and chimps both have the drive to acquire; both begin with the impulse to choose the bigger dish of candy. The chimps are clever and they know the results of their choices aren't making sense, but the human children have something different—an *independent* drive to comprehend. Because this drive is independent, it is able to check the drive to acquire, giving the prefrontal cortex a chance to hold off on grabbing the "obvious" dish and try to devise a different plan of action that will satisfice both drives by (a) making sense, as the present situation does not, and (b) getting the most candy. There appears to be nothing in the brains of the chimpanzees that can check their impulse to go for the most.

Checks and Balances Amongst the Drives

The impulse/check/balance process is an extremely powerful way to get along in the world. The four drives do not cancel each other out or fight themselves to a standstill; nor does any one of them attain permanent dominance in a healthy person. Instead, by their very clashes, they provide the impetus for an endless variety of possible problem-solving responses to the endless variety of the world. This works because the drives are (1) independent—one drive cannot be "bought off," so to speak, by fulfilling the others and (2) insatiable—all four criteria are always active and can never be fulfilled "once and for all." It also works because drives will act on satisficing ("good enough") solutions.

So important is the checking and balancing that we even seem to have evolved inherent skill sets for resolving tensions between the drives. For example, social scientist Jordan Peterson has focused his attention on a skill set for detecting and responding to novelty or surprises in the environment.[36] Upon the appearance of something new and unknown, a person will often feel both fear and curiosity—emotions representing the drive to defend and the drive to comprehend. Peterson believes we have a genetically built-in skill to manage this particular standoff.[37] The first step is to freeze all motion and focus intently on the novel event. Then make a small move that is safe, trying to elicit more information about the novel object. Step by step in this process we try to judge the object dangerous or not according to what it most closely resembles from our previous experience (stored in the neocortex). Of course, this first approximation may prove to be wrong, but on the whole, a mechanism for quickly and simultaneously satisfying both the drive to comprehend and the drive to defend—that is, to learn something that may be useful without getting hurt or killed in the process—would be an aid to survival for a species that relies on problem solving rather than instinct. And because it is a built-in skill, we do not have to figure out this basic mechanism, only the specific action plan that best fits the circumstances.

Social psychologist Alan Fiske's work has focused on four built-in skill sets that check the drive to acquire and the drive to bond against each other and achieve a balance.[38] These four skill sets are

(1) communal sharing—universally applied within family groups but also sometimes applied to the extended family and beyond; (2) hierarchy—agreement within a group on who has higher status, and thus deserves some deference; (3) reciprocity—willingness to do a favor now in expectation that the favor will eventually be returned; and (4) market pricing—simultaneous exchange of valued goods either by barter or with money. Expressed this way, they sound rather abstract, but Fiske's important point is that they are everyday behaviors, so natural to us that we don't even think about naming or categorizing them. Think, for example, of a group of college roommates. They freely share what's in the fridge (communal sharing) as long as no one is obviously freeloading (not reciprocating). They do not, however, help themselves to each other's computers. If Joe really wants to have Chris's computer, they might agree to a sale or a trade (market pricing). Joe would not get away with telling Chris what to wear to class, but Chris might dress more formally if Joe's parents were visiting (hierarchy). All of this would happen naturally, and violations of these unspoken rules would be immediately understood as "not being a good roommate." As Fiske puts it, "People understand their social life in terms of these four models, and they attempt to impose these relational structures on their social world. People want others to conform to the models."[39]

These skills help us balance the drive to get what we need with the drive to get along with each other well enough to meet most of our collective needs. Taken together, they are the alternative to getting what you need by constant fighting and stealing and fending off attack—the normal life of many animals—or to the total self-sufficiency and solitude of a Gila monster.

Fiske hypothesizes that these four skill sets are innate because they seem to be universal and there is some evidence that they surface spontaneously in children, without being taught. If Fiske is correct that these behaviors are genetically inherited skill sets, this is essential knowledge for leaders. For example, the relationships between a business firm and its employees are typically thought of by economists as strictly market transactions—the so-called "labor market." Mainstream economists—and the many business executives who have absorbed their ideas—simply do not recognize the other three skill sets as having anything to do with it. Such bosses

FIGURE 2.2. SKILL SETS ARRAYED ON A FOUR-DRIVE QUADRANGLE.

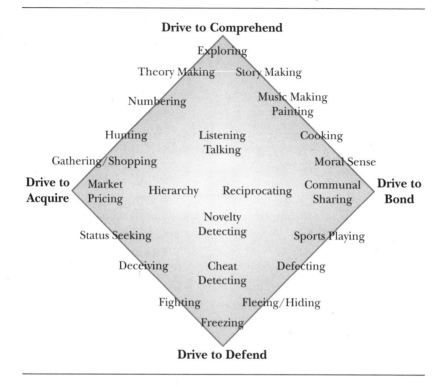

will be ignoring the many other ways, via the other three drives, they have available to reward employees and readily engage them in the collective effort. This limits their ability to provide good leadership.

In Figure 2.2, a variety of skill sets is arrayed to show how they could help the prefrontal cortex check and balance the four drives.

A COMPREHENSIVE TEST: THE ULTIMATUM GAME

One of the more effective demonstrations of the existence of drives in humans comes from the "ultimatum game," an experimental device carefully designed by behavioral economists to test for the existence not only of a human drive to acquire but also of other possible drives. It has turned out to be a surprisingly good test for the existence of all four of our hypothesized drives.

Two experimental subjects are randomly chosen to be the "Proposer" and the "Responder." The experimenter gives the Proposer some money—let's say it's twenty five-dollar bills—and both players can see how much it is. The Proposer is to place as much of the money as he chooses in front of the Responder as a "take it or leave it" offer. If the Responder accepts the offer, he or she keeps that money and the Proposer keeps the rest. If the Responder refuses the offer, neither party gets anything. Take a moment now before reading on to decide what you would offer as a Proposer. Learn below how your proposal would pay off.

Neoclassical economic theory predicts that any rational self-interested Proposer would offer the smallest possible amount— one five-dollar bill—knowing that any rational self-interested Responder would take it, since five dollars out of the blue is clearly better than nothing. In contrast, our four-drive model predicts that Proposers will try to satisfice all four of their drives. They will try to figure out (dC) how to end up with as much cash as possible (dA) while also staying on good terms with the other player (dB) or, at the very least, not making an enemy of the other player (dD). If the Proposer's offer leads to all four of these outcomes, it will be a real four-bagger, a home run in terms of all four drives. If the Proposer's offer is rejected, it will be a total strikeout, a loser by all four criteria: no money, no friend, a possible angry enemy, and a failure to comprehend the game.

Both players know that the $100 is an unearned windfall, which has arbitrarily given the Proposer a first-mover advantage. The Proposer will also reason, or at least sense, that the Responder has the same four drives he or she has and will therefore take a minimal offer as an insult. The reaction would likely be, "Stick that offer, you cheap bastard." What would be the minimum amount needed to earn an acceptance along with a pleased smile? The Proposer can't be sure, but it would be worth any reasonable cost to avoid a rejection, a four-way loss.

(You may be thinking that no one would actually be thinking all these things. That's true; the four drives are unconscious. But even if we don't sense them directly, we sense the conflict between them by means of the emotional markers attached to them in the limbic system and detected in the prefrontal cortex. We know we are having trouble making up our minds.)

When this experiment was actually run in industrial societies, the mean offer of Proposers was 44 percent of the total money. Virtually no Responders accepted offers of 20 percent or below. This result has come as a shock to mainline economists, since it dramatically contradicted the predictions of standard economic theory.

This consistent, but puzzling, finding led some behavioral economic researchers, joined by some anthropologists, to conduct a careful multicultural test designed to avoid a developed-country bias. Ultimatum game experiments were conducted in fifteen small nonindustrial cultures in twelve countries. Each experiment was set up as an economic exchange between two people who were members of the same culture but were strangers to each other. The experimenters offered rewards that were significant in local terms, worth several days of work. The average size of the proposals in each of the fifteen cultures ran from a low of 26 percent to a high of 58 percent. No group displayed the "rational" economic behavior—the lowest offer possible—predicted by standard economic theory. Something besides rational self-interest was influencing people's behavior, and on a worldwide basis. As the principal researcher, Joseph Henrich of the Institute for Advance Study in Berlin, concluded: "People everywhere put a social spin on economic exchanges."[40]

As I see it, people all around the world, both Proposers and Responders, seemed to be seeking what they defined as "fair" exchanges that actually served to satisfice all four drives. Proposers actually came out winners by having their offers accepted by Responders in 94 percent of all cases.[41] They were demonstrating a very high capacity to predict how the Responders would respond. They came away with a reasonable amount of cash (dA) and a good idea of how they won it (dC), having finished on good terms (dB), or at least not on bad terms (dD), with the other player. Fully indoctrinated economists would have been consistent losers. It does, however, offer significant support to our model, even though the designers of the experiment had never heard of it.

Later in the book, we will see that the impulse/check/balance algorithm has much wider applications; it provides a way to channel the clash of human individuals and groups into satisfactory

FIGURE 2.3. IMPULSES AND CHECKS.

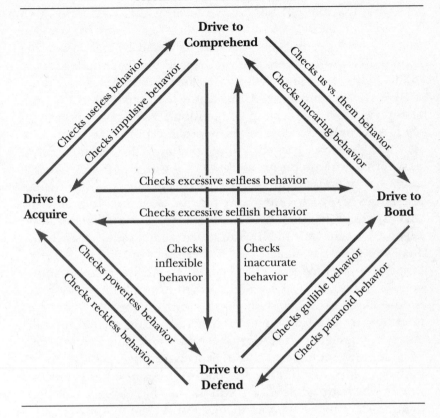

responses, just as it channels the clash of our innate drives into satisfactory responses. We will also see that some of the worst problems facing our society arise from the lack of an impulse/check/balance system, or the perversion of such a system.

Figure 2.3 presents examples in diagrammatic form of our hypotheses about the kind of check each drive gives the other three.

CONCLUSION

You can see now that the title of this section, "The Leadership Brain," is somewhat misleading. I certainly do not propose that people with a particular kind of brain will make the best leaders and that we should find out who they are and put them in charge. I propose that the normal human brain is the leadership brain and that we should all put our leadership brains to work, at the very least, leading ourselves in balanced lives and working cooperatively with others, and perhaps also becoming leaders of others in the usual sense—but if so, then good leaders.

We can be encouraged to have discovered that good leadership rests on such strong foundations. Helen has very tough choices to make, but her brain is designed to make them. Not necessarily easily or happily, but reasonably well. Speaking in ordinary terms, we would say "she's got a lot on her mind," "she'll weigh her options," and "she'll try to make the best of it." These are figures of speech, but now we see how accurately they describe what is actually happening in her brain. She has a lot on her mind because, like any normal human being, she has four basic drives, all of which have been activated by her situation, and because she has a neocortex loaded with personal memories, cultural knowledge, and know-how skills. She'll weigh her options because her prefrontal cortex will generate possible actions to take and use its impulse/check/balance mechanism (the ventromedial module, anterior cingulate cortex, dorsolateral module, and orbitofrontal module, plus input from the neocortex and feedback from the limbic system). She'll make the best of it because her prefrontal cortex will strive to send a solution that has satisfied all four drives for all the key people involved on to the motor cortex for action. Figure 2.4 is a schematic of how all of these brain parts work together to make leadership decisions.

Figure 2.4 offers a schematic summary of the theory of the leadership brain that this book offers—a theory that still needs a name. I have chosen to call it the Renewed Darwinian (RD) Theory of Human Behavior and Leadership. This name acknowledges that its major elements are built upon insights of Darwin's, drawn from his *Descent of Man*. His insights have, of course, been strengthened by many subsequent studies. Darwin's contributions are rounded out in the next chapter as we address the essential question of how the leadership brain, as described, could have evolved by Darwinian mechanisms.

FIGURE 2.4. SCHEMATIC OF HOW THE BRAIN WORKS
AS A DECISION-MAKING APPARATUS.

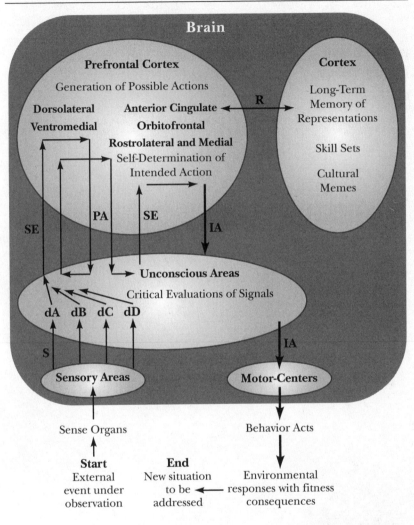

Finally, let me say that the fact that this is what the brain is designed to do is why I think the overall quality of leadership of all kinds can improve over time, much as the physical aspects of our lives have improved over time. Perfection will elude us— it is obvious every day that our leadership brains can make mistakes—but we can learn to use them better and to undermine them less often.

CHAPTER THREE

DARWIN REDISCOVERED
Did the Brain Evolve Leadership Capabilities?

Preference on the part of the women steadily acting in one direction, would ultimately affect the character of the tribe.[1]
— CHARLES DARWIN

With strictly social animals, natural selection sometimes acts on the individual, through the preservation of variations which are beneficial to the community.[2]
— CHARLES DARWIN

The following proposition seems to me in a high degree probable—namely, that any animal whatsoever, endowed with well-marked social instincts [dB], would inevitably acquire a moral sense of conscience, as soon as its intellectual powers [dC] had become as well, or nearly as well developed, as in man.[3]
— CHARLES DARWIN

Drawing heavily on Darwin's key insights, such as those above, along with recent findings from several disciplines, this chapter will piece together an answer to the query posed in its subtitle. The answer is my summary of a currently emerging scientific consensus. Future research undoubtedly will extend or even replace this story with a more accurate one, but for now I do not know of another answer that accounts for more empirical evidence.

As we saw in Chapter Two, human brains are capable of taking account of a vast array of *current* circumstances and finding a *unique survival solution* that meets not only their group's requirement for material resources (dA) but also their defensive requirements (dD), their requirements for group support (dB), and their requirements for finding more creative ways to adapt to their changing circumstances (dC). The solutions that meet this demanding test are, by definition, leadership solutions. They are acts of leading other people, not only in new directions that *fit* their *current* environment but also in a way that motivates them by satisficing all four of their drives. People who have learned to use their brains effectively in this regard will be better than others at leading their fellow humans and will be turned to for this special kind of help. This chapter will try to figure out how such a remarkable brain, with these leadership capabilities, could have evolved.

A Larger Brain—with a Price to Pay

Darwin said that humans survived, and largely dominated other creatures, because they are the most able to adapt to changing environments. I argued in Chapter Two that, in fact, humans have evolved a brain that can continually adapt to its *contemporary* environment, rather than banking on its adaptation to an *ancestral* environment. This brain was, in fact, an adaptation to a period of extreme and comparatively rapid climatic shifts.

Scientists have recently discovered that in East Africa, where several varieties of early hominids lived for millions of years, the climate was swinging fairly rapidly—every two hundred thousand years or so—between hot and dry conditions and cool and wet conditions. This seems slow to us, but it was too fast for hominids to adapt by waiting for genetic mutations to evolve appropriate survival instincts. One line of mutation that offered a way out of this trap was the development of a bigger brain with more information-processing capacity. And indeed, the fossil record shows that at some ancient point, which is difficult to date, the brains of hominids began to get bigger. This probably started even before the arrival of *H. habilis*. But it wasn't so simple as it sounds.

There seems to have been mutations which slowed down the maturation of the human brain and which made the skulls of human infants more pliable at birth than the skulls of chimpanzees. Our brains, unlike those of other animals, keep growing in size and complexity—*after* we are born—becoming much larger than the size of the female birth canal would have permitted at birth. But there was a price to pay. The fragility of the brain cases of human infants, along with other aspects of delayed maturation, meant that these infants were vulnerable, requiring a much longer period of intense nurturing by adults than other primate infants would need. Hominid mothers—unlike chimpanzee mothers, who do essentially all the nurturing of their young—now needed significant help from other adults.

One makes a similar trade-off buying, say, a bookcase at IKEA. On the one hand, the box fits in your car so you can take it right home; no more sitting at home waiting for the delivery truck. On the other hand, when you get home, you don't really have a bookcase until you assemble it.

A BETTER FOOD SUPPLY—WITH A PRICE TO PAY

The next big shift in hominid brains took place around two million years ago with the emergence of a new species, *Homo erectus*. Scholars know comparatively little about the shift from *H. habilis* to *Homo erectus* because the fossil and artifact record is limited, but it is known to have been a major step toward the evolution of the modern human brain.[4] Surprisingly, this may have been a result of cooking.

At some early point, hominids learned to control fire and subsequently discovered the utility of cooking. The date of this discovery is disputable, but its importance is hard to challenge. As physical anthropologist Richard Wrangham and his colleagues have pointed out, cooking increased the food supply by making it possible to consume plants, such as many roots, that were otherwise toxic or too tough to chew and by retarding spoiling, which allowed edibles to be stored.[5] The effects can be observed in the fossil record: *H. erectus* had smaller teeth than *H. habilis* and the body mass of females increased. Cooking would also have freed up considerable time that would have been spent chewing uncooked food (try eating an uncooked root some time); that extra time could have been spent in any number of useful ways, from finding more food to getting enough rest. However, since food would have to be brought to the fire and cooked before being eaten, it would be much more vulnerable to theft, particularly by the larger males. The females, who most probably gathered the vegetables, would be looking for help in guarding the food. There would have been a new advantage in mating with a reliable man who was willing to bond with a particular woman. Most important, mating with such a man would improve the odds that a woman's increasingly dependent offspring would survive and grow to maturity—the sine qua non of species survival.

Pair-Bonding Pays the Tab

Among the many misunderstandings of Darwin's theory of evolution (discussed further in the Appendix) is that it depends exclusively on natural selection; that is, the survival of genetic traits which allow the members of a species to overcome environmental obstacles including competition with other creatures and successful reproduction. In fact, Darwin proposed three methods of selection: natural selection, sexual selection, and group selection. Sexual selection is the survival of genetic traits that cause the members of one sex to be chosen as mates by members of the opposite sex, which will obviously cause those genetic traits to survive in future generations. Darwin's second epic book, *The Descent of Man,* provides dozens of examples of how sexual selection is a powerful process, even among humans.

Hominid females found themselves with two good reasons to favor males who would stay with them rather than straying after other available mates. While our hominid ancestors could not have known exactly how babies were made, their drive to acquire surely supplied an urge to experience the pleasures of sex after they reached puberty. They must have been observant enough to figure out that sex now often meant pregnancy later. Since human infants were maturing more slowly, the females figured out that it was not to their advantage to mate with the first male who expressed an interest in them, but to be selective. Looking ahead, with the help of their mothers and friends, they could anticipate nine months of pregnancy; two to four years of breast-feeding; and even more years of protecting, feeding, and training each child before it reached mature self-sufficiency. They could see that it would be difficult—sometimes impossible—to provide all the required nurturing themselves. A reliable mate would be a huge, perhaps decisive, advantage in the survival of the babies. With the advent of cooking, their need for a male to help guard the food was an additional reason to find a reliable mate.

Female hominids realized that they were acquiring more power in choosing which male they would mate with. They could be choosy simply because males were not as choosy. Males had far less at risk than females did by engaging in the pleasures of sex, and the females probably realized that they were the gatekeepers to what males so badly wanted.[6] Rape was probably becoming a less practical or attractive solution; females were closing the gap in size, and the males needed them more as cooks.

Given their power of mate selection, whom would the *H. habilis* females tend to select as a "good" mate? Their choice would determine which male genes made it into the next generation. I submit that the answer is rather obvious. They would select the kind of mate that, according to a study by evolutionary psychologist David Buss, women all over the world still prefer.[7] Obviously, they would select a likely breadwinner with ambition, a person with a robust drive to acquire (dA). But that is not all. These females would also be looking for someone who was healthy, strong, and prepared to help protect them and the children from all hazards (dD). But that is still not all. They would also select a male who was in love with them, a person who, beyond all obvious self-interest, simply felt driven to bond with them in a long-term commitment (dB). This was the new criterion. They wanted a hunter who would actually bring the bacon home because he loved his mate. They wanted a mate who had found the "sincerity" solution to the problem of making credible commitments, as discussed by the economist Robert Frank.[8]

Where were these choice male hominids with dB as well as dA and dD coming from? Of course we cannot really know, but they might have been the result of mutations that delayed switching off the genes that bonded infants to their mother. Such mutations would be similar to those that delayed the maturation of the brain, as discussed earlier. In any event, something happened that rendered a small minority of *H. habilis* adult males suitable for "domestication," a process that has been observed in several species. For example, Dmitri Belyaev, a Russian biologist, took a population of one hundred female and thirty male wild silver foxes to Siberia and started a careful process of interbreeding that favored the trait of "docility."[9] Amazingly quickly—by the thirtieth to thirty-fifth generation—70 to 80 percent of the foxes behaved as tamely as dogs. Interestingly, certain bodily changes paralleled this behavioral change, such as gracilization, the lightening of bone mass. Wrangham has pulled together the fossil evidence that gracilization has taken place in humans throughout history and is still proceeding.[10]

On the behavioral side, the family life of *Homo sapiens* is much more "domesticated" than that of our closest primate relative, the chimpanzees, amongst whom both males and females are entirely promiscuous. Careful observers of the behavior of chimpanzees in the wild and in captivity cannot determine the paternity of newborns except by laborious DNA testing, and there is no reason to believe the mothers or fathers can tell, either. Among humans, however, long-term mate bonding, monogamy, is the norm.

Given this evidence, this is what I believe took place. A mutation occurred which resulted in a minority of *H. habilis* adult males acquiring an *independent* drive to bond. On the basis of other, similar events, we can speculate that this may have occurred by the single step of freezing the genetic switch that was bonding male hominids to their mothers during their immature years. As long as the genes for bonding manifested themselves in ways that choosy females could spot, those maturing males would be chosen as mates (pure sexual selection) and those new genes would wind up in their offspring. In a small intermarrying group, this process could probably convert a population of totally promiscuous males into a population of good husbands and fathers in just a few thousand years. Eventually, these "domesticated" variants of late *H. habilis* would become a new species, *H. erectus,* whose stable family structure gave it a very strong competitive advantage: a higher percentage of *H. erectus* babies would grow to maturity than *H. habilis* babies. (And don't forgot, these babies also had bigger brains than anything else around.)

In short, a two-drive species (acquire and defend) had become something new—a three-drive species (acquire, defend, and bond, trusting and caring for each other). And indeed, paleoanthropologists report that monogamous pair-bonding and nuclear families seem to have been the pattern throughout human history in hunter-gatherer societies.[11] Among contemporary hunter-gatherers, we find that Australian aborigines, the Trobriand Islanders, pygmies, Kalahari Bushmen, and Amazonian Indian tribes all organize themselves into nuclear families.[12] In the historical period, polygamy has been widely practiced only among the elite ranks of highly stratified societies. While there seems to have always been marital infidelity, it has been a dangerous game subject to severe punishment. We can see why: monogamy in humans is founded primarily on an innate drive to bond—an indispensable component of our survival mechanism; the customs and laws which sanction monogamy are but reflections of the underlying non-negotiable drive to bond.

This was a radical development in another way. For billions of years, evolution had been a blind, mindless, trial-and-error process. Now female hominids, through the sexual selection process, were using their brains to select the brains of the next generation. Hominids were, in effect, pulling themselves up by their own bootstraps. And females, the "weaker sex," were in charge.[13]

I have to note that I am not attributing the transformation of *H. habilis* into *H. erectus* solely to sexual selection. A combination of natural selection and sexual selection achieved the result. But I would argue that any form of pair-bonding based only on the drive to acquire and selected for only by natural selection would have been a much more fragile, opportunistic, and short-lived alliance. True love, the long-lasting glue of pair-bonding, would have been missing.

The emergence of pair-bonding was, in all likelihood, essential to the survival of the hominid line. As the length of time during which children were totally dependent on their mother's care increased, the mortality rate of these children would have been creeping up on the birth rate. Eventually, there would have been a population crash and extinction. The creation of the nuclear family might very well have saved the entire hominid line from this fate; *H. habilis* did become extinct at about this time. *H. habilis,* with the two drives of acquiring and defending, must have been very individualistic folks—always and exclusively looking out for number one, in a constant struggle for existence with all others of their species (except for the bond of love between mother and infant). Any alliances between males would have been temporary and opportunistic, as they are among chimpanzees. Leadership could only have consisted of intimidating others into compliance. *H. erectus* operated in a new and very effective way. Parents could work as a team to sustain themselves and their offspring. For the first time, real leadership was called for, with both parents making real decisions that would influence the whole family.

THE UPPER PALEOLITHIC TRANSITION

The third major shift, to *H. sapiens,* known as the Upper Paleolithic Transition (UPT), has been difficult to date, but the current estimate places it around 200,000 years ago. *Homo erectus,* whose tools were probably limited to fairly simple ones made of wood and stone, evolved into modern *Homo sapiens,* the human species that developed language, sophisticated technologies, and complex tribal institutions and which developed civilization as we know it today.[14] Steven Pinker described the dramatic UPT shift in these terms:

> Calling it a revolution is no exaggeration. All other hominids come out of the comic strip *B.C.,* but the Upper Paleolithic people were the Flintstones. More than 45,000 years ago they somehow crossed sixty miles of open ocean to reach Australia, where they left behind hearths, cave paintings, the world's first polished tools, and today's aborigines. Europe (home of the Cro-Magnon) and the Middle East also saw unprecedented arts and technologies, which used new materials like antler, ivory, and bone as well as stone, sometimes transported hundreds of miles. The toolkit included fine blades, needles, awls, many kinds of axes and scrapers, spear points, spear throwers, bows and arrows, fishhooks, engravers, flutes, maybe even calendars. They built shelters, and

they slaughtered large animals by the thousands. They decorated
everything in sight—tools, cave walls, their bodies—and carved
knick-knacks in the shapes of animals and naked women, which
archeologists euphemistically call "fertility symbols." They were
us.... [This] first human revolution was not a cascade of changes
set off by a few key inventions. Ingenuity itself was the invention,
manifested in hundreds of innovations tens of thousands of miles
and years apart.[15]

Pinker's observation that "ingenuity itself was the invention"
suggests the emergence of an independent drive to comprehend.
If so, how and why did it happen?

Most scholars have been relying on natural selection to explain
the changes that created the new species, *H. sapiens*. I do not
disagree that natural selection played a major part, but so too, as
Darwin argued, did sexual selection (as discussed earlier regarding
the family), and a third selection mechanism proposed by Darwin,
"group" selection. How could this have happened?

THE ROLE OF LANGUAGE

I will start by asking, What could have been the final trigger,
the proximate cause—as cooking had been earlier—of this complex change process? Most scholars point to the emergence of
complex language. Physiologist Jared Diamond, for example,
attributes it to the development of an anatomy capable of complex spoken language—"the structure of the larynx, tongue, and
associated muscles that give us fine control over spoken sounds."[16]
Unfortunately, these vocal structures consist mostly of soft tissues
that quickly decay, rather than bones, making it very difficult to
date the origin of human language.

Terrance Deacon, a neuroscientist and evolutionary anthropologist, argues that the feature that distinguishes human
cognition from cognition in other species is the use of a complex system of multilevel symbolic representation.[17] This symbolic
system has developed from simpler forms of representation, such
as sketches and drawings,[18] in parallel with the long and gradual
development from simpler forms of communication—such as
facial expressions, verbal calls, hand sign language, and single
words—to complex verbal language with its sentence structure

and capacity for abstract conceptualization.[19] Moving language to higher levels of abstract representation greatly facilitated the hominids' social life and served, by mutual reinforcement, to gradually increase the size of the prefrontal area of the human brain where multiple ideas can be reviewed together (see Chapter Two on the role of the dorsolateral module). Symbolization created pressure for more working memory, and an enlarged working memory made more symbolization possible. Deacon concludes that the ability to use multiple levels of abstraction made humans much more versatile at solving problems—able to "think outside the box"—and became pre-wired or innate in our nature. To me, this suggests the emergence of a new innate, independent drive, the drive to comprehend (dC).

THE INTERMINGLING OF SKILL SETS

Archeologist Steven Mithen supports Pinker's case that the minds of the earlier hominids gradually became pre-wired with various specialized skill sets, but goes on to argue that the skill-set modules, originally disconnected from one another in the brain, eventually became directly connected via our working memory in the dorso-lateral module of the prefrontal cortex.[20] With this development, humans could use all their skills simultaneously to address complex, multidimensional problems which would have been beyond reach otherwise. Mithen concludes, quite persuasively, that it was the *intermingling* of our genetically based skill sets that made the UPT possible. And imagine where Helen would be if she had the ability to gauge other people's feelings and the ability to put her thoughts into words, but at any given moment could only use one or the other.

CHANGES IN THE DRIVES

I propose that the Upper Paleolithic Transition to *H. sapiens* was also brought on by two important changes in our set of innate drives.

As I have already suggested, our problem-solving ability evolved during the UPT into a fourth *independent* drive, the drive to comprehend (dC). I believe this was accomplished, as was the establishment of dB in males, primarily by female mate selection. And indeed, David Buss's aforementioned study found that women, and eventually men also, seek mates who, among other things, are intelligent.[21] To Buss, the widespread consistency of his findings suggests that these mate-selection criteria have been an innate skill set in all humans.

I also believe that, at some time during the UPT, the drive to bond was extended beyond the nuclear family. I propose that this happened primarily by a Darwinian process known as "group selection." Darwin pointed out that "although a high standard of morality gives but a slight or no advantage to each individual man and his children over the other men of the same tribe . . . yet an advancement in the standard of morality will certainly give an immense advantage to one tribe over another."[22] This remark led to a long-running controversy about whether an altruistic trait which could be disadvantageous to individual survival (for example, a willingness to risk one's life for someone else) could be incorporated into a species's genetic inheritance or would inevitably be eliminated in competition with those who lacked that trait and were out only for themselves (known to biologists as "free-riders"). This latter view became the dominate one among biologists. Only recently has this orthodox view been seriously challenged. The new view is that, while free-riders might out-compete altruists within a group, altruistic groups would clearly out-compete selfish groups.[23] Evolutionary biologists E. O. Wilson and David Sloan Wilson have demonstrated that this group selection process is not only theoretically possible but has occurred several times with great success among social insects.[24]

Critics, however, still point out that, with respect to humans, there is no explanation of how those within a group who exhibited altruistic behavior (in my terms, those with an independent drive to bond on equal footing with the drives to acquire and defend) could ever get the upper hand over the free-riders. It would seem the free-riders would have to prevail because they would have no scruples about how they did it. But, as explained earlier regarding pair-bonding, while males with an independent drive to bond would probably get less food and fewer chances at sex than males who had no such drive, more of their offspring would live to maturity. As far as evolution is concerned, that's the trump card and nothing else really matters. I would argue, therefore, that the independent drive to bond—first to the family and later to the tribe—emerged because, right from the start, it provided a genetic survival advantage to the *individuals* involved via the children who carried their genes. Selection could take hold at the inter-group level because sex selection, along with natural selection, had earlier made the dB males dominant within groups.

Sanctions to control free-riders could have been as simple as face-to-face social ostracism and isolation or as severe as exile and execution. Wrangham has pulled together evidence that many hunter-gatherer tribes have made use of capital punishment to eliminate free-rider traits from their communities.[25] But it has proven to be impossible to eliminate their genes from the gene pool. We will return to this issue in later chapters, which describe how the struggle with the free-riders in our midst has been played out over the centuries. As we will see, the biologists who predicted that free-riders would wipe out any altruistic tendencies were not entirely off the mark.

Once the drive to bond was extended to a group larger than the family, that group would take on the characteristics of a traditional tribe and would gain enormous competitive advantages over groups that had no such tribal character. Using their new tool of language and their enhanced cognitive capacity, these transitional hominids could conceptualize and *name* their collectives. Rituals of initiation and membership could be developed, along with all the symbols, songs, dances, and creation stories needed to reinforce the individual's commitment to the tribe. This would have been the start of the implicit (or explicit) social contract of mutual caring between individual members and their tribe. The ideal among members would be "all for one and one for all." All studies of contemporary tribes note the strength of the tribal bond. It is a lifetime commitment. It is not hard to imagine the superior strength of a committed tribe in direct competition with another tribe of equivalent size but made up of unbonded, uncommitted individuals.

Although we know little about the early development of the tribe as a social form—it left neither fossils nor documents—we can imagine the tribe's contribution to the development of leadership and governance as opposed to dominance. It simply wouldn't do to control the members of such a group by sheer violence; that would destroy the mutual trust and care which made the tribe successful in the competition for survival. We know that some tribes selected dual chiefs—a "peace" chief for handling domestic issues and a somewhat subordinate "war" chief to handle external affairs with other tribes. Many tribes made prominent use of a council of elders who would deliberate on important tribal issues and work toward a check-and-balance consensus decision. This council seemed to be selected informally by the tribal members on the basis of experience and signs of wisdom. Chiefs seemed in many cases to have been selected from the council. The historians E. Schultz and M. Tougiasw captured the essence of this new kind of leadership in their description of Massasoit, the Pokanoket chief who befriended the Pilgrims in Plymouth: "Massasoit's influence was extensive but his power far from absolute.... He maintained loyalty only by being a wise, compassionate leader."[26]

Further on, I will point out that the scope of the drive to bond continues to widen, and it will be an issue of increasing importance in Parts Two and Three of this book.

Trial by Fire

E. O. Wilson, whose career has been devoted to the study of social insects such as ants, bees, and termites, has evidence that it was severe environmental pressure that pushed a few social insect species into an entirely new level of social interdependence.[27] These species had already evolved what Wilson calls pre-adaptations toward such social behavior when they experienced a long period of extremely intensive environmental pressure. During this "trial by fire," these species developed group-oriented traits, hence their *eusociality*. This led these insect species to, in Wilson's language "a point of no return," a tipping point at which every individual's survival depended entirely on the survival of the group. These few species have since become very successful. They dominate all other species of their genera around the globe. Of course our hominid ancestors were not insects, but Wilson argues that something similar might have happened to humans.

What we now know, in regard to humans, is that, beginning around ninety thousand years ago, there was an extreme and persistent drought in East Africa which lasted about thirty thousand years. The early *H. sapiens* must have struggled mightily to avoid starvation, and the population must have shrunk considerably. Geneticists and evolutionary biologists now hypothesize, on the basis of the remarkable sameness of genes across all contemporary human populations, that our ancestors, around sixty thousand years ago—that is, around the end of the drought—were a group of as few as four to ten thousand people, living somewhere along the Rift Valley of Africa, and that key genetic changes that made the UPT possible took place amongst this relatively small group. Around fifty thousand years ago, *H. sapiens* began to expand out of Africa and around the globe.

On the basis of evidence such as Pinker has summarized regarding the UPT revolution, I suggest that the few bands who survived this terrible drought had done so by evolving a tribal moral code such as "all for one and one for all"—the human equivalent of the intense sociality of Wilson's insect survivors. They had emerged with a stronger drive to bond. Evidence from excavations in Zaire that date from around this time indicate that these early humans most likely lived in sophisticated, fairly egalitarian hunter-gatherer bands or tribes, probably equipped with wood, stone, bone, and fiber tools, and with shelters, clothing, fire, and cooking. To have created such artifacts and taught young people to create and use them, each tribe would probably have been a well-developed, tightly bonded organization with a common language and would probably have had a decision-making or governance system with a simple chain of command, a division of labor, a set of behavioral ground rules along with the appropriate rewards and punishments, and a belief system, including myths and rituals, that addressed the meaning of human existence. Such a group, so well equipped technologically, socially, and spiritually, would have had an enormous advantage over all other creatures, including other varieties of hominid.

In fact, the Sans people—the "bushmen" of the Kalahari desert in Namibia—who have been determined through genetic analysis to be the "oldest" human group, displayed all the features just cited before their way of life was seriously disrupted by the intrusion of modern life. The extensive early motion pictures that the Marshall family made of the life of the Sans people testify to these facts.

Figure 3.1 summarizes how the different selection mechanisms have cumulatively contributed to the transitions discussed so far. The reader will also note the addition of cultural selection and science selection as an indication of where the cutting edge of change in human affairs has moved. (The cultural impact was discussed in Chapter Two, but we will not be addressing the impact of science until Chapter Seven.) Here we find the variety/selection/retention process at work purely in the minds

FIGURE 3.1. ACCUMULATIVE SELECTION TIMELINE OF MAJOR HOMINID TRANSITIONS.

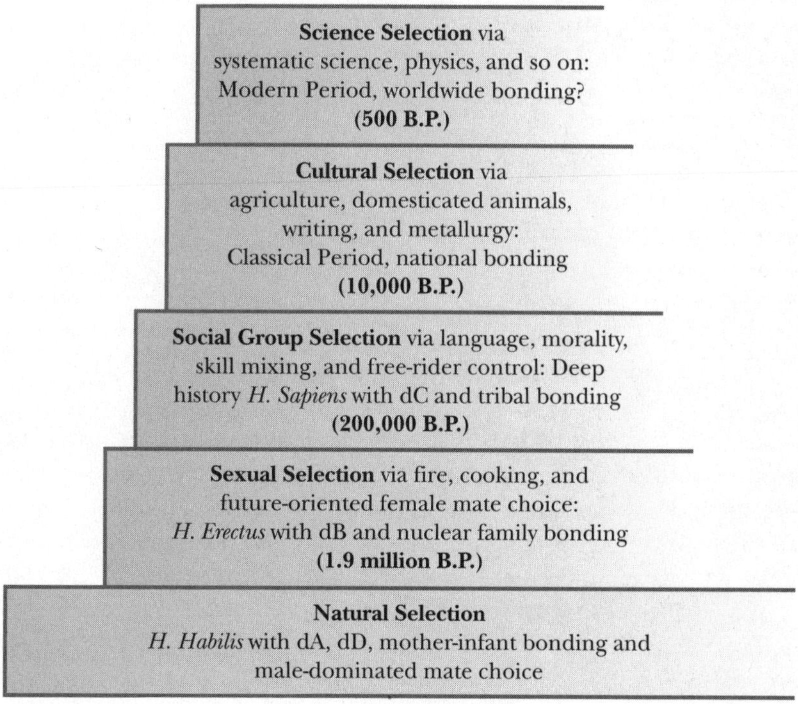

Science Selection via
systematic science, physics, and so on:
Modern Period, worldwide bonding?
(500 B.P.)

Cultural Selection via
agriculture, domesticated animals,
writing, and metallurgy:
Classical Period, national bonding
(10,000 B.P.)

Social Group Selection via language, morality,
skill mixing, and free-rider control: Deep
history *H. Sapiens* with dC and tribal bonding
(200,000 B.P.)

Sexual Selection via fire, cooking, and
future-oriented female mate choice:
H. Erectus with dB and nuclear family bonding
(1.9 million B.P.)

Natural Selection
H. Habilis with dA, dD, mother-infant bonding and
male-dominated mate choice

Note: Dates are approximate B.P. (before present).

of humans rather than moving through their genes. All five of these basic selection influences on human behavior are currently at work, and none of them can be stopped.

My description of tribal society indicates that *H. sapiens* emerged from the UPT, and in particular from the thirty-thousand-year drought, with something more than just a stronger drive to bond. The drive was not only stronger but smarter, more sophisticated, and versatile. We have already seen that, within an individual, the four drives are in continual conflict. Needless to say, within a group of people there will be continual conflicts of their various drives. The larger the group and the more different things it tries to do collectively—from hunting to teaching children to joking to arm wrestling to celebrating the turn of the seasons and the creation of the world—the more possibilities there are for conflict. Humans must have developed an ability to manage most of these conflicts well enough to maintain the solidarity of the tribe. And so, to complete our story, we must now show how humans could have evolved their moral sense or conscience.

THE DEVELOPMENT OF MORALITY

The issue of human morality has been a difficult one for the human sciences to deal with. Historically it has been left to philosophers and theologians. In fact, some scientists argue that science should have no voice in this matter. Stephen Jay Gould devoted an entire book to making this argument.[28] Nevertheless, this issue is now being studied systematically by evolutionary biologists and the various social sciences.

It may surprise you, as it did me, to learn that Darwin considered morality to be *the defining feature of H. sapiens.* He wrote, "I fully subscribe to the judgment of those writers who maintain that of all the differences between man and the lower animals, the moral sense of conscience is by far the most important."[29] As for how we acquired this moral sense, he thought it very likely that "any animal whatever, endowed with well-marked social instincts . . . would inevitably acquire a moral sense or conscience, as soon as its intellectual powers had become as well, or nearly as well, developed as in man."[30] These insights of Darwin's provide the foundation for the proposition that human morality is a genetically based skill set that evolved in humans during the UPT because it usefully enlisted the "new" drive to comprehend (Darwin's "intellectual powers") in supporting the expanding drive to bond (Darwin's "social instincts").

Morality as an Innate Skill Set

This view of morality is certainly not what any of us learned as we grew up. In fact, it is quite contrary to the common view of where morality comes from, yet entirely consistent with the common view of "doing the right thing." If morality is a skill set devised to coordinate two innate, unconscious, and potentially conflicting drives, it is rooted in emotions rather than cognitive principles. Indeed, several contemporary scholars from different disciplines have already come at this point from different directions. For example, primatologist Frans de Waal has written, "Aid to others in need would never be internalized as a duty without the fellow-feeling that drives people to take an interest in one another [what I would call the independent drive to bond]. Moral sentiments came first; moral principles, second."[31] E. O. Wilson writes that the evidence indicates that "moral concepts are derived from innate emotions" rather than being "constructed from mode and custom."[32]

If our moral skill set is, as Darwin explicitly said, the *inevitable* outcome of our possession of dC and dB, it should be possible to deduce the universal moral rules.[33] If one feels *driven* to establish a relationship of mutual trust and caring with another person, what kinds of behavior would help fulfill that drive? This question leads logically to the ancient and practical rule that one would treat the other person, most of the time, as one would desire to be treated oneself—the "Golden Rule," which has appeared in religious and philosophical teaching with regularity for three thousand years.[34] From this start, and presuming that the other person has the same innate independent drives to acquire, defend, bond, and comprehend, what behavior would help that person fulfill those four drives without violating one's own drives?

In support of the other's drive to acquire:

- Help enhance the other's capacity to acquire resources.
- Facilitate the other's pleasurable experiences.

In support of the other's drive to bond:

- Keep one's promises rather than breaking them.
- Seek fair exchanges rather than cheating exchanges.
- Return a favor with a favor.

In support of the other's drive to comprehend:

- Tell truths rather than falsehoods.
- Share useful information rather than withholding it.
- Respect the other's beliefs, even in disagreement, rather than ridiculing them.

In support of the other's drive to defend:

- Help protect the other, rather than harming or abandoning him or her.
- Help preserve the other's property rather than stealing or destroying it.

On the basis of this logic and of the existence of many other skill sets that support the other three basic drives, I hypothesized in my 2004 article "The Biological Basis of Morality" that moral intuitions such as these have become an innate (genetically based) skill set, applied whenever a person wishes to bond with another person or with a collective.[35] I will be referring to these rules in what follows as the *four-drive moral code*.

These rules are not always observed, of course. The other drives are always competing for preference, and sometimes they win. Therefore, the true confirmation of my hypothesis is not perfect observance of the rules but feelings of guilt—of a "bad conscience"—when they are knowingly broken.

The scholar who has gone the furthest in testing for the content of the moral intuitions of all humans is Marc Hauser.

His pathbreaking 2006 book, *Moral Minds: How Nature Designed Our Universal Sense of Right and Wrong*,[36] pulls together his own work on the subject and the widely scattered research of many others, mostly evolutionary psychologists and specialists in child development. He not only reports strong evidence of an innate moral sense in all humans but also presents empirical evidence for the existence of some specific moral rules, primarily the following:

- Help others rather than harm them.
- Tell truths, not lies—except for white lies.
- Keep promises.
- Seek fair exchanges that reflect merit differences.
- Detect and punish cheaters.

Hauser argues that human morality probably co-evolved gradually alongside the innate skill set(s) for language, a view which is consistent with my own analysis. He also reports the evidence that these moral rules appear in early childhood, leading him to argue that they are genetically based, although certainly subject to cultural variation. The Ultimatum Game experiments discussed in Chapter Two offer a clear example of both the universality of the sense of fairness and its cultural variation.

This combination of nature and nurture, instinct and culture, regarding morality was consistently pointed out by Darwin. As he said, "Although man has no special instincts to tell him how to aid his fellowmen, he still has the impulse, and with his improved intellectual faculties would naturally be much guided in this respect by reason and experience.[37] This entire line of theorizing about morality has recently been pulled together in a comprehensive way by an evolutionary psychologist, Jonathan Haidt, who argues that human morals are based on intuition and emotions and are subsequently elaborated and rationalized by reasoning. "The social intuitionist model ... proposed that morality, like language, is a major evolutionary adaptation for an intensely social species, built into multiple regions of the brain and body, that is better described as emergent than as learned, yet that requires input and shaping from a particular culture. Moral intuitions are therefore both innate and enculturated."[38]

DID THE BRAIN EVOLVE LEADERSHIP CAPABILITIES?

My answer to the question that gives this chapter its subtitle is, of course, yes. Every step of the evolutionary path we have been tracing involved a change in the human brain that has enhanced our capacity to adapt to contemporary changing environments. First we mutated to enable our brains to grow larger. Then we evolved an expanded memory, a place to store what we learned from our evolving cultures and our own experience. Then we evolved ever more sophisticated skill sets, each capable of further development with practice and experience. We developed new drives in our limbic systems—to bond and to comprehend. Much of our increased brain space was committed to the modules in the prefrontal cortex that check and balance our expanded collection of drives. (Although we don't know details on how this development happened, we know it did.) All of this enhanced our capacity to adapt to changes in our circumstances, which is to say, our capacity for leadership.

PEOPLE-W/O-CONSCIENCE

I argued earlier that, when hominid females began selecting mates for the drive to bond as an independent drive, *H. habilis* had begun its transition to *H. erectus* with its pair-bonded nuclear family. This mate-selection process started reducing the proportion of the male population who were "free-riders"—those who had no drive to bond. The later transition from *H. erectus* to *H. sapiens,* with its tribal bonding, depended on further reducing the proportion of free-riders to the tipping point at which they could be marginalized by various forms of face-to-face social control. But to marginalize such dangerous people must at first have been very difficult, and to eliminate them entirely might well have been impossible. Did the genes supporting bonding become universal, or were some genomes without dB still present in the *H. sapiens* pool, producing a small number of humans without a drive to bond and therefore without a healthy moral sense or conscience? If they survived then, are they still here?

Given current evidence, the answer is yes. And given the historical record, we can say that this fact appears to have had terrible consequences. Therefore, the continued existence of *people-w/o-conscience,* as I will call them, urgently needs to be confirmed or refuted by further research and, if confirmed, widely recognized. Darwin himself warned us about such people. In speaking of social instincts, he said, "A man who possessed no trace of such feelings would be an unnatural monster."[39]

As we will see, his use of the word *monster* was no exaggeration. Nevertheless, it is a word which implies that people such as Hitler are outside the natural order of things, unpredictable and incomprehensible. I don't think we need to see them that way anymore. Horrible they are, but not unpredictable and incomprehensible.

PSYCHOPATHY: A THREE-DRIVE GENETIC DEFECT

At the start of the nineteenth century, scientists and physicians began taking note of a strange type of person who was not insane in the "raving lunatic" sense and who often seemed quite intelligent, sociable, and well-adjusted, but who nevertheless committed acts of unprovoked violence, deception, and betrayal which defied comprehension. A term was coined for them — *psychopath* — composed of Greek roots meaning "suffering soul." This name was in fact a mistake; what makes psychopaths so incomprehensible is their complete lack of empathy, shame, or remorse. They are not suffering souls at all, only inflictors of suffering on others.

Psychologist Robert Hare, a leading researcher on psychopathy for more than twenty-five years, describes psychopaths as "social predators who charm, manipulate, and ruthlessly plow their way through life, leaving a broad trail of broken hearts, shattered expectations, and empty wallets. Completely lacking in conscience and in feelings for others, they selfishly take what they want and do as they please, violating social norms and expectations without the slightest sense of guilt or regret."[40] They have "an insatiable appetite for power and control"[41] combined with "a deeply disturbing inability to care about the pain and suffering experienced by others—in short, a complete lack of empathy."[42]

Without any knowledge of the theory of human drives presented in this book, Hare has identified psychopaths (whom biologists and economists call "free-riders" and whom sociologists and some psychologists tend to call "sociopaths") as human beings with a genetic defect—the lack of a drive to bond. It follows that they are incapable of empathy and have *no* skill set of conscience or morality. Their jaw-dropping selfishness and lack of empathy does not come from exaggerated drives to acquire and defend. Those drives are normal—which means they are innate, unconscious, independent, and *insatiable*—but are not checked and balanced by a drive to have trusting and caring relationships with others. In a sense, they are wild animals—motivated mainly by the two universal animal drives—but with all the advantages of a human drive to comprehend.

Hare has developed a preliminary set of conclusions about how the abnormality works, its genetically based nature, its locus in the limbic area of the brain, its likely forms of overt expression, its various effects on others, and the success and failure of various forms of corrective intervention. I will use Hare's own words to summarize these findings:

> Like the color-blind person, the psychopath lacks an important element of experience—in this case, emotional experience—but may have learned the words that others use to describe or mimic experiences that he cannot really understand.... Recent laboratory research provides convincing support for these clinical observations. This research is based on evidence that, for normal people, neutral words generally convey less information than do emotional words.... When we used this laboratory task with prison inmates [measuring their brain's response to both neutral and emotionally loaded words by means of electrodes on their scalp connected to an EEG recorder], the nonpsychopaths showed the normal pattern of responses... but the psychopaths did not: *They responded to emotional words as if they were neutral words.* This dramatic finding provided strong support for the argument that words do not have the same emotional or affective coloring for psychopaths as they do for other people.[43]

> It is the *emotionally charged* thoughts, images, and internal dialogue that give the "bite" to conscience, account for its powerful control over behavior, and generate guilt and remorse for transgressions. This is something that psychopaths cannot understand. For them conscience is little more than an intellectual awareness of rules others make up—empty words. The feelings needed to give clout to these rules are missing.[44]

Though psychopaths may talk a lot they are not necessarily skilled wordsmiths. It is primarily the "how," not eloquent use of language, that attracts our attention and cons us. Good looks, a touch of charisma, a flood of words, contrived distractions, a knack for knowing which buttons to press—all these can go a long way toward obscuring the fact that the psychopathic presentation is nothing more than a "line."[45]

Many people feel uncomfortable applying the term *psychopath* to children. They cite ethical and practical problems with pinning what amounts to a pejorative label on a youngster. But clinical experience and empirical research clearly indicate that the raw materials of the disorder can and do exist in children. Psychopathy does not suddenly spring, unannounced, into existence in adulthood. The precursors of the profile...first reveal themselves early in life.[46] ...Many adolescents go off track because of a poor social environment—abusive parents, poverty, lack of job opportunities, bad companions—but the psychopath seems off track from the start. Again: Why? Unfortunately, the forces that produce a psychopath are still obscure to researchers.[47] ...On balance,...I can find no convincing evidence that psychopathy is the direct result of early social or environmental factors.[48] ...There is no evidence that parental behavior causes psychopathy.[49]

Although psychopathy is not primarily the result of poor parenting or adverse childhood experiences, I think they play an important role in shaping what nature has provided. Social factors and parenting practices influence the way the disorder develops and is expressed in behavior. Thus, an individual with a mix of psychopathic personality traits who grows up in a stable family and has access to positive social and educational resources might become a con artist or white-collar criminal, or perhaps a somewhat shady entrepreneur, politician, or professional. Another individual, with much the same personality traits but from a deprived and disturbed background, might become a drifter, mercenary, or violent criminal.... No amount of social conditioning will by itself generate a capacity for caring about others or a powerful sense of right and wrong.[50]

[With] few exceptions, the traditional forms of psychotherapy, including psychoanalysis, group therapy, client-centered therapy, and psychodrama, have proved ineffective in the treatment of psychopathy. Nor have the biological therapies, including psychosurgery, electroshock therapy, and the use of various drugs, fared much better.[51]

A basic assumption of psychotherapy is that the patient needs and wants help for distressing or painful psychological and emotional problems.... Psychopaths don't feel they have psychological or emotional problems, and they see no reason to change their behavior to conform to societal standards with which they do not agree.... Psychopaths are not "fragile" individuals. What they think and do are extensions of a rock-solid personality structure that is extremely resistant to outside influence.[52]

To a large extent, the personalities of psychopaths are "carved in stone." There is little likelihood that anything you do will produce fundamental, sustained changes in how they see themselves or others.[53]

The fact is, compared with other major clinical disorders, little systematic research has been devoted to psychopathy, even though it is responsible for far more social distress and disruption than all other psychiatric disorders combined.[54]

I have quoted Hare at such length because so many of his details corroborate my argument that psychopathy is not something unaccountable but rather the predictable outcome of a particular genetic defect.

Three recent and independent twin studies provide conclusive evidence of the genetic basis of psychopathy.[55] (Twin studies are well established as the most reliable way to distinguish genetic influences on behavior from environmental influences.) A study using fMRI technology offers evidence that psychopaths' abnormality has to do with emotions, not with faulty reasoning, and that it originates in the limbic area of the brain. To quote the study's conclusion: "These data suggest that the *affective* [emotional] abnormalities so often observed in psychopathic offenders may be linked to deficient or weakened input from limbic structures."[56] The limbic area is, of course, exactly where the drive to bond is normally located and where its absence should be detected.

The behavior of someone without a drive to bond is so dramatically different from that of normal people that we find it very hard to see it accurately for what it is. (Recall, in Chapter Two, how baffled the human experimenters were by the chimps who could never take a helpful hint about which container held the food. Most of us are even more baffled by a fellow human who absolutely lacks the feelings and reactions that we experience in ourselves and others all day every day.) Hare himself tells the story of an article of his which was rejected; the editor objected that some of the EEGs in the article "couldn't have come from real people." In fact, they came from psychopaths.

But knowing the prehistoric origin of the small minority of psychopaths raises the question: What have they been up to all this time? The psychopaths studied by Hare seem to have played rather marginalized roles in society, albeit with painful results for the few people directly involved. This would be similar to the role hypothesized for them in hunter-gatherer tribes, as discussed earlier. But is this the whole story?

Hare estimates—conservatively, he insists—that "there are at least 2 million psychopaths in North America; the citizens of New York City have as many as 100,000 psychopaths among them."[57] In 2006, he and Paul Babiak coauthored a book, *Snakes in Suits,* that focuses on those clever psychopaths who manage to achieve powerful positions in business and government.

In Parts Two and Three, I will be emphasizing good leadership, but I will do this partly by contrasting it with the bad, and even evil, leadership practiced by people-w/o-conscience. In Part Two I will review the historic record of leadership in the spirit of a historical detective, trying to tease out the evidence indicating whether or not heads of state have displayed the behavior patterns of good leaders or that of people-w/o-conscience. Later in Part Two we will look for the presence or absence of such people among the CEOs of large corporations, as well as among the leaders of the institutions of religion, art, and science. Part Three will examine these same themes in contemporary organizations with more attention to critical problems and remedial action suggested by our understanding of the leadership brain.

HISTORIC
LEADERSHIP
PATTERNS

CHAPTER FOUR

ALL ABOUT LEADERS
Good, Bad, and Misguided

To do unto others as you would have them do unto
you—is the foundation stone of morality.
— CHARLES DARWIN[1]

DEFINITIONS OF LEADERSHIP

My general definition of leadership is a combination of two others. Jay Lorsch, a professor at Harvard Business School, defined a leader as "an individual who influences others to follow her lead." Lorsch pointed out that he chose to mention "influence" rather than "power" because leadership can be based on charisma (dB) or knowledge (dC) as well as on the power to reward (dA) and punish (dD) that often goes with hierarchical position.[2] This definition builds on the four innate drives of Renewed Darwinian Theory at work in our brains. To this I add the definition offered by Chatman and Kennedy: leadership is "a process of motivating people to work together collaboratively to accomplish great things."[3] This definition reinforces the key role of group collaboration, a cornerstone of the survival of our species, and, by mentioning motivation, introduces the element which will be a focus of this chapter: the leader's need to satisfice the four drives of those he or she leads. This definition of leadership applies at all levels, from parent-child relationships to the everyday relationships between friends to the relationships within companies and nations to the relationships between companies and the public and between one nation and another. They also apply to collective goals of all kinds, from running a car pool to running a corporation, and to leaders of impact ranging from Hitler to Gandhi.

But beyond a definition of leadership that is all-encompassing, we need criteria to make distinctions between good leadership, bad leadership, evil leadership, and misguided leadership. Our understanding of RD Theory—of the drives and the decision-making process within our brains—allows us to make these distinctions in a way that is not arbitrary and that is, in fact, both scientific and moral (value-oriented) at the same time:

- Good leadership is the exercise of influence over group stake-holders (acting as followers) that helps them satisfice all their four drives in a reasonably balanced and long-term sustainable manner, while also satisficing the leader's own four drives and keeping people-w/o-conscience out of power positions.
- Bad leadership is the exercise—by a person-w/o-conscience—of influence over followers so that the leader maximizes the fulfillment of his or her drive to acquire (while satisfying his or her dD and dC) by any means possible and without regard to the consequences for others.
- Evil leaders are the subset of bad leaders whose disregard for others extends to killing them.
- Misguided leadership is the exercise of influence over followers that helps them satisfy only one or two of their four drives while influencing them to ignore or suppress their other drives. Such leaders are typically misguided by following the example of bad or evil leaders, by being intimidated by such leaders, or by acting on incomplete leadership theories. This kind of leadership can also cause great damage by allowing people-w/o-conscience to assume positions of power over others.

These definitions of leadership should make it clear that each and every normal (with a conscience) human has the potential to be a good leader and that everybody, including people-w/o-conscience, will inevitably be a leader to some extent.

I realize that my definition of good leadership may sound unreasonable—like defining a good baseball player as one who hits a home run with bases loaded every time he's at bat. But we will see that good leadership is not really that extreme and not at all out of the question.

In my definition of good leadership, I used the adjective *long-term sustainable,* a term familiarized by the environmental movement. I want to emphasize this term's clear link to Darwin's overall theory of evolution. As explained in Chapter Two, the drive to bond was essential to the survival of our early ancestor, *Homo erectus,* and it still is essential to our own survival. Good leadership must satisfice and sustain the drive to bond going forward, and it is this long-term sustainable process that puts meaning and purpose into the human story. (More on this in Chapter Seven.)

EVIL LEADERSHIP: NAPOLEON'S RISE TO POWER BY ANY MEANS

Milton's *Paradise Lost* begins in Hell; the portrayals of God, Christ, Adam, Eve, and the angel Raphael do not come until we've had a good look at Satan and the other fallen angels. I, too, will begin in hell, with a look at leaders-w/o-conscience. Recall that these are leaders with a genetic defect: they lack the drive to bond and therefore have no inherent concern for the trust or care of others, only a practical concern to get along with (that is, manipulate) others in order to get what they want. However successful and civilized some of them seem, they are the psychopaths we met at the end of the previous chapter.

How common are such leaders? I mean this as a scientific question but I must admit I do not yet have a rigorous answer. Lacking that, I made a list of sixty-nine leaders who, in my judgment, are among the most impactful leaders of history and categorized them in the institutional tracks I will be following in Chapters Five, Six, and Seven (see Exhibit 4.1). I then rated them as good, misguided, bad, or evil, according to the criteria in the earlier list, and found I had forty good leaders, eight misguided leaders, and twenty-one bad or evil leaders. Given Hare's estimate that psychopaths constitute around 2 percent of the population—and that probably far less than 1 percent are the really bright ones who might, on a strictly random basis, achieve prominence as high-impact leaders in society—it is surely notable

EXHIBIT 4.1. IMPACTFUL LEADERS IN HUMAN HISTORY.

Political Leaders	Economic Leaders	Religious Leaders	Science Leaders
Hammurabi	di Medici	Moses	Plato
Ramses II	Rothschild	Confucius	Aristotle
Pericles	Vanderbilt	Jesus	Copernicus
Cyrus II	Carnegie	Muhammad	Galileo
Alexander	Gould	Luther	Bacon
Caesar	Rockefeller	Calvin	Machiavelli
Augustus	Edison	Gandhi	Newton
Cleopatra	Rhodes	King	Smith
Constantine	Ford	Dalai Lama	Watt
Charlemagne	Dupont		Faraday
Genghis Khan	Krupp		Darwin
Tamerlane	Sloan		Marx
Henry VIII	Watson		Maxwell
Elizabeth I			Bell
Isabella			Freud
Columbus			Einstein
Cortes			Bohr
Peter			
Catherine			
Louis XIV			
Washington			
Napoleon			
Lincoln			
T. Roosevelt			
Leopold II			
Churchill			
Stalin			
F. Roosevelt			
Hitler			
Mao			

that 30 percent of the people I rated as high-impact leaders throughout history struck me as bad or evil leaders, people-w/o-conscience. Since I am, obviously, not an expert on all these leaders, my ratings of them are not reliable at the individual level—which is why I don't categorize them in Exhibit 4.1. But I believe that my gross estimate of 30 percent is significant. This fits my argument that, if one's sole ambition in life is to acquire as much material wealth and power as possible, and if one has a clever brain, one has a better chance to get to the top of society's power and wealth hierarchies than normal four-drive humans with a balanced agenda. I believe that this 30 percent estimate also justifies the close attention I pay throughout this book to leaders-w/o-conscience.

It is also notable that, of my twenty-one leaders-w/o-conscience, fourteen were political leaders and six were economic leaders. Sheer ruthlessness could make Stalin a political leader or Jay Gould a business leader, but sheer ruthlessness could never have made Newton a scientific leader nor Jesus a spiritual leader.

Consider Napoleon, a figure of unending fascination, certainly a leader of many followers, even after his fall from power and even after his death. Emerson chose him for his book *Representative Men* as the exemplar of "the man of the world." But what kind of leader was Napoleon by our standards? Biographer Alan Schom[4] presents a stream of examples of ruthlessness, persistent and flagrant lying, and other actions without conscience. I offer only one of Schom's examples, Napoleon's withdrawal from his Egyptian campaign.

In 1798, Napoleon, at that time a divisional general, was authorized to launch a campaign to conquer Egypt. But in the process of landing in Egypt, he lost the entire French fleet that had been his troop transport. After the hard fighting required to, at least temporarily, subdue the Egyptian forces, he had to face up to his entrapment in Egypt. In desperation he decided to return to France by land, making his remaining men march and fight their way through Syria and Turkey. After his army forced the garrison at Jaffa to surrender, Napoleon found himself with four thousand prisoners on his hands. His aides-de-camp had promised the prisoners their lives, but Napoleon did not want to have to deal with them and finally had them all executed; some were even bayoneted along the edge of the sea rather than shot in order to save ammunition. His private secretary, Louis Bourrienne, later recalled, "As they stepped forward they found death and perished in the surf.... That atrocious scene still makes me shiver whenever I think about it ... the day of that blood-bath."[5]

Even though later Napoleon's advance was completely stopped at Acre and he was forced to retreat to Egypt, he claimed a total triumph. "Lies, every one of his claims, from beginning to end," Bourrienne later acknowledged. "I must confess I had found it painful recording these official works at his dictation." But when Bourrienne protested at the time, Napoleon replied with a smile, "*Mon cher,* you are a simpleton. You really don't understand a thing."[6]

Schom describes Napoleon's next move:

> Even before reaching Cairo with his defeated remnants, Napoleon had made up his mind to execute his long-prepared plans to abandon the army and return to France. The excuse he would use was that France was again at war with Austria and Russia—that French armies were faltering and needed his presence to recoup their recent losses. He had played all his cards [in Egypt] and failed completely. He had lost approximately three thousand men in the Syria campaign, in addition to the seven thousand or so lost earlier in Egypt.... The country had revolted against his rule.... And of course his navy had been sunk or captured. His splendid, ill-conceived expedition was a total failure.[7]

> And yet, this misadventure actually made possible the greatest event of his life. [His coup that secured his leadership of France as First Consul]. On returning to France, he was surprised to find himself greeted as a conquering hero. The French people knew little of his phenomenal disasters but much of the fact that he had captured Malta, the Pyramids, and Egypt, that he had taken Cairo from the heathens and won a resplendent victory over the Turks at the Battle of Abukir. It was in this light that he was permitted to rush to Paris as the conquering hero and sweep all before him.[8]

Schom makes the following comment in a medical appendix: "From a psychiatric viewpoint, all my medical friends confirm that Bonaparte—like so many dictatorial rulers—would according to the U.K. Mental Health Act of 1983 be described as a psychopath.... The combination of ... traits is reflected by the various kidnappings, murders, lies, and wars he perpetrated to the very end."

In short, Napoleon fits my definition of an evil leader, a leader-w/o-conscience who resorts to killing others to get his way. He exercised enormous influence over his followers in order to fulfill his own drives to acquire and then defend his own power and glory. He consistently did so by any means he could get away with, while inflicting vast harm on millions of innocent people.

I include this material neither to take Napoleon down a peg nor to guarantee that my book is unlikely to sell in France. Napoleon is here as an example of how dangerous leaders-w/o-conscience are, in part because we find it so hard to believe that anyone can behave so ruthlessly, especially people who *seem* to be so accomplished or admirable. When such behavior is brought to light, it is often treated as something mysterious, outside the normal workings of nature. (How *could* Bernie Madoff, who had so many friends and gave so much money to charities, ruin so many innocent people's lives? How is it possible?) But when we understand how the leadership brain works in normal people with four drives, we can understand how it must work in people-w/o-conscience, who are missing the drive to bond. As Bourrienne found, it is horrible to witness, but it does make sense. And if it makes sense, we have some hope of protecting ourselves from it. I will take that point up in Chapter Ten.

MISGUIDED LEADERSHIP ON OFFSHORE OIL PLATFORMS

Two psychologists, Robin Ely of the Harvard Business School and Debra Meyerson of Stanford University, heard about a pair of offshore oil rigs in the Gulf of Mexico on which a well-established ultra-macho culture had been transformed into something almost unbelievably different by a switch from misguided leadership to good leadership. The following account is based on their study.[9]

The employees and managers who work on these platforms range from very highly trained engineers to comparatively low-skilled high school graduates. Their environment has two salient features: it is very dangerous and very expensive. The culture in these all-male societies is macho; the assumption is that only really tough, roughneck men can handle these hazardous conditions. The men are expected to prove to their bosses every day how tough they are.

> Dangerous workplaces offer men a prime opportunity to continually assert and prove their masculinity, while also earning a living. Previous research had identified three main ways of demonstrating one's masculinity: *appearing* physically tough, *appearing* technically infallible, and *appearing* emotionally detached.
>
> And indeed, that's typically how it is on an oil rig. The men do physically tough work and avoid asking for help or asking to take a break; they avoid asking for help when something isn't working right or they're not sure what to do; and whatever happens—frustration, injury to themselves or their mates, a brush with death—they avoid letting on that it upsets them. As one might imagine, this was often unsafe or inefficient. An offshore installation manager (in charge of an offshore rig), a 27-year veteran of the company, described the life: "The field foremen were kind of like a pack of lions. The guy that was in charge was the one who could basically out-perform and out-shout and out-intimidate all the others. That's just how it worked out here on drilling rigs. So those people went to the top, over other people's bodies in some cases. Intimidation was the name of the game.... They decided who the driller was by fighting. If the job came open, the one that was left standing was the driller. It was that rowdy."
>
> Needless to say, the meanest sonofabitch on the rig was not necessarily the most competent manager of this billion-dollar facility. And as another worker noted, this was not a recipe for safety: "If you didn't bust your butt 110 percent, 12 hours a day, they sent you home because there were a lot of folks who wanted the job. A lot of unsafe things went on."

Here, I would say, is a fine example of what I call "misguided leadership," which I defined earlier in the chapter as "the exercise of influence over followers that helps them satisfice only one or two of their four drives while influencing them to ignore or suppress their other drives." Let's look at how the four drives were either satisficed or frustrated.

The oil rigs did function: oil was drilled, the company profited, and the men earned good pay with which to support themselves and their families. So dA was well taken care of.

As for dB, there was undoubtedly camaraderie and friendship, but at the same time, the drive to bond was constantly foiled by the imperative to neither ask for nor offer help and to show little or no concern for the difficulties or hazards experienced by one's workmates. To show such feelings would be "sissy stuff."

The drive to comprehend (dC) was being seriously short-changed because of the social restriction on admitting problems and seeking help. There was undoubtedly a treasure trove of knowledge and know-how scattered amongst these men, but too many opportunities to learn from each other were lost. As we will see, these macho men really did have the innate, independent drive to comprehend, but a powerful social force was suppressing it.

Certainly dD was being shortchanged. The work was inherently dangerous but the macho culture made it even more dangerous, both by pressuring workers to do dangerous things and to work themselves to exhaustion (to prove their manliness) and by keeping them from helping each other out of dangerous or overtaxing situations.

Finally, we have to note that, to the extent that dB, dC, and dD are frustrated, the men were forced to work less efficiently and less safely than they could have done and were therefore creating less of a valuable product than they could have done, so even dA was being shortchanged.

In sum, here was leadership which fulfilled dA fairly well but which shortchanged the other three drives, which in turn even shortchanged dA. This was not evil leadership. The ultimate goal was undoubtedly profit, but there was not a single-minded focus by the leadership on profit regardless of the cost to others. It's not that there was no concern for safety or competence at all, but that there was not as much as there could have been had the leadership taken a more balanced approach to all four drives.

My definition of misguided leadership included one final point: "This kind of leadership can also cause damage by allowing people-w/o-conscience to assume positions of power over others." We can see that the oil rig's promotion strategy was truly like a "pack of lions," as the top manager put it. Male lions do fight to pick the leader of their pride and so did these men. This process might well have allowed a person-w/o-conscience to gain power and do a significant amount of harm, while still being clever enough to conceal this behavior from his bosses.

You may ask why I call this type of leadership "misguided," as opposed to "unbalanced" or "one sided" or "poor but not bad." The oil rig crews, both the men and their bosses, tended to believe that their macho culture was necessary, that nothing less would get the job done. And this theory, although not the best, was plausible. The macho culture was working—the oil was being drilled—and certainly a physically weak, overly fearful, or mechanically inept man would not have been a successful leader on the rig. Both leaders and followers were making what seemed to them to be reasonable trade-offs between dA (the need to get the job done and make a living along with the need for status and self-esteem) and dD (the need not to sink too low in status and become subject to disrespect and hazardous harassment), between dA and dB, and between dA and dC. These men simply were misguided into following the macho leadership style without understanding that a much better method, good four-drive leadership, was available.

GOOD LEADERSHIP: DISPLACING MACHO CULTURE ON OFFSHORE OIL PLATFORMS

As I indicated, Ely and Meyerson were intrigued by the reported transformation of this culture on two new rigs, which they refer to in their (as yet unpublished) study as Rex and Comus. As they put it:

> Rex and Comus, built in the mid 1990s, were designed from the start to reflect the company's new priorities. A senior manager described the company's initiative as follows: "We were more and more frustrated with the fact that people kept getting hurt. In the early nineties we made the commitment to reduce injuries that became known as 'Safety 200'." Organizational changes resulted in an 84 percent decline in the company's accident rate; in the same period, the company's level of productivity (number of

barrels), efficiency (cost per barrel), and reliability (production "up" time) came to exceed the industry's previous benchmark.

Everyone—workers, managers, contractors—attributed the difference to the company-wide initiative to make safety its highest priority. Macho behavior was unsafe and therefore simply unacceptable. Ely and Meyerson suggest that the company's safety initiative was indeed a catalyst that made Rex and Comus different from their predecessors, but they also conclude that the difference represented more than a response to prohibitions about acting in unsafe ways—it arose from a transformation in how the men experienced themselves and their relationships with one another. This transformation—prompted by organizational conditions stemming from the safety initiative—released the men from the role of masculinity commonly associated with dangerous work. In contrast to other dangerous workplaces, here was a place where tough strong workers readily conceded their physical limitations and their mistakes and openly shared their fears and anxieties, while demonstrating sensitivity to others.

As Darwin said, our uniquely human strategy for survival is not simply to win the fight or flee for our own lives (dA) or (dD) but *to figure out* (dC)—right on the spot, if necessary—how to keep ourselves *and each other* (dB) safe from harm. Safety, then, is an issue that tends to bring all four drives to the fore (since it is often an attempt to meet dA needs that puts someone in danger in the first place). A number of companies have found that an all-out attempt to bring down the accident rate of dangerous work brings all kinds of other success along with it,[10] and the RD Theory has shown us why this is to be expected.

With this in mind, let's look in more detail—through Ely and Meyerson's eyes—at what happened on the Rex and Comus oil rigs.

The leadership of Rex and Comus worked to orient its workers to at least three purposes that connected them to others: ensuring each other's safety [dD]; building a sense of community, trust, and teamwork [dB]; and learning about and contributing to the work as a valuable activity in its own right [dC and dA]. In the past, these workers had found little meaning in their work, partly because they perceived the company as indifferent to their welfare, but their experience on Rex and Comus was different.

Rex's goal statements, *generated by the employees themselves* and conspicuously posted in every meeting room, included "no one gets hurt," "people supporting people," "respect and protect the environment," "every drop as fast as possible," and "not a penny more than it takes." Of these goals, safety was clearly the highest priority, and company policies convinced the workers that the company took this goal seriously as an end in itself. For example, *everyone* who entered the facility received instructions on how to shut the platform down—in other words, halt the flow of gas and oil—if safety demanded it. The instructions were clear: at first sight of a potentially hazardous situation—for example, a spark or a flame—shut the platform down; no questions asked and no repercussions for a mistaken judgment, even though shutdowns were costly. The company's socialization of recruits emphasized this policy. As one veteran operator explained, "We set them down at orientation when they first get here, and we tell them that you've got the right to shut down anything if you feel it is unsafe."

One production operator noted, "What keeps us together is our goals. Sometimes we have to make trade-offs between them—for example, 'safety' and 'every drop.' But we never compromise safety." Another explained, "It makes you feel good to know that they're more worried about your safety than they are about getting the job done." He contrasted today's commitment to safety with the lip service of the past.

Other organizational features were designed to develop and sustain a sense of community. For example, every meeting began with the ritual of "recognitions"—recognizing workers who got up in the middle of the night to help solve a problem, went out of their way to help a coworker, sacrificed a family visit when duty unexpectedly called, and so on. As a production operator noted, "It's a necessity because we have to support each other and give positive reinforcement daily." One worker described the change in culture this way: "The culture at these other places was mistrust and people watching their backs. We went from living in that world to living in a good world."

It was leadership—what I would call *good* leadership—that brought such changes about. One worker described Rex's senior manager as follows: "He opened our eyes to the personal side of things. He knows that the work's going to get done, but he cared more about the relationship side of everything. And the fact that he was able to take that vision and make us all see it without thinking that it was top-down, driven down our throats, gave us the tools and allowed us to open our own eyes to it." In this one bit of testimony, one hears dA ("the work's going to get done"), dB ("the personal side of things"), dC ("make us see [the vision]," "open our eyes"), and dD (not "driven down our throats"). That's four-drive leadership, but it's also four-drive followership because the employee recognizes that all four of his basic human drives are being addressed, even if he doesn't think of it in those terms.

Organizational features designed to enhance safety and a sense of community and which communicated that the company cared about its workers may in turn have prompted workers to recognize and invest in the intrinsic value of their work—producing gas and oil for consumers. Ely and Meyerson observed workers going out of their way to increase productivity. At morning meetings, they actively discussed productivity metrics and exchanged ideas about how they could increase output, sometimes seeking data beyond the standard reports. While the motivations for such behavior were probably complex, there was some evidence that they felt proud to make a difference to company stakeholders, such as consumers. A drilling foreman described feeling "great when I drive down the street and see people putting gas in their cars so they can get to work and take their kids to school. It may sound funny, but that just makes me think this is a great thing I get to do out here." A mechanic explained why he went to the trouble to get guidance on a task: "It gives you that warm fuzzy feeling to know that you looked at everything [carefully] and ensured you don't lose a half-million dollars in the process."

One might wonder—as evolutionary biologists have traditionally wondered about the rise of a "domesticated" human species—how the lambs survived among the macho wolves. Ely and Meyerson were told that "men who behaved too aggressively failed to move up in the company ... because their behavior made it unsafe for others to express themselves openly" and therefore literally unsafe to work. Had the company ignored this crucial issue, its effort to transform the oil rig culture might well have failed. Because the company did take this issue seriously, it may well have prevented some people-w/o-conscience from "earning" power positions by means of their own aggression and cleverness rather than by helping others to satisfice all four of their natural drives.

Just as concern for employees' safety involves a uniquely human blend of dA, dD, dB, and dC, training also tends to be an occasion for the addressing of all four drives. In a business setting, dA is often—but not always—the initial motivation for training. But training can also address the trainees' innate, independent dC, which is not the exact same thing as fulfilling the organization's need for employees with a particular skill. And by addressing an individual's dC, leaders show that they care about the individuals themselves, which fulfills dB on both sides of the bargain. As for dD, training may address it directly if people are being taught how to avoid or handle a particular danger, but training may also address dD by making individuals more economically valuable and less likely to find themselves underpaid or unemployed. One manager, having attended a team-building program, was struck by the fact that the company "spent *overtime,* spent *money* for you to go."

The title of Ely and Meyerson's paper is *The Organizational Reconstruction of Men's Identity.* The authors conclude that the company's leaders changed not only the work culture of these platforms but even the personalities of the platform workers. And the change these researchers see is, to my eyes, clearly in a direction that fits the RD Theory. In response to leadership behaviors, the workers' behaviors changed in such ways as

- Welcoming training opportunities to become safer and more effective workers
- Expressing their concerns and fears publicly so that these can be addressed to increase safety and effectiveness

- Acknowledging their mistakes openly so that all can learn
- Responding to opportunities to help other workers be safe and effective
- Becoming involved with and identifying with the larger purpose of the firm, which is to be of service to customers and the wider society; in other words, to act and feel more like owners and less like hired hands
- Reporting that they felt they were becoming better people, "kinder and gentler," and appreciating what their leaders had done for them in this regard
- Reporting that they were still quietly proud of their strength and courage in the face of unavoidable danger, but no longer felt required to prove it every day
- Reporting that they were proud of the skills they were learning, proud to "know what I'm doing"
- Reporting that they had acquired a "sense of community" with people "who trusted each other"

These men were discovering *within themselves, at work,* their innate drive to bond with their coworkers in long-term relationships of mutual trust and caring and their innate drive to comprehend themselves and their environment—half of their fourfold humanity. (Their awareness of their other two drives was already obvious.) Management's role was primarily to *stop* suppressing these feelings, which they did by acknowledging the workers' feelings as legitimate and by speaking openly of their own similar feelings. Management was not, as the one worker put it, driving these things down their throats.

It seems safe to say that the change in leadership behavior had an important influence on these observed and self-reported changes in worker behavior and, in turn, on the various overall performance indicators of the entire system. I would explain it by saying that we humans have evolved to survive by fulfilling and defending our needs in groups and by constantly figuring out the best way to deal with each situation (as opposed to obeying a limited set of instincts in every situation). This is how we function best. Leadership that keeps us from fulfilling all four of our own and each other's independent drives does not allow us to function at our best. Leadership that encourages and enables us to fulfill all four of our own and each other's independent drives will, most of the time and in the long run, get better results. That's what happened on Rex and Comus. It is also a long-term sustainable strategy.

Other Evidence of the Effectiveness of Good/Moral Leadership

That the Rex and Comus outcome was not a lucky result but a scientifically predictable result is strongly indicated (it's too soon to say "proven") by a study conducted by my former coauthor Nitin Nohria and his Harvard colleagues, Boris Groysberg and Linda-Eling Lee. Their survey of a large sample of multinational firms found that an organization's ability to meet the four fundamental drives explains, on average, about 60 percent of employee variance on motivational indicators of their emotional involvement and attachment to the work of their organization (previous models have explained about 30 percent). As the authors put it, "A company can best improve overall motivational scores by satisfying all four drives in concert." And as the RD Theory would predict, "The whole is more than the sum of its parts. A poor showing on just one drive substantially diminishes the impact of the other three drives."[11]

An important wave of current research, known as "positive psychology" and centered around the University of Michigan, sheds light on good leadership from a different direction. There is abundant empirical evidence that when *positive* factors (such as friendship, pride, safety, or appreciation) are given greater emphasis than *negative* factors (such as disapproval, insecurity, or disappointment), people are more inclined to engage in positive change (such as innovation or greater teamwork).[12] Our four-drive model of the brain tells us that what is universally "positive" for human beings is the balanced satisficing of our four innate drives. So even from the perspective of positive psychology, if the leaders of Rex and Comus wanted to make a positive change—safer work practices—they went about it in just the right way.

MORAL LEADERSHIP

Morality has been a controversial term to apply to leadership. Some liberal scientists are suspicious of what seems to be a forced merger between science and religion. It reminds them of the rejected medieval connection of church with state. Religions, after all, have always seemed to have a monopoly on the subject of morals. But not anymore. In Chapter Three, I cited some of the breakthrough findings which argue that humans have an innate and universal moral sense, as Darwin himself said. Science is making progress in understanding this observation, not only in behavioral terms but even in flesh-and-blood biological terms. As evidence of this new trend, several books have recently appeared with the word *moral* in their titles, including *Moral Markets, Moral Minds, Moral Machines, Moral Intelligence,* and *Moral Leadership.* Such books can be placed alongside earlier classics, *The Moral Animal* and *Moral Sense.*

Consider again the four-drive moral code which I deduced in Chapter Three as a logical, *inevitable* consequence of the existence of our innate cognitive powers (dC) and our social instincts (dB). Much of this "ideal" moral behavior is, in fact, to be found in Ely and Meyerson's description of Rex and Comus, indicating that these are not utopian rules crafted by ideal philosopher-kings but that the behavior described is indeed natural to human beings. (Natural, but not always followed—obviously it can be thwarted and distorted.)

I do not hesitate, then, to say that what I have called good leadership is in fact moral leadership. And with science getting into the morality issue in a big way, we need to begin treating the propositions that (1) good leadership is the same as moral leadership, (2) misguided leadership is amoral leadership, and (3) bad and evil leadership is immoral leadership as *scientific* propositions. This new role for science does not turn out to be in opposition to the enduring insights of religion. A very distinguished rabbi, asked about the essence of religion, replied, "The Golden Rule says it all. All the rest is commentary."

Of course, there are technical aspects of leadership that one need not classify as moral or immoral, but even these elements need to be guided by moral standards because they will either fulfill or frustrate one or more of the four drives present in all stakeholders. For example, deciding how to carry out all the necessary steps for a U.S. auto firm to manufacture an auto part overseas is not in itself a moral issue, but any decision to outsource that replaces workers receiving a living wage with workers receiving a less-than-living wage is a moral issue. And if it is an immoral decision, then even those who participate in the purely technical aspects of the outsourcing (filing permits, for example) will, if they know about it, feel their drive to bond being violated rather than fulfilled. A very great many middle- and low-level people who participated in subprime mortgage lending and in the creation and sale of subprime-mortgage-backed securities (to be discussed in Chapter Nine) must now be feeling violated in just this way.

My original definition of good leadership now needs to be clarified in the following way. Good/moral leadership is the process of influencing followers by practicing the Golden Rule with all stakeholders in a particular way—that is, by helping them satisfice their four drives in a balanced manner and helping oneself do so as well—while keeping people-w/o-conscience out of power positions.

Easier said than done, of course. In each concrete situation, the facts about the various stakeholders and the environment they face must be taken into account to find the path from the status quo position to greater four-drive fulfillment for every stakeholder. This will make great demands on the prefrontal cortex's ability to respond to conflicting emotional markers from the four drives and on the neocortex's treasure of memories and skill sets. The greater the number and diversity of the stakeholders, the greater the leadership challenge. But I propose that when a significant fraction of the people in leadership positions at all levels have learned to see what they are doing in these four-drive and impulse/check/balance terms, we can enjoy a steady improvement in leadership and the consequences that flow from it, akin to the steady improvement we have grown accustomed to seeing in science, technology, and medicine.

PREVIEW OF CHAPTERS FIVE THROUGH SEVEN

The next three chapters examine critical leadership episodes in the evolution of broad clusters of human institutions that have channeled and expressed our four innate independent drives in historic times.

In Chapter Five, I will discuss leadership episodes in the evolution of political institutions from tribes to city-states, nations, empires, and eventually to constitutional republics. These institutions reflect primarily the human drive to bond and secondarily the drive to defend. We will see that the biggest success so far in the history of political systems, the Constitution of the United States, was achieved by using the impulse/check/balance process in ways that closely resemble the balancing process used by our prefrontal cortex.

In Chapter Six, I take a similar approach to the evolution of economic institutions, which reflect primarily the drive to acquire. We will see how the biggest success so far in the history of economic systems, the modern corporation, is itself seriously flawed by its failure to take a four-drive balancing form as is done in the human brain.

In Chapter Seven, I address the leadership of the institutions of religion, art, and science, which reflect primarily the drive to comprehend—to give meaning to human life.

In all three chapters, I will pay particular attention to the interplay between the vast majority of humans who have an innate, independent drive to bond (and the resulting sturdy conscience) and that small minority of humans who do not—the people-w/o-conscience. As was suggested by my informal tally of high-impact leaders early in this chapter, it is in the political and economic realms—the realms most clearly dedicated to fulfilling dA and dD—that we will find that such people have made and are still making a huge and disastrous difference. This finding may help us make sense of the cryptic comment of James Joyce's Stephen in *Ulysses*, "history is a nightmare from which I am trying to awake." I would generalize this to all of us. "Human history is a nightmare from which all of us are trying to awake." I hope to provide a clear wake-up call.

CHAPTER FIVE

LEADERSHIP AND THE HISTORIC EVOLUTION OF POLITICAL INSTITUTIONS

A man who wishes to make a vocation of being good at all times will come to ruin among so many who are not good. Hence it is necessary for a prince who wishes to maintain his position to learn how not to be good, and to use this knowledge or not to use it according to necessity.
— MACHIAVELLI[1]

THE FALL AND THE RISE OF LEADERS-W/O-CONSCIENCE

To understand leadership we need to understand how it has evolved in political institutions. I think most observers would agree that human political institutions in historical times have moved—however slowly and unevenly and with however many setbacks—toward vesting political power in wider and wider segments of the population. We seem to be gradually evolving from a world of tyrants, despots, emperors, and absolute monarchs toward a world of constitutional republics. In Renewed Darwinian Theory terms, we might say that we are gradually evolving from a world of misguided, bad, or downright evil leaders toward a world of good/moral leaders—"good/moral" in the technical RD Theory sense that they at least try to address all four drives for all citizens.

All to the good, but why is this evolution necessary? How did four-drive humanity come to find itself in a world of tyrants, despots, emperors, and absolute monarchs. in the first place? And why has it been so hard to replace that with a world of constitutional republics? For that matter, why have constitutional republics been the replacement of choice (in cases in which one despotism wasn't simply replaced by another)? I believe that the RD Theory concept of good/moral leadership sheds new, important, and practical light on these fundamental leadership questions.

In Chapter Three, I presented the argument of many mainstream evolutionary biologists that *altruism* (their term for our drive to bond), although it undeniably exists, could not possibly have been the product of Darwinian evolution. Individuals driven exclusively by a genetically based drive of self-interest (our drive to acquire) would have outcompeted any individuals with genetically based impulses to help others (our drive to bond), eliminating any such genetic predisposition from the gene pool. Altruism, biologists argue, can only be learned, not inherent.

The RD Theory, in common with biologists E. O. Wilson, David Sloan Wilson, and others, argues that a genetically based drive to bond could indeed have evolved, not by Darwinian natural selection alone, but by a combination of natural selection, sexual selection, and group selection. As we saw in Chapter Three, early *H. erectus* took the initial steps by establishing pair-bonding. Early *H. sapiens* completed the transformation by extending bonding to the tribe. One might expect that people missing the dB genes—the people I am calling "people-w/o-conscience"—would have disappeared from the population, but the evidence says this did not happen. Where, then, have they been all this time? And if they have been among us all this time, why haven't they managed to outcompete four-drive humans and drive us to extinction?

I argued that, within tribes, people-w/o-conscience could be marginalized by the face-to-face social controls possible in such a society. But the transition to "civilization," with its population explosion, let the genie back out of the bottle, poisoning the ranks of leadership at all levels to this very day. It created an opening for people-w/o-conscience to gain enormous power in large-scale political institutions, and the frequent success of such people has misguided or intimidated many other people into imitating them.

THE CULTURAL SHIFT TO CIVILIZATION AND THE RISE OF LEADERS-W/O-CONSCIENCE

The population explosion was partly an effect of the spread of *H. sapiens* tribes around the globe. But it was also the specific result of four big cultural or technical innovations—settled agriculture, animal and plant domestication, metallurgy, and writing—which ingenious humans, motivated by their dC, began to develop some ten thousand years ago. Civilization had arrived, and the effects have been obvious and spectacular. Among the many developments were the rise of cities as trading centers and the transfer of valuable arable land from collective ownership to private ownership. Those who gained control of the trading centers and arable land gained enormously in wealth—far beyond their individual powers of acquisition—so that societies became much more stratified. It appears that the combination of population increase and stratification meant that face-to-face social control of the remaining people-w/o-conscience began to break down. In this environment, an individual whose drive to acquire (dA) was unchecked by a normal drive to bond (dB) was likely to be more successful at gaining power and thereby wealth by any and all means. Such people would have no qualms about taking advantage of the "naive" drive to bond embedded in the limbic brains of the vast majority. Such people could also take full advantage of the common dD tendency to be intimidated by and deferential to powerful authority figures. (This tendency was dramatically demonstrated in the Milgram experiments.[2]) Such people, unburdened by the internal restraint of a healthy conscience, would not hesitate to manipulate and exploit the drives of the majority in order to gratify their own insatiable drives to acquire wealth and power. (Keep in mind that we all have an insatiable drive to acquire, but most of us have a strong counterforce in the drive to bond.)

And exploit they did. As cities grew into city-states, nations, and empires, leaders-w/o-conscience could marshal ever-greater military and legal power (the latter backed by the former); they themselves were typically above the law. Slavery and its near equivalent, serfdom, flourished. Some leaders-w/o-conscience co-opted the symbols, ideologies, and social structures of various religions in order to augment their own power. (Further on, we will see what was probably history's greatest example of that.) The general pattern of monogamous pair-bonding shifted somewhat back toward polygamy among the elite, which inevitably would have increased the proportion of people-w/o-conscience in the population (or at least, amongst the elite).

In a way, then, the biologists were right: under certain social or technical conditions, people-w/o-conscience can indeed out-compete ordinary four-drive people. Extinction, however, is not an option. The tyrant who kills all his subjects must go back to picking berries and throwing rocks at squirrels.

The historical record of early empires, though limited, sup-ports this story of dominance by people-w/o-conscience. Cognitive psychologist David Geary describes despots as "individuals who have considerable social power and whose behavior is not typ-ically constrained by affective or social consequences; they are also likely to differ from other people in terms of empathy for others [missing their dB], and in terms of the intensity of their need for social dominance [unchecked dA]." Geary then points out that "[these] individuals and their coalitions gained control of the first six human civilizations—ancient Mesopotamia, Egypt, the Aztec and Inca empires, and imperial India and China. Across these and many other civilizations, the activities of despots were centered on diverting the material and social resources of the culture to themselves, and to their kin, typically to the detriment of many other people. On the basis of the historical record, they lived in opulence, and the men almost always had exclusive sexual access to scores—sometimes thousands—of women."[3] Geary has, perhaps inadvertently, offered a succinct description of people-w/o-conscience and their conduct as leaders. We will see much more of this further on.

The Dark Ages as an Age of Leaders-w/o-Conscience

The aptly named "Dark Ages" (roughly 300 A.D. to 1000 A.D.)[4] offer many examples of leaders-w/o-conscience, an aspect of that period which has been carefully described but poorly understood. Perhaps the supreme example is the history of the Byzantine Empire, which lasted from 330 A.D. to 1453 A.D. In J. J. Norwich's excellent book, *A Short History of Byzantium*,[5] the author acknowledges that he admires much about the Dark Ages and feels that it does not deserve its name and reputation, yet we will see how well even his account supports my argument that, for many centuries, much of human civilization was largely under the control of leaders-w/o-conscience.

The story of the Byzantine Empire begins with Constantine the Great, born around 274 A.D. His father, Constantius Chlorus, was one of the Roman Empire's most successful generals and in 305 became one of two joint emperors. By 311, both joint emperors had died, and Constantine found himself one of three rivals for the emperor's purple toga. The rivalry soon turned to war. Constantine quickly negotiated a truce with one rival, Licinius, then destroyed his other rival, Maxentius, in a famous battle. He later instigated a civil war with Licinius and, after nine long years of vicious war, he finally defeated him and promptly put him to death. He also managed to rid himself of his wife, the Empress Fausta, his oldest son, Cripus, and the son of Licinius; no reasons for their executions were ever made known. Constantine was clearly above the law.

At that time, Christianity, although spreading rapidly throughout the Empire, was a persecuted movement, considered by the Roman elite to be the dregs of society. Nevertheless, its hour had come. Constantine reported much later to his official biographer that, just before the battle with Maxentius, he saw a vision of a cross in the sky bearing the motto "Hoc Vince" ("Conquer by This"). From that time on, he placed the cross on the shields of his soldiers and apparently decided to be the protector and patron of his Christian subjects. Constantine issued the Edict of

Milan, granting Christianity full legal recognition throughout the Empire. To further signal his new support, Constantine presented the Christian Pope Melchiodes with an elegant palace as the papal residence in Rome. The pope accepted the gift, and Christianity was on its way to power.

Constantine then undertook to unify a split in the Christian church, primarily over the critical question of the divinity of Jesus, in order to rule the empire with the help of a unified church. He presided over the Council of Nicea (the influence of which is felt to this day) and successfully "established a great confederacy of the Eastern and Western Churches and his own moral supremacy over it."[6] When a group of Christians known as Gnostics disagreed with the Council's conclusions, Constantine used his troops to brutally eliminate them (see more about this in Chapter Seven).[7] Back in Rome, Constantine built great basilicas dedicated to St. Paul and St. Peter, enhancing Christianity's status as the established church of the Empire.

But Constantine seems to have concluded that Rome was too pagan and too republican to be an appropriate capital of his new Christian Empire.[8] He began the construction of a fabulous new capital in the small town of Byzantium, in what is now western Turkey, which was renamed Constantinople (and is now Istanbul). At its center stood a hundred-foot column of Egyptian porphyry. "On its summit stood a statue. Its body was that of an Apollo by Phidias but its head, which was surrounded by a metal halo with a representation of the sun's beams radiating from it, was that of Constantine himself."[9] Constantine was not the first Roman emperor to represent himself as divine, but he was certainly the first to do so as a Christian.[10]

I will stop here, having reached only page 21 of Norwich's 431-page book. But the pattern is already clear and, as Norwich covers the subsequent eleven centuries, it does not change much. The end of an emperor's reign—often by palace assassination or military revolt and only occasionally by natural death—almost always triggered a bloody multiyear struggle among rival contenders. Whoever came out on top could expect uprisings by local warlords in outlying provinces, major wars with adjacent empires, or struggles—sometimes ideological but sometimes military—between the eastern and western branches of the

Christian Church, not to mention the chaos and disruption of the Holy Crusades. Warfare of one kind or another was virtually continuous. That much of this violence was committed in the name of Jesus, who taught people to love not only their neighbors but even strangers, shows the degree to which Christianity had been co-opted by Constantine the Great.

Since records of this period almost exclusively concern the elite, we have to exercise our imaginations to visualize what life must have been like for an ordinary person suffering the consequences of rule by leaders-w/o-conscience which Norwich has described. What would it have been like to be coerced into the military under such leaders? What would it have been like to be a craftsman in a city with the local leader-w/o-conscience as your only protector? What would it have been like to have been a well-to-do merchant with the emperor's minions out scouting for treasures to confiscate for his palace? And finally, what would it have been like to have been a slave or a serf at the mercy of leaders-w/o–conscience? Life in hunter-gatherer bands would undoubtedly have been rough, but healthy adults would almost certainly have had more control over their own fates during the Paleolithic Age than during the Dark Ages.

MACHIAVELLI'S CLEAR VIEW OF LEADERS-W/O-CONSCIENCE

Were Constantine and his successors actually people-w/o-conscience—people genetically lacking the drive to bond and the conscience that comes with it? It is obviously impossible to do any clinical testing, but we can try judging them against a list of twelve behavioral symptoms that Robert Hare carefully developed and that has been widely used as a diagnostic tool. I would judge Constantine, for example, as displaying eight of the twelve behaviors, with no information regarding the other four. Certainly this is not definitive, but it is highly suggestive. We have, in addition, another window into such leaders—a guide to practical leadership written by the foremost leadership scholar of his day, the famous Niccolò Machiavelli.

Machiavelli was born just fourteen years after the Byzantine Empire ended with the fall of Constantinople. He came from a middle-class family of Florence whose members had held a number of minor offices in the city's government. Eventually he became the trusted first assistant of Piero Soderini, the gonfaloniere (head of state) of Florence. Fourteen years of service in this post gave Machiavelli the opportunity to observe firsthand the major European political figures of his time. He was also a careful student of the available histories of earlier governments, going back to ancient Greece.

When his mentor, Soderini, was ousted from power by the return of the Medici in 1512, Machiavelli was purged, imprisoned, tortured, and forced into retirement. At this point he undertook the writing of his treatise, *The Prince,* dedicated to Florence's new head of state, Lorenzo de Medici, and offering him practical advice on how to achieve his goals.

What was this knowledge and what were those goals? Machiavelli took it for granted that "great men" were "ruled by an insatiable desire for material gain and driven by the principle of self-interest."[11] In RD Theory terms, Machiavelli assumed that ambitious leaders were leaders-w/o-conscience. His advice to this clientele was entirely to the point:

> How praiseworthy it is for a prince to keep his word and to live by integrity and not by deceit everyone knows; nevertheless, one sees from the experience of our times that the princes who have accomplished great deeds are those who have cared little for keeping their promises and who have known how to manipulate the minds of men by shrewdness; and in the end they have surpassed those who laid their foundations upon honesty.... A wise ruler, therefore, cannot and should not keep his word when such an observance of faith would be to his disadvantage.... But it is necessary to know how to disguise this nature well and to be a great hypocrite and a liar; and men are so simpleminded and so controlled by their present necessities that one who deceives will always find another who will allow himself to be deceived.... A prince, therefore, must be very careful never to let anything slip from his lips which is not full of the five qualities mentioned above; he should appear, upon seeing and hearing him, to be all mercy, all faithfulness, all integrity, all kindness, all religion. And there is nothing more necessary than to seem to possess this last quality.... Everyone sees what you seem to be, few perceive what you are, and those few do not dare to contradict

the opinion of the many who have the majesty of the state to defend them.[12]

From this arises an argument; whether it is better to be loved than to be feared, or the contrary. I reply that one should like to be both one and the other; but since it is difficult to join them together, it is much safer to be feared than to be loved when one of the two must be lacking.... Men are less hesitant about harming someone who makes himself loved than one who makes himself feared because love is held together by a chain of obligation which, since men are a sorry lot, is broken on every occasion in which their own self-interest is concerned; but fear is held together by a dread of punishment which will never abandon you.[13]

Well used are those cruelties (if it is permitted to speak well of evil) that are carried out in a single stroke, done out of necessity to protect oneself, and are not continued but are instead converted into the greatest possible benefits for the subjects. Badly used are those cruelties which, although being few at the outset, grow with the passing of time instead of disappearing.[14]

To illustrate the proper and improper use of "cruelty," Machiavelli cited Agathocles of Syracuse and Oliverotto of Fermo. Both of these men were successful generals who were ambitious to be princes. Each lured all the powerful and wealthy leaders of his city-state into a closed space, locked them in, and had his soldiers kill them all. Agathocles subsequently adhered to Machiavelli's advice and had a long and prosperous reign. Oliverotto did not and met a quick and bloody end.

A SOLUTION TO THE PROBLEM OF LEADERS-W/O-CONSCIENCE?

The recovery of civil life from the devastation of the Dark Ages was slow. Under the influence of Enlightenment thinkers such as Thomas Hobbes, John Locke, Montesquieu, and David Hume, nations throughout Europe struggled to find more humane ways to govern, but with limited success. It was in the new world of America that this process reached an important turning point in the formation of the United States government under its Constitution, a governance structure based significantly on the work of the Enlightenment thinkers and expressly designed to avoid the concentration of political power in any one leader's hands and thus end the rule of "tyrants," the Framers' term for our leaders-w/o-conscience. It was a bid to overturn and reverse the long march of one despotic government after another. As one participant, Simeon Baldwin, said, "Revolutions in government have in general been the tumultuous exchange of one tyrant for another.... Never before has the collected wisdom of a nation been permitted quietly to deliberate, and determine upon the form of government best adapted to the genius, views and circumstances of the citizens. Never before have the people of any nation been permitted, candidly to examine, and then deliberately to adopt or reject the constitution proposed."[15] (Think of Helen's deliberation versus the lunge of a shark.)

We are fortunate that the Framers of the Constitution left us with an amazingly complete record of this examination and deliberation, and I will make extensive use of it here. The two most amazing aspects of the story, from the standpoint of this book, are the way the Framers zeroed in on controlling the leadership of people-w/o-conscience and the way their approach to political decision making mirrors the impulse/check/balance decision-making process of the human prefrontal cortex (described in Chapter Two). James Madison, one of the principal authors of the Constitution, captured this point in his oft-quoted sentence, "What is government itself, but the greatest of all reflections on human nature." The Framers were quite consciously trying to construct a durable, effective, beneficent government based on the most up-to-date knowledge of what they referred to as *human nature,* a term which appears fifteen times in *The Federalist Papers*[16] and which corresponds to what I have been referring to as the innate features of the brain.

The Framers needed to figure out what "being human" meant—what ultimate drives made people tick—because they recognized that they would have to guide and constrain these drives if they hoped to fashion a government that functioned for the benefit of all the people. The Framers knew that the informal social controls which worked fairly well within a family and amongst neighbors were not sufficient to govern a populous and growing nation. They were keenly aware of Montesquieu's observation, echoing Aristotle's, that republican governments tended to fail as they grew larger.

All traditional governments at that time, and all earlier governments that anyone knew about, stood on three foundations: the monarchy, the aristocracy, and the established church. These institutions were considered essential for civilization and for social order among the masses. But the Framers saw, from their own observations of Europe, that these three pillars supported governments which consistently oppressed the many for the benefit of the elite. (We now know that even the empires in the New World, such as the Inca and the Aztec, which had no connection at all to European history, used the same three pillars to control the masses for the benefit of the elite.) The Framers agreed that they wanted to abandon all three of these institutions as building blocks for their new government. But how could it be done without replacing the evils of tyranny with the evils of anarchy?

The Framers began with the premise that government was absolutely essential if human beings were going to live together in peace and prosperity. As John Jay said, "Nothing is more certain than the indispensable necessity of Government, and it is equally undeniable, that whenever and however it is instituted, the people must cede to it some of their natural rights, in order to vest it with requisite powers."[17] Hamilton made this same point with an added slap at the "exceptionalist" attitude some Americans had about themselves:

> Men are ambitious...has it not invariably been found, that momentary passions and immediate interests have a more active and imperious control over human conduct than general or remote considerations of policy, utility or justice? ... Have we not already seen enough of the fallacy and extravagance of those idle theories which have amused us with promises of an exemption from the imperfections, weaknesses and evils incident to society in every shape? Is it not time to awake from the deceitful dream of a golden age, and to adopt as a practical maxim for the direction of our political conduct, that we, as well as other inhabitants of the globe, are yet remote from the happy empire of perfect wisdom and perfect virtue?[18]

This starting premise was critical to all that was to follow. It pushed aside any arguments that the best government was the least government. As there were for the Framers no divine rights of kings, neither was there to be libertarianism or anarchy. In terms of RD Theory, the Framers were saying that humans have reasonable capacities for self-governance, given their prefrontal cortex and four generally balanced drives, but this mechanism is by no means foolproof. We therefore need a strong and stable—albeit limited—governance system to support, and even to supplement if needed, the internal checks and balances of our innate drives. We need to use our creative capacities (dC) to design a government that can strike a reasonable balance between private individual property rights (dA) and the common good (dB), while guarding us against internal and external enemies (dD).

The Framers were conscious that they were discarding many of the useful materials out of which Europeans had built their governments. They hoped instead to use the raw drives of human nature—the *passions,* a term used sixty-eight times in *The Federalist Papers*—turning these often disruptive human emotions to the work of upholding republican government. This was by no means a utopian faith in the innate goodness of humanity. The Framers were deeply distrustful of human nature and warned, in particular, that people were driven by what they called *ambition.* This term appears forty-seven times in *The Federalist Papers* and always in the negative sense of a constant hunger for power and wealth; it did not have the positive connotations the word has today. *Ambition,* as they understood the term, was something government needed to check. Hamilton warns against "the ambitious enterprise and vainglorious pursuits of a monarchy" and "the ambitious intrigues of... Executive magistrates."[19] Madison warns against "the intrigues of the ambitious or the bribes of the rich."[20]

The Framers also feared what they called "factions," which Madison defined as "a number of citizens... who are united and actuated by some common impulse of passion, or of interest, adverse to the rights of other citizens, or to the permanent and aggregate interests of the community."[21] They recognized both the innate and the insatiable aspects of these factions; groups will naturally have special interests, and different groups will have different special interests. Somehow, this normal source of conflict must be made constructive rather than destructive; as Madison wrote, "The regulation of these various and interfering interests forms the principal task of modern legislation, and involves the spirit of party and faction in the necessary and ordinary operations of the government."[22]

Above all, the Framers, who knew their Machiavelli, feared the concentration of political power in the hands of any clever men with unrestrained "ambition"—our people-w/o-conscience. What, then, could counter such people, who seemed to have had their way all through history? Who but a man of "ambition" could stand in the way of another man of "ambition"?

But the Framers were too realistic to be entirely pessimistic. They knew that human nature could be grasping and corrupt, but they also knew that people could be wise, virtuous, and public-spirited. The passion they looked to as a check on ambition (dA, in our terms) was called *virtue,* a term that appears thirty-nine times in *The Federalist Papers.* This term signified for them a public-mindedness and an instinct to act for the common good. In other words, people became "virtuous" as they put aside particular, selfish interests and bonded broadly to the collective (dB, in our terms). The Framers hoped to create a government that would tap into this drive.

CHECKS AND BALANCES

The Framers were aware that people were both "ambitious" and "virtuous," but were also aware that people managed to balance these drives—not always, but most of the time—and were therefore capable of self-government. Facing on a national scale the problem we all face individually—how to reconcile our conflicting legitimate impulses into constructive action—the Framers believed they had found a way to protect society from the exceptions (the people-w/o-conscience) while taking advantage of the historical opportunity for a government that balanced ambition and virtue (acquisition and bonding).

They arrived at a solution very like the human brain's solution to the clash of innate, insatiable drives. They tried to create a centralized national government that would contain and channel the drive of ambition into publicly constructive paths, balancing various powers within the government even while consolidating enough power into the government with which to oppose the powers outside it (including the power of the populace itself).

The government they created, embodied in the Constitution, was anything but streamlined. It was designed, in fact, to be cumbersome, intricate, complicated, and studded with process and procedure. It was deliberately designed to force dialogue and debate. The Framers wanted to delay any hasty lawmaking. Even though the Constitution grew out of an effort to draw power into a new national government, it also very much reflected the Framers' instincts against concentrating power.

The Framers worked carefully to prevent consolidation of authority in the hands of any single dominant office or institution. The phrase "checks and balances," used over and over in creating the constitutional structure, sums up the one organizing algorithm, the one design mechanism, on which the Framers relied consistently. "Checks and balances" meant counterbalancing the impulses of the various drives of human nature with other drives. The counterbalancing was to be carried out through reasoned debate (playing a role similar to that of the prefrontal cortex). This was the high road, the only road, to wisdom in public affairs. Each governmental element was positioned as a check upon the other governmental elements, so as to sustain a dynamic balance. The Framers poised the voting rights of the people as a check on the entire governmental apparatus, even as the government and its laws were to check the impulsive behavior of the individual citizen. The legislature, judiciary, and executive branches of government were each designed to balance any rash and hasty action by the other branches. The president commanded the army, but Congress funded it. The Congress declared war and the president, as commander in chief, waged it. The president negotiated treaties, the Senate ratified them. The House was given the power to bring articles of impeachment, the Senate to try them. The federal right to levy taxes, incur debts, and regulate foreign and interstate commerce served to check the individual states, while the states explicitly retained all other rights not conferred on the federal government.

Religion posed a unique problem which resulted in a unique solution. While Americans were certain they could do without a monarchy and an aristocracy, they had no intention of doing away with religion—they only wanted to stop using it as a pillar of government. But how was religion to be checked; with what could it be balanced? There was no answer except the balancing of other religions. So for perhaps the first time in history, a government explicitly denied itself the right to name an established religion.

The final masterstroke of the system of checks and balances was the Bill of Rights, which wasn't added until 1790 but which has become, in most Americans' minds, the very heart of the Constitution. The Bill of Rights explicitly checked the rights of the government as a whole by defining what it could not do.

The United States Constitution remains the preeminent example in human history of wisdom embedded in a large-scale human institution. Its parallels with the design of the human brain are truly amazing. Translating the Framers' eighteenth-century language into RD Theory terms is almost too easy. Their "human nature" is our group of genetically based features of the brain. More specifically, their "passions" and "impulses" are our innate drives: their "ambition" is our drive to acquire, their "virtue" is our drive to bond, their "reason" is our drive to comprehend. Their "wisdom" is our state of dynamic balance between the drives. For the Framers, impulses are checked by other impulses and by the process of dialogue; in the brain, drives are checked by other drives and by the neural exchanges—the dialogue—between the unconscious and conscious brain. Amazingly, the Framers created a government that, in essence, serves the American people as a prefrontal cortex in relation to the drives.

LINCOLN'S GOOD/MORAL LEADERSHIP

At the time of American independence, the South was already becoming less reliant on a slave economy, and some slave owners were already looking for a way to phase it out. But in the early nineteenth century, a new wave of English immigrants settled into the virgin lands of the Gulf states, creating a fresh demand for slaves. Jefferson Davis, who became the president of the

Confederacy, was typical of this new breed of slave owner. He was able to acquire large holdings of rich delta land along with all the slaves he needed to create a large cotton-producing business. He and others like him became extremely rich and became political leaders in their own states and to some extent in Washington. Even though these men were already rich and reasonably powerful, there was even more money to be made by moving the slavery system farther west at the expense to those unlucky enough to be black instead of white. They were the kind of ambitious factional leaders that the Framers had worried about.

Foiled in their ambitions by Lincoln's election, these men precipitated the Civil War. They had few doubts about their ability to manipulate the vast majority of Southerners, who were not slave owners, into making heroic and bloody sacrifices by appealing to their drive to bond with others of their region in defense of their families, their home states, and their way of life. Some of these leaders may even have been people-w/o-conscience, entirely lacking the drive to bond, but they were well aware of how it worked in other people.

We have already seen how Constantine would have dealt with such a factional threat. Manipulation, threat, or pure violence—whichever looked likeliest to succeed. Pure dA and dD, with a powerful dC completely in their service. Lincoln, however, used all four of his drives, in amazingly intense but balanced ways, to defend the nation, to integrate rather than destroy the factions which were opposed to his goal, and to bring the South back into the nation once it was no longer a threat to the nation's existence. All along, he was determined to care as well as possible for those who suffered the most: the slaves and the soldiers, including those who fought for the South.

Lincoln's drive to acquire was never in doubt. By the age of twenty-three, he already knew what he wanted to achieve—not wealth or fame but the high esteem of his countrymen, esteem that would outlast his own lifetime.[23] He seemed to sense that the only way he could do this was by doing his best to make the world a better place; in RD Theory terms, by helping others to fulfill their four drives. He also sensed early on that he had a special potential for leadership and moved gracefully into one leadership role after another as a young soldier in the Blackhawk War, a young political leader in Salem, a young lawyer on the Illinois trial circuit, and a freshman Congressman. In these various roles he was practicing and developing his skills in dealing with a wide variety of people, resolving their four-drive conflicts. At the national Republican Convention of 1860, Lincoln carefully positioned himself to be the number two choice of the delegates backing the leading candidates. When the favorites faltered, one by one, he moved to the front. This was the path he chose to satisfice his powerful ambition to gain the lasting high esteem of others.

Lincoln's drive to bond in long-lasting caring relationships was truly remarkable. Throughout his life he created lasting friendships. He was unusually gregarious. His humor was spontaneous and infectious. His stories were loaded with sound folk wisdom. His strength as a listener was based on his empathy for people's deeper feelings, and people were astounded by his ability to remember their personal situations. But the true depth of his capacity for compassion came forth during the Civil War in his regular visits to frontline soldiers and to the bedsides of the wounded. The strength of his bond with these men made itself known in the absentee soldier vote which created his landslide victory in 1864.

Lincoln had a powerful drive to comprehend. Having almost no formal education, he early on developed both the habit of thinking things out for himself and a devotion to books. In his youth, the few books he got his hands on were mostly classics which he read over and over until they became part of his own way of comprehending the world. His dC capacities came into full view with his carefully-thought-out positions in the famous senatorial campaign debates with Stephen Douglas. Here he first displayed his grasp of the meaning to the wider world of the American experiment in republican government. His ability to articulate his deep beliefs on this issue were to come into full flower in his Gettysburg Address and the Second Inaugural Address.

Lincoln's drive to defend may have been his most powerful drive. I am surprised to have reached this conclusion, since it is well known that he was almost careless about his own personal safety. But he reached a white-hot intensity in his defense of the Union, the cause that dominated his life. During the war, he took a few measures which were (and still are) Constitutionally debatable. Whatever one's judgment on their legality, though, it seems clear they were motivated by his desire to defend his country from partition; none seems to have been for his own political advantage.

He realized at the start of his presidency that, if he were going to succeed in defending the Union, he had to build and sustain bonds with all the regional factions, especially the border states. In RD terms, he had to satisfice two innate and independent drives, dD and dB, rather than sacrifice one for the other, which an evil leader would have done as a matter of course and which a misguided leader might have done, feeling there was no other practical choice. He therefore made the strategic choice to recruit his presidential rivals into the key offices of his cabinet. He knew if he could engage their full efforts in the struggle, he had a chance of drawing their many followers in as well. Lincoln had to use his full array of social skills to recruit these men. He then had to gradually convince them that his vision for success in the war could work and show how each of them could make his own significant contribution to it. Bonding these men into an effective team subsequently helped Lincoln bond the people in their regions to the war effort. Whenever events strained Lincoln's ties with any particular region, he turned to the relevant member of his cabinet team for advice and help in holding things together.

As the war drew toward a close, Lincoln's focus shifted to the massive problem of rebuilding the bonds with the Confederate states. He was keenly aware of what a long and painful process this would be, extending far beyond his administration. Yet a beginning must be made. How to turn the nation's attention to this task in the right way? Lincoln started in his Second Inaugural Address. His words of reconciliation are well known: "With malice toward none; with charity for all; with firmness in the right, as God gives us to see the right... to do all which may achieve and cherish a just, and a lasting peace, among ourselves, and with all nations." Yet it is forgotten that these final words were preceded by Lincoln's most concise and blunt articulation of the cause of the war:

> One eighth of the whole population were colored slaves, not
> distributed generally over the union, but localized in the Southern

part of it. These slaves constituted a peculiar and powerful interest [a private property (dA) interest]. All knew that this interest was, somehow, the cause of the war. To strengthen, perpetuate, and extend this interest was the object for which the insurgents would rend the Union, even by war; while the government claimed no right to do more than to restrict the territorial enlargement of it.

Further on, he added, "It may seem strange that any men should dare to ask a just God's assistance in wringing their bread from the sweat of other men's faces; but let us judge not that we be not judged." Lincoln's speech was by no means all sweetness and light. He asked his fellow countrymen to recognize some hard truths and, *in spite of these truths,* proposed charity for all. To me, this is a spectacular display of four-drive leadership.

When news came that Lee had surrendered to Grant, a jubilant crowd gathered on the lawn of the White House. A band was playing Union fight songs. The cheering crowd called for Lincoln to speak. He quieted them and spoke briefly of a day of thanksgiving being planned, then paused and asked the band to play one of his favorite tunes—"Dixie." What a simple, powerful act of good and moral leadership. With that insight and the courage to act on it at such an emotional moment, he had turned the nation's attention to the long hard road of reconciliation that lay ahead. Four evenings later he was shot.

Humans will probably always need the help of especially gifted moral leaders in order to extend the bonds of caring and trust beyond the easy range of the family and the face-to-face community. Such bonds have become essential to the future of humanity. Lincoln has shown us the way.

PROGRESS AND REGRESS IN THE TWENTIETH AND TWENTY-FIRST CENTURIES

The twentieth century dawned with a real hope that political institutions worldwide could evolve into humane mechanisms for helping their citizens fulfill all four innate drives. Of course, this hope would not have been expressed in RD Theory terms, but political institutions were frequently seen as collectives committed to mutual caring (dB), as providers of opportunities for all to achieve some reasonable material success (dA), as guarantors of security (dD), and as givers of meaning to people's lives (dC). The United States had served the wider world as an example of such governance throughout the nineteenth century, despite its shortcomings (particularly slavery). While most European nations were still monarchies, many had become constitutional monarchies with elected parliaments and prime ministers, as had Japan. European colonial powers were ostensibly spreading democratic systems among the developing nations. It seemed that only in the Chinese and Ottoman empires were the despots still in place, and even they were tottering.

This rosy picture was shattered by the shock of World War I. Yet that horrible bloodbath at least brought the fall of the German, Austro-Hungarian, Russian, Chinese, and Ottoman empires and the birth of many new republics. The rest of the twentieth century, however, brought a parade of mass-murdering dictators—Hitler, Stalin, Pol Pot, Idi Amin, Mao Zedung, and others. And even as we move into the twenty-first century, we can see a frightening number of heads of state who are acting like leaders-w/o-conscience. Why is this still possible?

We have seen that the rise and fall of evil three-drive leadership is, at least to some extent, a by-product of our amazing four-drive adaptability. Our physical and social conditions keep changing—whether one thinks of it as progress or mere flux—and this sometimes creates new openings for the smartest of the people-w/o-conscience. The rise of the city and of other social groups larger than the tribe was one such opening. Any period of social turmoil tends to provide such openings as well. The social turmoil in Africa, for example, continues to provide opportunities for people-w/o-conscience to gain power. Journalist Jean-Claude Tonme wrote that the biggest problem in Africa is its plague of bad national leaders. "In Africa, our leaders have led us into misery, and we need to rid ourselves of these cancers.... What is at issue is an Africa where dictators kill, steal and usurp power yet are treated like heroes at meetings of the African Union with no danger that they will lose their seat at the United Nations."[24] He draws particular attention to the dictatorial leaders of Chad, Togo, the Central African Republic, Uganda, Gabon, and his own country, Cameroon. He does not even bother to mention Robert Mugabe of Zimbabwe or the leaders of Sudan and Libya. All these leaders are at least candidate people-w/o-conscience who have opportunistically gained power in the midst of civil turmoil.

I have devoted much of this chapter to leaders-w/o-conscience. Their existence was an unpleasant surprise to me, discovered in the course of my research for this book. I know others will find it hard to believe, as I did myself. Baffled by such men, we are often reduced to calling them "monsters," as if they were inexplicable, outside the reach of scientific explanation. (No one had noticed that Darwin had already used the very same term to scientifically characterize a hypothetical person with no social instincts (dB) and, therefore, no conscience.) This is just where Hare and other psychologists and psychiatrists have been stuck in regard to the psychopaths they have studied. While systematically observing the behavior of psychopaths, they cannot account for it. Recall the editor who rejected Hare's electroencephalograms because he did not believe that humans could have produced them.

I believe that the Renewed Darwinian Theory enables us to reclassify these "inexplicable" people as human beings genetically lacking the innate, independent drive to bond—rare but entirely understandable products of the history of the human gene pool. This recognition allows us to see leaders-w/o-conscience as a massive public health problem that has been afflicting our species throughout recorded history. This recognition, in turn, creates the possibility of taking the biggest step since the framing of the Constitution toward freeing humanity from such leaders. How to take this step in a humane manner is not at all clear. But recognizing that evil leadership is caused by a natural process allows one to at least explore the possibilities of constraining or avoiding it, fully aware that marginalizing the likes of Constantine, Napoleon, and Hitler will never be easy.

In the mid-nineteenth century, a new development—comparable in significance to the invention of cooking and the rise of cities—created yet another new opening for leaders-w/o-conscience to acquire enormous wealth and power. In the next chapter, we will see what the RD Theory tells us about corporations and their leaders.

CHAPTER SIX

LEADERSHIP OF ECONOMIC INSTITUTIONS
The Rise of Corporations

*The social responsibility of business is to increase
its profits.*
— MILTON FRIEDMAN[1]

*Every man holds his property subject to the general
right of the community to regulate its use to whatever
degree the public welfare may require it.*
— THEODORE ROOSEVELT[2]

OVERVIEW OF ECONOMIC INSTITUTIONS

Having cast the light of the Renewed Darwinian Theory on the leadership of political institutions in the previous chapter, I will now turn that light upon the leadership of an institution that rivals government in its influence over people's lives around the world—the corporation. But first I must briefly put the corporation and its leadership issues in historical perspective. Only by considering where the corporation came from can we understand what special kind of institution it is and what its special leadership issues are.

In late Stone Age tribes, the primary "economic institutions" were the gathering party and the hunting party. When certain animals became domesticated, the nomadic pastoral life became dominant and these domesticated animals became the primary forms of wealth. Then, of course, agriculture took over as the dominant way of "making a living," and the individual ownership of arable land became the chief basis of wealth.

Not much is known about the patterns of land ownership during the transition to the earliest empires of the Middle East. However, since hunting and foraging land seems to have been collectively "owned" by the tribe and since, during the transition to individual ownership, arable land would probably have changed hands primarily by armed conquest, it is likely that conquered land would have been treated as the property of the tribal warlord or, later, the king or emperor. He, of course, would then have had the power to award large parcels of conquered land to others, such as successful generals. The people who were living on the land at the time of the conquest were probably treated as landless serfs with some rights but not many. Clearly this was the established "feudal" system during the Dark Ages and on into the Middle Ages in Europe. It was by this process that arable land, the primary means of production at the time, became subject to individual ownership and was usually held in large parcels. The labor needed to work these large parcels would have been secured by arrangements such as slavery, serfdom, indentured servitude, day labor, and tenantry. The RD Theory predicts that, wherever people-w/o-conscience managed to secure the ownership of large parcels of land, they would seek the least costly form of labor available—slavery, if they could get away with it.

These traditional land-ownership arrangements were brought to the English colonies in America when the King of England granted large parcels to favored members of the aristocracy. In the Southern tidewater region, these parcels were of a large "plantation" size; while individual families could certainly own them, a significant number of landless laborers were needed to work them. The fact that most of these landless laborers were eventually secured by a slavery system suggests that some of the early landowners were people-w/o-conscience. The English landowners were learning about slavery from the Spanish and Portuguese colonists in other parts of the Americas, and English law at the time was essentially silent about slavery. In the New England and mid-Atlantic colonies, however, the pattern of land ownership took a different turn. For various complex reasons, the original large parcels of land were broken up into smaller parcels that could often be worked by a single landowning family. To cite just one example, William Penn, who secured a large land grant as an eligible aristocrat, persuaded a group of his fellow citizens in England to join him in the New World by promising them land of their own.

Meanwhile, in Europe, manufacturing workshops with skilled artisans had been steadily growing in number since the start of the Renaissance. Over time, workshops clustered into craft guilds, which established and enforced the terms of trade and of employment for each craft. Trade expanded from the local market to a national market and even to an international market. But each workshop remained small, never employing as many people as agriculture did, and therefore maintained the kind of face-to-face relationships that probably kept people-w/o-conscience from gaining control. Only when workshops evolved into factories in Europe, and shortly afterwards in the newly established United States, did manufacturing gradually replace agriculture as the dominant form of employment and factories become the setting in which most people fulfilled their dA drive.

Thus the concept of private ownership of the physical means of production of goods and services was carried forward from the ownership of arable land to the ownership of workshops to the ownership of factories and finally on to corporations. And the laws which legitimated private ownership of land more or less "went along for the ride," legitimating the private ownership of workshops, factories, and then corporations of ever-greater size, taking no official notice that an ever-smaller minority owned the settings in which an ever-larger majority tried to fulfill its basic drive to acquire. And this ever-smaller minority was gaining power not only over employees but also over competitors, customers, people living near the factories, constituents of politicians who had been paid off by corporate owners . . . but we are getting ahead of our story.

Corporations, much less large corporations, were essentially unknown to the Framers of the Constitution. In fact, for Locke and for the Framers of the U.S. Constitution, private ownership was the very essence of liberty, but the ownership they had in mind was ownership of the family farm. The U.S. Constitution was one of the legal documents in which private property rights to the physical means of production were explicitly established. Amendment V of the Bill of Rights states, "No person shall . . .

be deprived of life, liberty, or property, without due process of law; nor shall private property be taken for public use, without just compensation.'' The Framers assumed that ownership of the means of production would be widely dispersed amongst many private farmers working their own land. But this was not how it turned out.

Overview of the Corporation

Today's corporations are legally established collectives that have been empowered primarily to fulfill the human drive to acquire. The positive results of this particular means of organizing the fulfillment of the drive to acquire are conspicuous and impressive. Compared to other ways of organizing economic activity, corporations are, by and large, vastly more cost-efficient and innovative. The reasons for this success are complex, but scholars generally agree on the two most important reasons. First, the corporate system, in contrast to individual ownership, makes it possible to quickly assemble enough capital to achieve economies of scale. Second, the corporate system makes it possible for multiple firms to start up in a given industry, creating the competitive striving (dA) that leads each firm to continually improve and innovate.[3]

As a result, corporations have been able to marshal economic resources on an unprecedented scale and put those resources to work in patient, long-term undertakings which no individual or small group could accomplish. Corporations have so increased our ability to produce useful goods and services that they have become the dominant means for doing so all over the world.

Unfortunately, the harm they can do has also been impressive, generally taking the form of (1) exploiting and harming employees, (2) promoting the sale of wasteful or even harmful products, (3) defrauding small investors and creditors, (4) competing unfairly with competitors and dealing unfairly with suppliers and distributors, (5) damaging the physical and biological environment, or (6) corrupting the government. When corporations are successful in corrupting the government, they can control policies and laws to the point of evading taxes, securing unfair subsidies, and shirking responsibility for any harm they do to others. Of course, such abuses can help the corporation's large investors and top executives acquire enormous wealth.

How can the same institutions be so beneficent and also, at times, so abusive? How can they be both Mr. Hyde and Dr. Jekyll? What does the RD Theory suggest about this puzzle?

In industrial countries, corporations have become the primary institutional means by which to fulfill the drive to acquire, but dA is not the only drive. Today's corporation is a highly complex collective, typically drawing together the participation of hundreds, thousands, or even millions of employees, customers, suppliers, and shareholders. To various degrees, these people are drawn into bonds of mutual caring or there would be no team effort, no brand loyalty, no creative spark, no corporate esprit, and no management motivational tools other than financial rewards and threats. In other words, although corporations are organized primarily to fulfill the drive to acquire, they could not accomplish this without relying heavily on the human drive to bond, the human drive to comprehend, and even the drive to defend.

With our grounding in the RD Theory, we should already hear some alarms going off in our minds:

- A corporation, given the way it has been chartered and legally defined, is essentially unbalanced in terms of our four innate drives. In some corporations, the drive to bond is treated strictly as a means of fulfilling dA. These corporations treat employees well, play fair with competitors, and give customers and suppliers an honest deal because that's good for the dA bottom line—and only to the extent that it is good for the dA bottom line—not because it is what humans are innately designed to do in relation to one another. (And we must remember that, in the end, the "corporation" is not a conscious being and can do nothing; only its individual members can make decisions and take actions.) Seen in terms of what we learned in Part One about the functioning of the human brain, every corporation has to address the stubborn fact that all four human drives are in the heads of each and every normal person involved. But legally, the four drives do not have equal voices. In some corporations, the dA drives of individuals are deliberately and expertly stimulated and magnified, while the dB drives of individuals are largely ignored. In these corporations there is one all-powerful faction—the coalition of large shareholders (represented by the directors) and their top management with their laser-like focus on maximizing profits—with little in the way of checks and balances.

- A corporation is legally defined as an "individual" with all the rights and responsibilities that entails. But what kind of individual are we talking about? The courts often seem to be supporting the view of the neoclassical economists that corporate "individuals" have only dA wired into their brains and have no mandated responsibilities to address drives other than dA or segments of society other than their owners. At times, the courts have even insisted that corporate leaders put maximum profitability above every other concern or else face financial penalties from suits brought by stockholders. In fact, the World Trade Organization seems to be concluding that any national government's effort to enact and enforce laws to constrain multinational corporations from abusive behavior within their own national boundaries is to be judged a "restraint of trade" and hence illegal under emerging international trade law. Far from encouraging a healthy balance of dA with dB and the other drives, that balance is discouraged and may even be penalized—by the marketplace, if not by the authorities. From this legal perspective, then, the corporation is expected to behave like a person-w/o-conscience—in fact, like a superhuman person-w/o-conscience, with the combined power of hundreds, thousands, or even tens of thousands of ordinary people. And so it sometimes does. The abuses of such corporations are precisely the abuses we expect of a person-w/o-conscience—doing anything they can get away with to acquire wealth and to acquire the power needed to acquire wealth.
- The very conspicuous success and power of corporations acts as a powerful magnet attracting the people-w/o-conscience in our midst who maintain a single-minded focus on gaining power and thereby wealth. Corporations seem fairly vulnerable to being taken over by a small clever group drawn from

the tiny minority of "monsters" in the population. It is important to remember that a person-w/o-conscience at the helm of a collective is dangerous not only because he or she is a person-w/o-conscience, but because practically everyone else is not a person-w/o-conscience. A person-w/o-conscience CEO with ten thousand people-w/o-conscience employees would not pose that much of a threat; they wouldn't begin to have the coherence and effectiveness of a normal company. But any real company, even with a person-w/o-conscience group at the top, is mainly composed of four-drive humans who feel friendly toward fellow workers, grateful for favors done, sympathetic toward a coworker struggling with an obstacle, concerned for the welfare of their families, and loyal to their employing firm. A reasonably well-organized collection of such people is capable of performing remarkable feats but, with a person-w/o-conscience at the top, these might be feats of manufacturing and selling defective products or driving someone else out of business by underhanded means. They might even be feats of manufacturing, rating, or selling bonds backed by mortgages which, unbeknownst to most of the people involved, are close to worthless.

A person-w/o-conscience who works his or her way into a top leadership position of a major corporation can change its entire business culture. Employees at lower levels have no choice but to go along with their leader's tactics or quit their jobs. Such a leader-w/o-conscience can even change the culture of an entire industry. In such circumstances, any normal four-drive leader of a competitive firm is put on the defensive and is pressured into imitating the leader-w/o-conscience or selling out on unfavorable terms. Top-level executives who are people-w/o-conscience can exercise power on a scale that is far beyond face-to-face social controls. They can command the help of sophisticated lawyers, accountants, and public relations experts in abusing the rights of others and in subverting the public interest. They command vast financial resources that can go far toward corrupting the governmental process itself. They can make a finely tuned analysis of whether dollars spent on lobbying or on campaign contributions return the most value in special favors, greatly complicating the already difficult job of regulating corporations. Thus they can, at times, even gain control over the drafting of laws designed to regulate their own behavior.

We saw in the previous chapter that when the rise of civilization brought about larger and highly stratified collectives, such as city-states, the people-w/o-conscience genie was let out of the bottle in which it had been largely confined since the transformation to *Homo sapiens*. Seen from the point of view of the RD Theory of human behavior, the rise of corporations—of collectives legally sanctioned and socially encouraged to fulfill dA without having to balance it with an equally powerful dB—was a serious mistake. What more perfect vehicle for acquiring personal wealth can a person-w/o-conscience imagine, especially in the United States, where the government has been designed to keep people-w/o-conscience politicians under control and where there was no experience with regulating corporations? *How did this situation come to pass?*

James Madison could not have predicted the rise of corporations, but he did foresee that political factions would organize around the narrow economic interests of an elite few: "Those who hold and those who are without property have ever formed distinct interests in society."[4] Madison believed that the acquisitive drive was deeply human, a powerful drive that no political structure would be able to ignore. Any government trying to wrestle it under control by brute force would cease to be a republic. The only solution—the only "republican remedy"—Madison could see was to turn the acquisitive drive against itself, not only by checking the acquisitive passion (dA) with the passion for the common good (dB), but also by checking the raw, irrepressible dA energy of one individual with that of another. This was also Madison's solution for those people-w/o-conscience—those without a dB—who could be counted on to try to work their way into top government positions.

The Framers created a remarkable set of institutions—with a powerfully adaptive capacity for balance and growth—in the political sphere, where it has been able to constrain the "monsters" reasonably well. But in the business sphere, the Framers took only the first steps of what has proven to be a painful, protracted, and limited search for effective check-and-balance mechanisms.

In effect, the corporation as we know it flew in under the radar of the Framers and the Constitution. The corporate structure was never given the kind of impulse/check/balance embodiment that the government itself received. There was never a constitutional convention dedicated to shaping the corporation. It was never provided with the structural mechanisms to constrain the damage that people-w/o-conscience could do from top corporate power positions. Despite the Framers' concern to control factions, this particular type of faction was allowed to become so powerful that, at times, it could overwhelm the government's regulatory powers, first at the state level and then at the federal level.

The Rise of American Corporations and the Struggle to Regulate Them

Early European corporations were chartered *one at a time* as joint-stock firms by the crown and constrained to undertake a *single* tightly defined job such as building a specified road or bridge. But post-Revolution Americans so distrusted the idea of broad executive powers that this power was instead given to the state legislatures, as elected guardians of "the people." An 1804 Supreme Court decision confirmed that corporations were "mere creature[s]" of the state legislatures, holding only those powers of operation expressly granted by their charters.[5] This made it possible to reshape the concept of the corporation from a privileged grant of power over a very specific economic opportunity to a vehicle of unbounded economic opportunity. State legislatures granted charters increasingly freely as the pace of economic activity quickened.

By the middle of the nineteenth century, the largest American corporations were already operating across state boundaries, while the federal government was only belatedly and tentatively assuming comparable proportions and powers and was facing intense resistance, particularly to federal control of slavery. Concerns about corporations' growing abuse of their growing power coalesced at the time into the concept that governments should police (rather than directly initiate, sponsor, or run) corporations, but *only* when a corporation's actions conflicted with the property rights of others.

THE FIRST CORPORATIONS WITH NATIONAL SCOPE: THE RAILROADS

The railroads were the first American businesses to reach massive scale and thus the first to outgrow state regulatory structures. The first American railroad charter was granted by New Jersey in 1815 to support the construction of a railroad from Trenton to New Brunswick. The railroad idea slowly gathered momentum. By the 1840s and 1850s, states were granting numerous charters to railroad corporations, and railroads began to spread across the country. Meanwhile, consistent with Madison's warning about the "bribes of the rich," the emergence of these new enterprises led to systematic efforts to corrupt the political process. The railroads were acquiring preponderant influence within state legislatures and the state courts. The railroads depended on favorable policies and rulings in order to increase their profits, and they exerted as much pressure as they could bring to bear when critical decisions had to be made. Shaping and bending policy via "factions" was an ancient art, but it was the railroads that made it into a quintessential American scandal. The nation's earliest professional lobbyists were spawned from this industry; graft and corruption took hold in a significant way.[6]

Jay Gould—to judge by his behavior pattern—was the first and most clear-cut candidate for the leader-w/o-conscience label to appear on the national railroad scene as a major player. Gould began speculating in railroad securities during the Civil War, buying up run-down roads, cobbling them together, and selling them off at huge profits. Whenever he achieved a local monopoly he raised the rates. He used predatory pricing to force competitive roads to sell out to him at rock-bottom prices. By 1881, at the peak of his power, his railroad empire spread across the continent. Along the way, he issued millions of dollars in fraudulent securities and dispensed thousands of dollars in bribes to judges and legislators. He was utterly unscrupulous as a highly skilled financier, although he proved less adept at actually operating railroads. In fact, railroads weren't his only business, but his schemes were consistently large scale and his methods consistently dishonest. He bribed Grant administration officials with hundreds of thousands of dollars just to warn him if any policy change might affect his 1869 attempt to corner the gold market.[7] All told, his record closely matches Hare's list of the defining characteristics of psychopaths.

Meanwhile, Cornelius Vanderbilt, another railroad tycoon, was establishing his own record as a candidate person-w/o-conscience. A set of reports issued in 1871 exposed Vanderbilt's business methods, concluding that "through stock waterings, fictitious construction costs, and profits on land grants, the four roads, controlled by Commodore Vanderbilt, realized profits of $135 million in excess of the actual cost of these roads."[8] Vanderbilt said things like "What do I care about the law? Don't I got the power?" and "The public be damned." He acknowledged, "I have been insane on the subject of money making my entire life" and told an opponent, "You have undertaken to cheat me. I won't sue you, the law takes too long. I will ruin you." Vanderbilt and Gould competed to corrupt the government; on one occasion, Vanderbilt was "dismissed by legislators for [his] 'paltry' offer of only $1,000 (and only half in cash), while Jay Gould was paying between $2,000 and $3,000 for a vote."[9] Quite literally, this was a people-w/o-conscience race to the bottom.

By the 1870s, the abuses of the railroads had become a serious national political problem. Early efforts at regulation were sporadic and unevenly effective. But as railroads became increasingly indispensable economic lifelines to surrounding communities, there was growing popular agitation over the very high rates that the railroads were charging for freight whenever they secured a local monopoly. A number of states (mainly in the agricultural Midwest) passed Granger laws in the 1870s, attempting to regulate railroad rates. However, these efforts were checked in the Granger cases of 1877, in which the U.S. Supreme Court, while upholding the principle of government regulation over railroads and other industries "affected with a public interest," nonetheless insisted that state regulatory authority ended at state lines—which, of course, most railroads crossed and left behind. Then, in 1886, the Supreme Court issued the *Wabash, St. Louis and Pacific Railroad Company v. Illinois* decision, which held that commerce originating or ending outside the boundaries of a given state could not be regulated by that state.

The Federal Response

The *Wabash* decision made the need for federal regulation clear. As progressive reformer Henry Demarest Lloyd observed, "Our laws and commissions to regulate the railroads are but toddling steps in a path in which we need to walk like men."[10] Accordingly, in 1887, Congress created the Interstate Commerce Commission. The statute authorizing the ICC outlawed rebating, pooling, and most forms of rate discrimination between long- and short-haul traffic. Congress also held that rates had to be "just and reasonable," a determination the ICC was empowered to adjudicate. It took the federal government several decades, in other words, to assert the authority of full regulation over the railroads.

Meanwhile, other businesses were reaching comparable scale. As the national infrastructure (particularly railroad and telegraph networks) welded together a national market, and as technologies of mass production emerged in a series of industries over the 1870s, 1880s, and 1890s, manufacturing businesses grew bigger in scale and in scope of operation until they were doing business on a national—and sometimes international—scale. Like the railroads, moreover, they assumed corporate form as they grew.

But for these new large-scale manufacturers, the regulatory context was even more tentative. The states that had chartered them held jurisdiction over their behavior—at least theoretically. But as these manufacturers expanded their operations to a national scale, state governments handled the situation gingerly—if they handled it at all. Although, by the 1880s, most states had set up advisory commissions to oversee the activities of corporations engaged in transportation, banking, and insurance, it wasn't until 1903 that any state except Massachusetts had a commission to oversee its manufacturing firms.[11] And while state laws were beginning to affirm the right of regulation in theory, there were virtually no effective policing mechanisms.

By the end of the 1880s, big business seemed to be running amok and, in 1890, Congress responded with the Sherman Act, which outlawed "every contract, combination in form of trust or otherwise, or conspiracy, in restraint of trade or commerce" and criminalized "every person who shall monopolize, or attempt to monopolize, or combine or conspire with any other person or persons, to monopolize any part of the trade or commerce among the several States, or with foreign nations." Yet the act set up no new machinery of execution, and its limits became clear in 1895 when the Supreme Court ruled that the American Sugar Refining Company, although it controlled 98 percent of its market, was not in violation of the law because it manufactured sugar rather than selling it, and so was not engaged in interstate commerce.

By the end of the nineteenth century, then, a tightly cohesive and politically powerful cluster of corporate leaders had formed a faction which had outgrown the reach of republican governance. In terms of this book's theory, this small set of men, several of whom were probably dA-driven people-w/o-conscience, had control of wonderful new vehicles for the acquisition of power and money and were operating without restraining dB mechanisms, either personal or institutional. (There were no income or estate taxes to constrain their accumulation of wealth.)

Meanwhile, social tensions were rising. Confrontations between organized labor and big business were escalating. In 1886, a man attending a rally of striking workers in Haymarket Square in Chicago hurled a bomb, provoking the police to open fire on the gathering. In 1894, armed conflict again enveloped Chicago when a strike at the Pullman plant spurred President Cleveland to send federal troops to the city. The ensuing melee left thirteen dead and dozens more wounded. Over thirteen hundred strikes erupted that year, many of them violent, as the United States plunged deeper into a national depression that made fears of "insurrection" all the sharper. By the mid-1890s, many Americans feared that the nation was coming apart.

One figure confronting the specter of insurrection and republican collapse was Theodore Roosevelt. "The time of the great social revolutions has come," he declared as a rising political figure in 1894. And indeed, it was insurrectionary violence that thrust Roosevelt onto center stage. On September 6, 1901, less than a year after being reelected president, William McKinley was assassinated while attending the Pan-American Exposition, ushering Roosevelt into the presidency.[12]

McKinley's assassin, Leon Czolgosz, explained his act bluntly: "McKinley was going around the country shouting about prosperity when there was no prosperity for the poor man."[13] Here was class warfare embodied. Indeed, Czolgosz was a professed anarchist. Anarchism, at the time, was an inchoate creed. Emma Goldman, in the journal *Mother Earth,* came as close to codifying the movement as anyone when she defined anarchism as "the theory that [because] all forms of government rest on violence," government itself is illegitimate.

The anarchists were few, disorganized, and scattered. Still, they were genuine in their belief and fully determined to act. A prime minister of Spain, a president of France, a king of Italy, and the Hapsburg Empress Elizabeth had already been assassinated by anarchists when McKinley was killed.[14] The social strain these terrorists signified—the sense that republican government itself was breaking down if not already broken—was also very real. McKinley's assassination was the violent action of one man, but it was also a symptom of a widening crisis.

Roosevelt feared this crisis acutely. In his first message to Congress as president, he called for legislation banning anarchists from immigrating into the United States. He called for aggressive police action to track down the American anarchists behind acts of violence and to bring them to trial. But he also recognized that American government, indeed American society, faced a deeper, graver task. Pressing social issues had to be addressed. Mechanisms of governance and government had to be revitalized. A social system had to be restored. And these challenges meant, in turn, imposing meaningful regulatory structures on society's engines of acquisition—the corporations. Their abuses had to be curbed. In RD Theory terms, the drive to acquire had to be brought in line with the drive to bond. Industrialization was creating massive business organizations and a class of workers that was becoming increasingly exploited and alienated. What Roosevelt feared was the very real prospect of class warfare. This fear dominated his thinking about the issue of business regulation.

This situation confronting Roosevelt was quite different from that which had confronted the Framers, yet the issues were familiar. In Madisonian terms, the class warfare Roosevelt feared was a war of two inimically opposed "factions." If Americans were to retain self-government, the national government had to rise above any particular class interest. Roosevelt observed in a speech that "many republics have risen, have flourished for a less or greater time, and then have fallen because their citizens lost the power of governing themselves and thereby of governing their state; and in no way has this loss of power been so often and so clearly shown as in the tendency to turn the government into a government primarily for the benefit of one class instead of a government for the benefit of the people as a whole.... The outcome was equally fatal, whether the country fell into the hands of a wealthy oligarchy which exploited the poor or whether it fell under the domination of a turbulent mob which plundered the rich."[15] In either case, it would be dA overwhelming dB on a national scale. Instead, Roosevelt urged awareness of a "community of interest," an awareness he considered vital to American civic functionality. "The welfare of each of us is dependent fundamentally upon the welfare of all of us."[16] This can be dismissed as a platitude, but the RD Theory shows us that this is actually how we are designed to survive. It is what our innate and insatiable drive to bond is telling us every time we make a decision that involves or could involve both our own wishes and those of others.

Roosevelt made the specific point about corporate regulation to Congress: "Experience has shown conclusively that it is useless to try to get any adequate regulation and supervision of these great corporations by state action. Such regulation and supervision can only be effectually exercised by a sovereign whose jurisdiction is coextensive with the work of the corporations—that is, by national government."[17]

Standard Oil

Under Theodore Roosevelt, the government intensified enforcement of the Sherman Antitrust Act as a basis for methodical federal corporate regulation. Symbolically most important was the case brought in 1906 against Standard Oil, founded and led by John D. Rockefeller. Standard refined 87 percent of all kerosene in the United States and marketed 89 percent of it. According to a 1907 ICC report, the company was pressuring the railroads into giving it significant secret rebates (in violation of the Elkins and Hepburn Acts), spying on competitors, and engaging in predatory pricing to drive competitors into selling out to Standard at fire-sale prices. Twenty-one states eventually joined in the proceedings against the corporation. Roosevelt stepped up his attack rhetorically in a special message to Congress in January 1908, decrying "the speculative folly and flagrant dishonesty of a few great men of wealth."

The federal circuit court ruled against Standard in 1909, ordering the breakup of the company. The U.S. Supreme Court upheld the breakup in 1911, forcing the corporation to dismantle itself. In Ron Chernow's apt assessment, "Thus ended the longest running morality play in American business history."[18]

Yet the larger "morality play" was far from over. Regulation through judicial action was highly unwieldy and useful only after the fact. It was a reactive response to the problem, rather than a proactive one. The basic imbalance of dA and dB remained. The law granted much more power to the necessary impulse for acquisition than it granted to the equally necessary impulse for cooperation. As Roosevelt wrote: "The power of the mighty industrial overlords of the country had increased with giant strides, while the methods of controlling them, or checking abuses by them, on the part of the people, through the Government, remained archaic and therefore practically impotent."[19]

Corporate Abuses Leading into the Great Depression

As the twentieth century moved on, policymakers fretted over the extent to which the federal government should "intervene" in the business sphere. The corporate abuses that resurfaced during the boom of the 1920s seem to have been a Wall Street variety—stock price manipulation which enriched a few investor people-w/o-conscience while ruining many ordinary investors.

An episode of the TV program *American Experience,* narrated by no less eminent an economist than John Kenneth Galbraith, suggested that this is just what happened. I do not have the historical expertise to judge whether or not its analysis is conclusive, but it fits so startlingly with the RD Theory (and with current events on Wall Street, which I will discuss in Chapter Nine) that I will offer it here. I hope it will be further tested by historians of the Depression. A few Wall Street traders discovered that they could, by closely coordinating their trades, manipulate stock prices up and down to their great advantage. For instance, by carefully timing their purchases of RCA stock they could, over a short period of time, lead the stock to 150 percent of its initial price. Then by carefully timing their sales, they could quickly unload the stock and pocket their profits. At times they could even go short on the stock to gain additional profits as the price collapsed. William C. Durant, founder of General Motors, was one of these traders. Another was Jesse Livermore, well known at the time for organizing pools of investors to coordinate their stock manipulations and a conspicuously wealthy man. When he returned home at the close of Black Tuesday—October 29, 1929, the day of the biggest drop of the market—he found his wife, Dorothy, very worried. Hearing the terrible news about the market, Dorothy was already engaged in moving out all of their furniture. Jesse quickly reassured her that he had just had the "biggest money-making day of his entire life." Given what we know about Livermore, it seems likely that he had been unloading his stock holdings for some time and perhaps going short the week before. Such evidence is anecdotal, but the show did make a plausible argument that, during the long bull market of the 1920s, such coordinated manipulation could have sucked enough money out of the market to undermine stock values, making them vulnerable to the tipping event of a final big sell-off by insider traders. And once the entire market started to fall, automatic margin calls and shorted stocks would speed it into a major collapse. Such a collapse came with the Crash of 1929.

But why would men who were already wealthy and under no particular financial pressure themselves be willing to devastate millions of other people's lives just to make even more money? I don't think normal people would be willing. The trade-off of additional wealth gained versus the vast suffering caused just wouldn't make sense for a normal four-drive person. But for people-w/o-conscience, there would be no such trade-off. The drive to acquire would be fulfilled spectacularly, the drive to comprehend would be fulfilled by the ingenuity of the scheme, and the drive to defend would be fulfilled by not getting caught. As for the suffering caused, first we have to remember that even the perpetrators, if they existed, would not have known the history of the Depression in advance. But more to the point is the fact that, even if they could have known, it wouldn't have mattered. The drive to bond—to care about other people—simply wouldn't exist for these people, so the suffering they created for others would be neither a pleasure nor a deterrent; it would be irrelevant. The skeptic might finally say, "I just do not believe such people exist." To which I would have to respond, "I have good reason to think they do, but I wish that science would give us a definitive DNA-based answer. Meanwhile, my hypothesis is sufficiently well grounded that we need to pay attention to the available circumstantial evidence and keep an open mind about this 'unbelievable' possibility."

PROGRESS AND REGRESS SINCE THE GREAT DEPRESSION

There was no sustainable consensus regarding the regulation of Wall Street until Franklin Roosevelt took office in March 1933. Roosevelt immediately went to work developing new regulations for the securities business. "The big objective is to restore the old idea that a person who uses other people's money does so in a fiduciary capacity," Roosevelt explained in a press conference on March 29. "A person who works in either a stock or a commodity exchange is acting as the agent for other people. This being so, the agent has a responsibility to be as honest and forthcoming as possible."[20] The David, dB, was at last being armed for his battle with the Goliath, dA.

Congress established the Securities and Exchange Commission, which, for a time at least, severely curbed stock manipulation. It certainly put Jesse Livermore out of business. In 1940, a broken Jesse walked into the cloakroom of a Manhattan hotel and shot himself.

FDR's New Deal went on to establish a further set of regulatory commissions, including the Federal Trade Commission and the Federal Communications Commission. Most notably, the National Labor Relations Act (or Wagner Act) of 1935 asserted the positive right of labor to organize into unions and bargain collectively with corporations—and in the process legitimated the ongoing federal oversight of labor relations. Finally, after considerable experimentation, policymakers were developing a set of regulatory tools and institutions to check abuses on an industry-by-industry basis. Such institutions had the potential to tailor their regulations to the unique features of each industry, curb its major abuses, and bring its affairs into balance.[21]

But progress has not been uniform or linear. Some industries have proven less amenable to regulation. Coal mining, for example, probably had the most flagrant and persistent employee abuses until nearly mid-century. Miners were inadequately protected from cave-ins, methane explosions, carbon monoxide poisoning, and the pervasive coal dust that leads to black lung disease. Mining companies pushed wages below a sustainable living level, engaged in violent union-busting, and even subjected children to deadly working conditions. There was nothing inevitable about these manifold abuses; they have all been corrected and the coal mines are still in business. But that only happened by means of governmental regulation and in spite of the persistent resistance of the mine owners, who argued that governmental regulations were violating their property rights. It was as if in a land of plenty, an honest, hard-working miner had no right to expect living wages and safe working conditions that enabled him to survive and support the life of his family. Or in RD Theory terms, it was as if dA existed but dB were only a figment of someone's imagination.

There have been episodes of serious backsliding. The irrational fad for deregulation in the 1980s and 1990s was a significant retreat from the responsibilities of federal corporate regulation, with such disastrous consequences as the savings and loan collapse of the late 1980s. More recently, the outbreak of massive scandals such as Enron, WorldCom, and Tyco in the first few years of the twenty-first century points to the dangers of lapsed vigilance. Enron, a case we will return to later, seems to have managed to carry out all six forms of abuse that were cited earlier.

Large multinationals are now overreaching the capacity of even national governments to regulate them; their behavior frequently reflects the knowledge of their top managements that nobody can police them. Like Constantine, although more discretely, they are above the law. Just as the railroads earlier overran the capacity of states to regulate them, so Tyco can evade U.S. taxes by deciding it is based in Bermuda. Our Congress as yet has not been able to stop this kind of abuse. Nor are there any adequate international institutions in place to address these problems, as will be discussed further in Chapter Nine.

What does the Renewed Darwinian Theory suggest to us about corporations and the ongoing problem of adequate regulation? Corporations are not inherently destructive or dysfunctional. They are able to produce a wealth of valuable goods and services that can enhance the lives of all. They arise in response to—and they can productively channel—the basic drives that shape us all. However, balance among the drives is difficult to maintain in a corporate context. One point is obvious, but easily overlooked. Corporations are not just engines of acquisition. To be sure, they are profit-driven, which is to say, they are manifestations of our drive to acquire. But, because they depend on the cooperation of large numbers of people to perform the necessary work, they are totally dependent on the human drive to bond. The etymology is instructive: *corporation* derives from the Latin word *corpus,* or "body," signifying a collective enterprise.

To sum up: because corporations did not become important until after the framing of the Constitution, a chance was missed to give them the impulse/check/balance form that would have balanced their power to marshal the acquisitive drives of large groups of investors with the obligation to honor the implicit, conscience-driven dB ground rules of mutual caring. Instead, the second half of that equation is no more than a peripheral part of the makeup of many corporations, entirely outweighed by the drive to acquire. This has left corporations vulnerable to person-w/o-conscience leadership, and each society in which such a corporation operates—often the entire world—is vulnerable to the resulting corporate abuses. This is my answer to the Jekyll and Hyde mystery. We will come back to this issue in Chapters Eight and Nine as we consider the kinds of reforms that might better achieve morally balanced leadership in corporations.

CHAPTER SEVEN

LEADERSHIP IN INSTITUTIONS OF HUMAN MEANING
Religion, Art, and Science

> As soon as the important faculties of the
> imagination, wonder, and curiosity, together with
> some power of reasoning, had become partially
> developed, man would naturally crave to understand
> what was passing around him, and would have
> vaguely speculated on his own existence.
> — CHARLES DARWIN[1]

The drive to comprehend is one of our four innate, independent drives, and the institutions of religion, art, and science are three of the most prevalent and powerful means by which many people fulfill that drive. These institutions contribute powerfully to our understanding of the meaning of human life and effort. For religion and art, this is an obvious part of their missions while, for science, this is a somewhat inadvertent by-product of its mission. The quality of leadership in all three fields, then, must be of some significance.

THE INSTITUTION OF RELIGION AND HUMAN MEANING

Given the mental capacity of humans and their drive to comprehend, it was inevitable, as Darwin observed, that they would ask the ultimate questions. When natural explanations were lacking, it was inevitable that people would turn to supernatural explanations; hence the occurrence of religion in every known society.

While religion has risen primarily in response to the independent drive to comprehend, it also plays a role in fulfilling the other three drives. Religion is intimately connected to the drive to bond; all religions are closely associated with morals and ethics, a necessary skill set for the fulfillment of dB. Religion has also been inevitably involved, in a lesser way, with the drives to acquire and to defend. It is probably universal that people are taught to pray for their "daily bread" (dA). In regard to dD, we have only to think of the many wars that have been fought to defend or propagate the faith or, if fought for some other reason, at least fought "with God on our side."

This should not be surprising. A four-drive human is always balancing all four innate, independent, and insatiable drives, so anything as important as explaining our purpose in life is bound to involve all four drives, not just the drive to comprehend, just as something as important as earning a living or choosing a mate involves all four drives, not just the drive to acquire.

It follows then that religious leadership, like any other kind of leadership, needs to be what I have defined as good leadership, guided by the four-drive moral code. This can be as challenging for religious leaders as it is for government and business leaders. A fairly obscure episode of history—the clash of the Gnostics and the Orthodox Christians in the second, third, and fourth centuries A.D.—sheds a most interesting, although disturbing, light on how the four-drive nature of human beings can play out in religious leadership.

GOOD/MORAL LEADERSHIP AND THE GNOSTIC CHALLENGE TO ORTHODOX CHRISTIANITY

Gnosticism was a religious movement in the early Christian era which, for a time, was in competition with Orthodox Christianity but which came to be considered a heresy and was eventually crushed by Constantine's legions. *The Gnostic Gospels,* by Elaine Pagels, a leading historian of the Gnostics, is especially useful for the purpose of this book because Pagels analyzes the Gnostic interpretation of Christ's life and teachings by contrasting it to the Orthodox version of Christianity that eventually prevailed, indirectly illuminating some of the issues of religious leadership in terms of our four drives.[2] Her discussion of these ancient texts will probably challenge the assumptions of many readers on the sensitive issue of religious doctrine, so I will quote extensively in order to assure the reader that I am not tilting the story.

As Pagels explains:

> According to the Gnostic teacher Theodotus, writing in Asia Minor (c. 140–160), the Gnostic is one who has come to understand "who we were, and what we have become; where we were...whither we are hastening; from what we are being released; what birth is, and what is rebirth. Yet to know oneself, at the deepest level, is simultaneously to know God; this is the secret of *gnosis*."[3]

Clearly the Gnostics were focusing intensely on the ultimate questions of the meaning of human existence, primarily by means of knowing one's inner self. In terms of this book, they were focusing on the role of the unconscious in conscious behavior. Pagels explains why the Gnostics were considered heretical by the Christians of the day who became known as Orthodox:

> Gnostic Christians undoubtedly expressed ideas that the Orthodox abhorred. For example, some of these Gnostic texts question whether all suffering, labor and death derive from human sin, which, in the orthodox version, marred an originally perfect creation. Others speak of the feminine element in the divine, celebrating God as Father *and* Mother. Still others suggest that Christ's resurrection is to be understood symbolically, not literally.[4]

Even more offensive or threatening to Orthodox Christian leaders, Pagels believes, was the Gnostics' challenge to the emerging church hierarchy of bishops, priests, deacons, and laity. According to one Gnostic author, the Gnostics "join together as equals, enjoying mutual love, spontaneously helping one another. But the ... ordinary Christians wanted to command one another, outrivaling one another in their empty ambition; they are inflated with lust for power, each one imaging that he is superior to the others." The Orthodox bishop Iranaeus confirmed the difference, although with quite a different slant: "When they [the Gnostics] met, all the members first participated in drawing lots. Whoever received a certain lot apparently was designated to take the role of *priest;* another was to offer the sacrament as *bishop;* another would read the Scriptures for worship, and others would address the group as a *prophet*, offering extemporaneous spiritual instruction. The next time the group met, they would throw lots again so that the persons taking each role changed continually."[5] Given such radically different views of the proper authority structure of the church, Pagels argues, it is no mystery that the Orthodox hierarchy opposed the Gnostics.

But an even more fundamental difference between the Orthodox and Gnostic views struck deeper at the legitimacy of the Orthodox church and its hierarchy. In the gospel of John, Thomas asks Jesus, "Lord, we do not know where you are going, how can we know the way?" Jesus replies, "I am the way, the truth, and the light; no one comes to the Father, but by me." But in the Gnostic *Gospel of Thomas,* Jesus' answer is very different: "There is light within a man of light, and it lights up the whole world. If he does not shine, he is darkness." As Pagels explains, "Far from legitimizing any institution, this [Gnostic] saying directs one instead to oneself—to one's inner capacity to find one's own direction, to the 'light within'." She then adds,

> According to the [Gnostic] *Gospel of Thomas,* Jesus ridiculed those who thought of the "Kingdom of God" in literal terms, as if it were a specific place. Instead, it is a state of self-discovery: Rather, the "Kingdom is inside of you, and it is outside of you. When you come to know yourselves, then you will be known, and you will realize that you are the sons of the living Father." That "Kingdom," then, symbolizes a state of transformed consciousness.[6]

The tensions around such fundamental differences in doctrine built to a crisis between the two branches of the church.

By the year 200, the battle lines had been drawn: both Orthodox and Gnostic Christians claimed to represent the true church and accused one another of being outsiders, false brethren, and hypocrites. How was a believer to tell true Christians from false ones? Orthodox and Gnostic Christians offered different answers, as each group attempted to define the church in ways that excluded the other. Gnostic Christians ... pointed to qualitative criteria ... Quoting a saying of Jesus ("By their fruits you shall know them") that required evidence of spiritual maturity to demonstrate that a person belonged to the true church. But Orthodox Christians, by the late second century, had begun to establish objective criteria for church membership. Whoever confessed the creed, accepted the ritual of baptism, participated in worship, and obeyed the clergy was accepted as a fellow Christian. So the Orthodox Ignatius, Bishop of Antioch, defines the church in terms of the bishop, who represents that system: "Let no one do anything pertaining to the church without the bishop.... To join with the bishop is to join the church; to separate oneself from the bishop is to separate oneself not only from the church, but from God himself." Apart from the church hierarchy, "there is nothing that can be called a church."[7]

The two sides of this dispute had pushed each other to extreme positions. The Orthodox insisted that the religious faith of ordinary people must be entirely guided and ruled by an institutional authority. In contrast, the Gnostics insisted that there was no religious value at all in an institutional authority. (They both could have profited from the insights of the Framers of the Constitution, who saw the innate potential for goodness in humans but also recognized that humans were flawed, "not angels," and therefore needed the institutional aids of government to stay on track.)

In the end, the Gnostics were totally and brutally suppressed, and the Roman Catholic Church ruled through its hierarchy in dual harness with the Byzantine emperors, beginning with Constantine. In time, the position of the pope, imbued with great power and wealth, very likely became a tempting target for gifted people-w/o-conscience, as we have already seen with positions such as emperor, king, and CEO. There have been a few popes who seem to fit the description.

What, then, can this historical episode teach us about four-drive leadership? The disagreement between the Orthodox church and the Gnostics seems to have been a matter of pure dC—how does one gain true knowledge of God and oneself? But even this question has an important dB element. Most knowledge, after all, is passed on by people to other people, either directly or indirectly (through books, for example). Any large question of what knowledge is essential and how such knowledge is to be gained will therefore have social ramifications. (Think of the contemporary debates over what children should learn from their parents versus what they should or should not learn in school—that is, from the government—versus what they should or should not learn from TV, the Web, and so on. The ramifications for family and social life are many and serious.)

Although I believe Constantine to have been a person-w/o-conscience, he seems to have had a canny understanding of how dB worked in other people; more so, I would say, than the Gnostics. While the defeat of the Gnostics might seem, from the passages of Pagels I have quoted, to have been a defeat for dB, that was only true in the short run. In the long run, it seems to me to have been a victory for dB, perhaps even too great a victory. While the original Roman "converts" to Christianity were probably being coerced to accept the Nicene Creed out of their fear of Roman power, their descendents would have learned to accept the tenets of the church as a matter of sacred faith. The resulting creation of a Christendom encompassing nearly all of Europe was a case of the fulfillment of bonding on a huge scale. Constantine seems to have understood how important shared religious beliefs could be in binding his empire together and in securing loyalty to himself and future emperors.

In taking this decisive step, Constantine made Christianity so strong an institution—in large part because its members were so powerfully bonded to each other—that it not only supported the Byzantine and Roman empires but long outlived them. But at what cost? By forcing obedience to a frozen creed, he danger-ously shut down the spirit of open inquiry implicit in the drive to comprehend—something the Gnostics emphasized. This threw off the balance of the four-drive system. Any search for more accurate answers to any question was a threat; all answers were to come from the state-church hierarchy. This blocked the development of science and the search for new ways to increase economic productivity—two of the less fortunate hallmarks of the medieval period. In the following sections of this chapter, we will see that today it helps block the convergence of science and religion, thus significantly blocking humanity's drive to comprehend its nature and purpose.

I hope that religious scholars not only will check out the accuracy of this interpretation of Christian history, but will also reexamine the histories of other major religions to look for parallel events. For example, did Islam go through a comparable passage from an early stage of insightful observations about human nature to a stage of militaristic expansion (providing opportunities for leaders-w/o-conscience) and then to a stage comparable to the Protestant Reformation? Looking this way at all the major religions could lay the groundwork for a fresh approach to ecumenical reconciliation.

THE INSTITUTION OF ART AND HUMAN MEANING

Art in its many forms has been found in all cultures of all times, a strong indication that our hypothesized drive to comprehend— a drive to make sense of the world and give meaning to it—is genetically innate. Artistic representation manifests a conscious awareness of the people, creatures, and things around us—what they look like, what they do, what makes them important or interesting. Much of art brings out the human response, the feelings that these external signals evoke in us. The fact that a particular thing is singled out to be portrayed seems to confer some kind of meaning on it. The universality of representational decoration is a strong indicator that the drive to comprehend is not only innate but independent. Put simply, there is no discernable dA, dB, or dD value in drawing a picture of a tree on one's leather water bag, but every culture does something like that.

Art has been used to represent the full range of human emotions and an ever-widening range of human experiences. This may indicate not only the postulated independence of dC from the other drives but also the wide scope of dC itself. It seems that we are interested in making sense of as many of our human traits and experiences as possible, whether or not those traits and experiences or our comprehension of them have any particular survival value. Put another way, everything about us has the potential to be meaningful.

Some forms of art are more explicit than others about putting meaning into people's lives. Art has been used to evoke the sacred; to induce or declare or bemoan love; to acknowledge and respond to beauty; to praise, condemn, and satirize; to spread joy and express sorrow; to formulate intuitions about emerging social hazards—in short, to declare what *matters,* what has meaning.

Given the artistic sophistication displayed forty thousand years ago in the caves at Lescaux, art might well have been a part of hominid life as far back as late *H. erectus*. It has been argued that art might well have predated language. Evolutionary psychologists are developing evidence that some of the arts, such as music, constitute an innate skill set. Perhaps there are also innate latent skills for painting, poetry, and so on.

The question of the meaning of human existence is latent as a theme in many works of art. Religious paintings are an obvious example. Poetry often addresses these questions. Among well-known modern painters, Paul Gauguin has probably been the most explicit in addressing the ultimate questions. Gauguin went to the South Pacific seeking his dream of a perfect utopian society. Of course, he did not find his "noble savages," yet his paintings reflect his vision of the serenity of what island life might have been like before the disrupting effect of civilization. The amazing impact that Gauguin's most famous painting can have on contemporary people, even of a very different culture, is clear in the article that follows. I quote it here as a way to summarize the limited amount that I have to say about art in a book about human behavior and leadership.

On Loan, Sublime Awe
A Jewel of the MFA Staggers Crowds in Japan

Nagoya, Japan—One woman in the throng of admirers stood in front of the painting and cried. Another had just driven 2-1/2 hours from Osaka to be among the first to get close to it. "I felt goose bumps in my skin," she said after she did. A third, in halting English, struggled to explain the significance of the work. "The picture purifies us," she said exuberantly, "It gives us power and energy."

The painting is one of the Museum of Fine Arts' treasures, Paul Gauguin's monumental "Where Do We Come From? What Are We? Where Are We Going?" The enormous painting is set in Tahiti and has never been seen before in Asia. But when the painting got here, the Japanese people were ready. Its arrival was heralded on national prime time TV. The image was reproduced on street banners.... The governor of the region showed up to see it, and so did the mayor of Nagoya and the top guns at Toyota.... In the first week more than 15,000 people saw it, compared with an average of about 4,000 for other shows....

One of the many opening events featured the celebrated Tokyo writer Rei Nakanishi, who gave an impassioned speech called "The Painting that Changed My Life." Dr. Shunkichi Baba, the director of the Nagoya museum, explained why Gauguin is much admired in Japan. "We believe he tried to pursue what had to be done in his short life, He cared about the meaning of life and what could be done in life. That trait has particular relevance now. He is asking us to consider these same questions. It is a confused time in the 21st century, economically and politically. He is asking us to go back to the basics."[8]

The institution of art is, in a fundamental way, different from the other institutions being discussed. There are no powerful leaders in the same sense that there are in the other institutions. There are no Caesars here. Art is basically an individualistic process, even though its influence and impact is vast. Art is not an organized process, even though the help between artists flows between bonded relationship, as elsewhere. Therefore, the institution of art has, as I see it, little to say about leadership in general, even though it has so often spoken so loudly, so effectively, and so usefully about specific leaders. And, as can be seen in the example above, it can so powerfully speak to the meaning of human existence.

The Institution of Science and Human Meaning

As indicated in Figure 3.1, the transition to civilization—the first big change in human affairs created and transmitted exclusively by culture—was initiated by four major technical innovations: settled agriculture, domestication of animals, metallurgy, and writing. These triggers of massive change can be ranked in importance with three earlier triggers: the control of fire for cooking, the development of language, and the development of conscience. The final transition of comparable importance (so far) was the emergence of systematic science, the current cutting edge of change.

While science had long played a role in human affairs, it became a trigger of significant change only in the past five centuries. The period known as the Enlightenment brought a flowering of scientific thinkers who built on one another's insights, addressing the whole range of topics that we now submit to systematic scientific inquiry.

Listing chronologically even a few of their names and their scientific fields of study will show the astonishing scope of the emerging sciences:

Copernicus (1473–1543)	The first modern astrophysicist; revolutionized thinking about the solar system
Bacon (1561–1626)	A philosopher and scientist who provided the first explanation of the scientific method
Galileo (1564–1642)	The first systematic practitioner of physics and general science
Harvey (1578–1657)	A physician who first described blood circulation and launched the science of physiology
Hobbes (1588–1679)	The first modern political scientist
Descartes (1596–1650)	A gifted mathematician and father of modern philosophy
Willis (1621–1675)	The father of modern neuroscience and neurology
Boyle (1627–1691)	The originator of modern chemistry
Locke (1632–1704)	A philosopher of cultural determinism; proposed the first modern model of constitutional government
Newton (1642–1727)	The first scientist to combine physics and advanced mathematics

Montesquieu (1689–1755)	The first modern political historian
Hume (1711–1776)	A skeptical political scientist who influenced the Framers of the Constitution
Thomas Reid (1719–1796)	A pioneer of psychology who argued that all humans have the capacity to understand their environment with "common sense"
Adam Smith (1723–1790)	The first scientific economist; also a moral philosopher
Darwin (1809–1882)	The first to propose a general scientific theory of biology

From this sustained burst of creativity, science has flowered and become so powerful an influence in human affairs that it is fair to say that it is now *the* cutting edge of change in the world. The benefits have been enormous. Science made possible the industrial and information revolutions as well as the revolution in health care. It has doubled the life span of the average human and triggered another wave of population growth. It has greatly increased human economic productivity, with corresponding increases in the standard of living. It has enabled people to use their bodies less as machines for heavy labor and more as equipment with which to guide machinery and to create new ideas, artifacts, and knowledge. It has enabled us to understand the smallest units of matter as well as the remotest objects in space and time. It has led to the mapping of the genome and of the details of the human body, most recently the brain.

Science has also brought great risks to humankind. Starting with the controlled use of gunpowder, it has escalated our capacity to harm each other, finally arriving at what seems to be the ultimate weapon of mass self-destruction, the nuclear bomb.

Throughout its comparatively short history, science has had a very different role to play in society than religion, even though it is clearly energized by the same drive to comprehend. Science, as an institution, has never explicitly taken upon itself the task of giving meaning to human life in the way that religion and art do. It has undertaken the specialized role of pursuing *natural* explanations of *all* phenomena, including the nature of humans. Yet science's string of successes, on its own more limited terms, have been so spectacular—and not only continuous but accelerating—that it has become a giver of human meaning in spite of itself. It is science that has made it possible for humanity to set goals for itself such as continual material progress, mastery of the world and even our solar system, and the defeat of—rather than submission to—the major ills that have always beset us. Such goals were unimaginable before the rise of science; they seem both natural and uplifting now. Science, as an institution, has indeed made a profound impact on what it means to be human.

For a time, the various natural sciences were split out into separate disciplines, each pursuing its own specialized questions. But over the past fifty years this fragmentation has reversed, and great progress has been made in unifying these sciences—the goal that E. O. Wilson calls "consilience."[9] Now physicists, chemists, and biologists can generally work back and forth between their disciplines and explain a phenomenon of mutual interest in a shared language of scientifically tested propositions.

Although human behavior is only one of the many phenomena that science has undertaken to explain, it is the topic that has brought science into its most intense conflict with religion. For here, too, science confers meaning without meaning to. As science advances in its search for natural causes, religion is inevitably forced to retreat as it loses its basis for one supernatural answer after another. Copernicus destroyed religion's supernatural belief in the earth as the center of the universe with the sun and stars revolving around it. Darwin's theory of evolution undercut religious belief in the direct and separate Divine creation of each and every species, especially humans. This process has been extremely distressing to the leaders and followers of all religions, as is painfully clear in the continuing rejection of Darwin's theory of human evolution by many religious leaders.

Let me pose a leadership question: Is this distress and mutual aggravation necessary? Could careful four-drive leadership—both religious and scientific—bring about a convergence of these two crucial but contentious players in modern life? Is any agreement even imaginable on the ultimate questions?

POSSIBLE CONVERGENCE OF RELIGION AND SCIENCE ON THE MEANING OF HUMAN EXISTENCE?

Kenneth Miller, a biologist at Brown University, is the latest scholar to systematically address this issue. His book, *Finding Darwin's God: A Scientist's Search for Common Ground Between God and Evolution*,[10] is a comprehensive report on the current dialogue between science and religion. Miller works his way through all of the various religious attacks on evolutionary theory, assembling the detailed scientific evidence and totally discrediting the religious objections.[11] Miller concludes that "it is no longer possible to sustain scientifically the view that living things did not evolve from earlier forms or that the human species was not produced by the same evolutionary mechanisms that apply to the rest of the living world."[12] The evidence is solid: evolution is a fact, a proven theory.

Why, then, are the religious attacks on evolutionary theory so persistent and so deeply felt? Miller points out that it is partly because some evolutionary biologists have openly attacked basic religious doctrines. For example:

- The late-nineteenth-century German naturalist, Ernst Haeckel, wrote, "The cell consists of matter called protoplasm, composed chiefly of carbon with an admixture of hydrogen, nitrogen, and sulfur. These component parts, properly united, produce the soul and body of the animated world, and suitably nursed became man. With this single argument the mystery of the universe is explained, the Deity annulled, and a new era of infinite knowledge ushered in."[13] So much for the doctrine that God is the ultimate and original Creator.
- David Hull wrote, "Whatever the God implied by evolutionary theory and the data of natural history may be like, He is not the Protestant God of waste not, want not. He is also not a loving God who cares about His productions. He is not even the awful God portrayed in the book of Job. The God of the Galapagos is careless, wasteful, indifferent, almost diabolical. He is certainly not the sort of God to whom anyone would be inclined

to pray."[14] So much for the doctrine that God is good, caring, and loving.

- Richard Dawkins argues that a world ruled by evolution is very different from one designed by a Creator. Such a world "would be neither evil nor good in intention. It would manifest no intentions of any kind. In a universe of physical forces and genetic replication, some people are going to get hurt, other people are going to get lucky, and you won't find any rhyme or reason in it, nor any justice. The universe that we observe has precisely the properties we should expect if there is, at bottom, no design, no purpose, no evil and no good, nothing but blind, pitiless indifference."[15] So much for God the purposeful Creator.

- Stephen Jay Gould, in his book, *Wonderful Life*, calls the existence of humans "a wildly improbable evolutionary event," "a detail, not a purpose," and "a cosmic accident."[16] So much for the idea that God created humans in His likeness.

This is extreme ideological warfare. Is it any wonder that religious leaders fight back? They feel, with the deepest conviction, that the view of the universe offered by Haeckel, Hull, Dawkins, Gould, and others is false at the most fundamental level. How can there be any convergence of these positions?

Miller then reverses his story and develops a step-by-step case for a possible convergence based on *scientific findings* that the biologists quoted above had not taken into account. He begins with Newton's law of gravitation. The attraction between bodies is proportional to their masses and inversely proportional to the distance between them. The ratio between the attraction and these other factors is a so-called "constant of nature," which is a physicist's way of saying, "It is what it is. The universe just comes that way."

What it is, at least to fifteen decimal places, is 0.000000000066732 meters cubed per kilogram per second squared. But it is perfectly fair to ask: "Why is it that and not something else? What would happen if it *were* something else?" According to Miller, "It turns out that the consequences of even very small changes in the gravitational constant would be profound. If the constant were even slightly larger, it would have increased the force of gravity just enough to slow expansion after the Big Bang."[17] Miller then quotes the world-famous mathematical physicist, Stephen Hawking: "If the rate of expansion one second after the Big Bang had been smaller [because of a larger gravitational constant] by even one part in a hundred thousand million million, the universe would have collapsed back into itself before it reached its present size."[18] Conversely, Miller continues, "If it [the gravitational constant] had been smaller, the dust from the Big Bang would just have continued to expand, never coalescing into galaxies, stars, planets—or us. Moreover, gravity is only one of four fundamental forces in the universe. If any of the other three, the strong nuclear force, electromagnetism, and the resonance level of electrons, were of a different absolute value than they in fact are, life as we know it would be impossible."[19] In summary, he quotes Hawking again: "The odds against a universe like ours emerging out of something like the Big Bang are enormous. I think there are clearly religious implications."[20]

Hawking went on to make his implications even clearer: "This means that the initial state of the universe must have been very carefully chosen indeed if the hot big bang model was correct right back to the beginning of time. It would be very difficult to explain why the universe should have begun in just this way, except as the act of a God who intended to create beings like us."[21] This amazing conclusion of Hawking's is due to the incomprehensible enormousness of the odds *against any natural explanation.* Hawking came to this conclusion in his book *A Brief History of Time.* After discussing in detail all the available natural explanations of the Big Bang, he finds each of them seriously flawed. While he does not totally rule out the possibility of finding a viable natural explanation of the Big Bang, he does not see *any* prospects.[22]

Where does this leave the scientifically minded? The failure of one explanation certainly does not prove the truth of whatever alternative happens to be available. Fatal flaws in the Big Bang theory do not, in themselves, validate the account of creation in Genesis. Some people, probably many scientists, would declare themselves agnostics in the face of an unknowable mystery. Some people—certainly many religionists but also a growing number of scientists—would declare for a supernatural Creator of the universe, if not as an absolute certainty, at least as the more probable hypothesis. I think these people would accurately be called Deists. (I confess that Hawking's arguments have moved me from the ranks of the agnostics to the ranks of the Deists.) Certainly no one who agrees with Hawking's analysis would still be scientifically justified in dogmatically claiming to be an atheist or even a theist who believes that the Creator is constantly intervening in the affairs of our world. Both agnostics and Deists, however, might be able to agree that neither position can *ever* be disproved by scientific testing and might therefore be able to agree to respect the other group's way of thinking. Miller argues, and I agree, that this might be the basis for a limited—but very important—form of reconciliation between science and religion.

Of course, there are enormous social and psychological obstacles to even such a limited agreement. The trouble for scientists is that the proposed resolution clearly violates the code of most scientists that they should *never* resort to supernatural explanations of events. They have been taught that, with sufficient creativity, persistent hard work, and some inspiration, someone can eventually find a natural explanation for *every* phenomenon. This assumption is accepted as a matter of faith, of course, since no one can yet claim to have all the evidence needed to support it. But the record of science so far has supported this faith—all the way up to the Big Bang Theory.

And there the record of success seems to hit a wall. Here is how the astrophysicist Robert Jastrow expresses the dilemma scientists face: "For the scientist, who has lived by his faith in the power of reason, the story ends as a bad dream. He has scaled the mountains of ignorance; he is about to conquer the highest peak; as he pulls himself over the final rock; he is greeted by a band of theologians who have been sitting there for centuries."[23] Jastrow's story makes it clear why it will be so very difficult for scientists to acknowledge the implications of their own Big Bang Theory of the creation of the universe. Other drives than dC are involved. There is loyalty to the community of scientists and its code and history of success (dB) and there is the possible loss of status (dA). There are also fears of a defeat by a traditional adversary (dD).

Some scientists are responding by desperately searching for alternative explanations which, for instance, postulate millions upon millions of universes popping off endlessly in the random search for a relatively stable, life-supporting universe like ours. But as other scientists point out, even such multiverse theories still raise the question of the "first mover." The dogmatic belief of most scientists that they can explain *every* phenomenon is, I argue, the key belief that is currently leading science off track.

Obviously, Miller is one of the scientists who endorse the supernatural Creator hypothesis, but his argument moves on directly to the issue addressed in this book—the evolution and meaning of human behavior. Miller first cites Ian Barbour, the physicist and religious scholar: "Natural laws and choice may equally be instruments of God's intentions. These can be purposeful without an exact predetermined plan."[24] This argument gets Miller around the teleological or deterministic hurdle. Miller then goes on to say, "Given evolution's ability to adapt, to innovate, to test and to experiment, sooner or later it would have given the Creator exactly what He was looking for—a creature like us."[25] This argument puts Miller clearly on the side of putting meaning into human existence. But his use of the word *looking* opens the door again to the teleological problem by suggesting that the Creator has a divinely willed end-state which we will eventually reach.

I would change one word in Miller's sentence. I would replace the word *looking* with the word *hoping*. And I say this, not as a religionist acting on faith, but as a scientist exploring the logical implications of the hypothesis, derived from the Big Bang Theory, that the universe had a supernatural Creator.

The Renewed Darwinian Theory of Human Behavior and Leadership proposes that the human who emerged from the evolutionary process has a pre-wired *requirement* to make morally significant choices in a way that is *not* predetermined. It is as much within our power to make choices that lead to the destruction of our species as it is to make choices which keep us on the track of continued life and development. If it were the Creator's *will* that we "succeed," it does not seem logical that we would have been created with a capacity to fail. Logically, then, it must be the

Creator's *hope*—but not the Creator's *will*—that we stay on the path of life.

It follows that the Creator can *never* intervene directly in human affairs; it would clearly signal a failure of the Creator's experiment. A hope that is guaranteed or enforced is not a hope. This is the sound reason that many religious leaders have offered us as an explanation for the existence of evil and suffering. We have been given the freedom to make mistakes, and even to be evil, as the price of having the freedom of choice in the first place. But the Darwinian theory of human behavior identifies us as a species which has *evolved* to be a moral actor, a maker of hard choices, capable of sin but not doomed to it.

While we as humans cannot expect to envision the Creator's long-term *hope* for us, the RD Theory tells us that we can trust our moral skill set as a guide to whether or not we are staying on track toward a better life for all. It is like a gyroscope, which cannot tell you where you are going but can warn you that you are about to tip over. Are we—as individuals, as members of collectives, or as an entire species—working to fulfill, for ourselves and for others, all four drives? Are we becoming more peaceable, more healthy, more prosperous, more knowledgeable, more caring, more just, more creative, and more secure in a sustainable relation with each other and our earthly environment? And are we raising the next generation to do even better by these hard-wired yet infinitely flexible criteria? Or are we becoming more violent, more exploitive, more addicted, more impoverished, more ignorant, more paranoid, and more destructive to each other and our environment?

THE CONVERGENCE OF RELIGION AND SCIENCE AS A LEADERSHIP CHALLENGE

While the RD Theory argues that our brains are designed (by the processes of evolution) to try to stay on track, history shows us that humans have always needed gifted leadership to help them recognize and fulfill the universal moral sense we all have (except people-w/o-conscience), to see the opportunities to move forward on track, to see the potential of worldwide bonding. I believe, then, that the ultimate test for the scientific and religious leaders of our time is to overcome their reluctance to acknowledge each other's shares of the truth and then to help others acknowledge and live according to this combined understanding.

It will be a hard test indeed. Miller has reported, in a private conversation, that his book has generated about as much hate mail from scientists as from religious believers. The former would excommunicate him from the scientific community while the latter would dispatch him to hell. I have already discussed what makes it hard for scientists to accept convergence. What are the main mental sticking points for religious believers?

First, how can *all* religions come to believe they are *all* worshiping the same Creator? In this regard, science can help by providing the Big Bang Theory as the ultimate argument for a single supernatural Creator. Every religious believer can potentially see that our one and only universe is the product of a single Big Bang (in fact, the scientific term for it is a "singularity"), so if the universe was produced by a Creator at all, it must have been produced by a *single* Creator. Each religion can still use its traditional symbols and rituals to worship the one Creator.

The second sticking point may be more difficult to deal with. Most religious traditions have produced some ancient sacred documents. In some religions, these documents are seen as the revealed word of God, not as their human authors' understanding of God's word. This belief in direct, infallible, divine revelation chains religions to the particular words chosen by particular writers at particular (and generally remote) times. I agree with many writers that this belief in the frozen literal truth of ancient sacred texts is the key misleading belief that blocks religious leadership from embracing evolution and other well-established scientific findings. This blockage is very similar to that of scientists (see Jastrow's description earlier) who simply can't bear the thought that a religious account of the beginnings of the universe might have been right all along.

Many religious scholars have avoided the freezing of scriptures and made them open to reinterpretation based on newer, verifiable knowledge. As an example of this, I refer the interested reader to *The Science of God*, by Gerald Schroeder,[26] which demonstrates how the story of creation in Genesis can be reinterpreted as a symbolic story that is amazingly consistent with the understanding of the creation developed by contemporary science. Or consider Genesis 3:4–7:

> And the serpent said unto the woman, ye shall not surely die: For God doth know that in the day ye eat [the fruit from the forbidden tree], then your eyes shall be opened, and ye shall be as gods, knowing good and evil. And when the woman saw that the tree was good for food, and that it was pleasant to the eyes, and a tree to be desired to make one wise, she took of the fruit thereof, and did eat, and gave also unto her husband with her: and he did eat. And the eyes of them both were opened, and they knew that they were naked.

My argument is that when hominids evolved dB and dC, they lost their innocence and were forced to make moral choices between good and evil—the hard choices, God-like choices. And it was Eve's deliberate choice of her "husband," Adam, as the one with whom to share the forbidden fruit that pulled the men into sharing this state of the "knowledge of good and evil."

The Dalai Lama displayed the kind of openness to current scientific findings I'm talking about at a conference held between a group of distinguished mind and brain scholars and a group of equally distinguished Buddhist scholars. To quote the Dalai Lama,

> For instance, when it comes to the workings of the mind, Buddhism has a centuries-old science that has been of practical interest to researchers in the cognitive and neurosciences and in the study of emotions, offering significant contributions to their understanding.... On the other hand, Buddhism can learn from science as well. I have often said that if science proves facts that conflict with Buddhist understanding, Buddhism must change accordingly. We should always adopt a view that accords with the facts.[27]

Each major religion has subgroups that cover the spectrum from openness to science, as expressed by the Dalai Lama, to insistence on the literal interpretation of ancient texts in the face of all contradictory scientific evidence. In this regard, I would urge religious leaders to bear in mind that there have been some few religious leaders who were probably people-w/o-conscience and that their single-minded concerns for power might have shaped some aspects of ancient religious texts. Constantine, after all, played a major role in drafting the Nicene Creed and it is by no means clear that he was exclusively motivated by a drive to understand God. With this in mind, one task of religious leadership would be to purge religious literature of such dubious influences, just as one task of scientific leadership should be to purge inaccurate theories from scientific literature.

No discussion of the current dialogue between religion and science can ignore Richard Dawkins's provocatively titled book, *The God Delusion*.[28] I am sorry to have to judge it a rather painful example of misguided scientific leadership. "Painful" because I find myself in total agreement with almost all of the lesser conclusions Dawkins makes on the way to stating his final conclusion, made clear in the book's title. "Misguided leadership" because he assumes that, because science has in so many cases found natural explanations of phenomena that supersede the supernatural religious explanations, it follows that science can go all the way and displace all supernatural explanations. Dawkins actually quotes *A Brief History of Time*, in which Hawking says "for then we should know the mind of God," and still goes on to declare that Hawking is an atheist. How is this consistent with Hawking's quotations earlier in this chapter? Dawkins also makes very favorable mention of Miller's contributions to refuting the arguments of creationists and proceeds to label him an atheist. But in doing so, he totally ignores Miller's arguments (following Hawking and Darwin) for a supernatural origin of the universe and even the title of Miller's book, *Finding Darwin's God*. Dawkins may have sound scientific grounds for totally ignoring the arguments of these two authorities, but he has not stated them. Is he so committed to the scientific code of *no supernatural explanations permitted* that he simply cannot perceive their evidence that argues for making a single, albeit important, exception in regard to the Big Bang?

The RD Theory asserts that the drive to comprehend is an innate drive for all human beings. And like all the drives, dC is significantly fulfilled for most of us as members of cultures. It is culture that passes on knowledge across time. Cultural institutions dedicated to fulfilling dC are essential and, in turn, the leadership of these institutions is vitally important. I think the two chief institutions dedicated to dC—religion and science—are, in some mirrored way, currently going off track. There is heightened tension between them, particularly between some leading evolutionary biologists and some leaders of the fundamentalist wings of the major religions. The latter is expressed as a backlash against the growing dominance of the materialistic, secular, science-oriented aspects of Western culture. Some of these religious leaders are still trying to harness the power of government to force their particular religious beliefs on others, as Constantine did long ago. On the scientific side, some prominent leaders are taking highly provocative, arrogant positions that simply reinforce the worst fears of the fundamentalists. It is up to the leaders of each side to break up this dangerous tit-for-tat cycle.

Yet I think there is hope that, with the help of good/moral leadership, both science and religion can acknowledge that each has a historical record that deserves respect; not as politically correct "tolerance" but as a genuine acknowledgment of the truth. We can all be grateful that scientists have so diligently pursued natural explanations of all phenomena, all the way to the Big Bang, and that religious leaders have so tenaciously argued for the existence of a supernatural Creator of the universe. As we reflect on the meaning of human existence in light of the mystery of the Big Bang and of the extreme unlikelihood that the Big Bang randomly created a universe with precisely the right four physical constants, we might hear an inner voice clearly say, "Be still, and *know* that I am the Creator." Then we might realize that we must all be members of the Creator's hoped-for species on earth and must all be worshipping the one Creator of our one and only universe.

Moving toward such a reconciliation can be an essential part of the larger human mission of helping our species keep on track. It would clear the way for our collective dC to advance in directions that are blocked by the current science versus religion impasse. Bringing that about would be the essence of good/moral leadership.

FIGURE 7.1. DRIVEN TO LEAD.

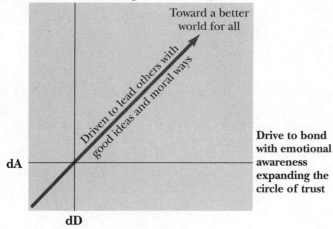

Drive to comprehend with conscious cognition expanding the frontiers of knowledge

Toward a better world for all

Driven to lead others with good ideas and moral ways

dA

Drive to bond with emotional awareness expanding the circle of trust

dD

More generally the theme of "keeping on track" will be used for the rest of this book. It is, of course, the journey metaphor, and journeys through time into the unknown future require good/moral leaders who combine the unique human drives to comprehend and bond, and thereby lead the way toward satisficing all four drives, toward a better world for all. Figure 7.1 is an attempt to capture this process in diagrammatic form.

PART THREE

LEADERSHIP IN CONTEMPORARY AFFAIRS

CHAPTER EIGHT

KEEPING ON TRACK
Leadership in Contemporary Corporations

> *We have always known that heedless self-interest was*
> *bad morals; we know now that it is bad economics.*
> — FRANKLIN DELANO ROOSEVELT[1]

CAN CORPORATIONS EVER BE HUMANE? GOOD/MORAL LEADERSHIP OF CORPORATIONS

We find it hard today to imagine the CEO of a cigarette company sponsoring basic scientific research on the suspected health risk of his company's product, assuring himself of the dire results, immediately warning the public to stop smoking, stopping the promotion of smoking, and letting his company's sales drop, even as he searches for ways to find new employment for most of its employees. But should we be so pessimistic? In fact, British Tobacco has, essentially, been doing this very thing for many years. I had the good fortune to be a faculty member for a Harvard Business School action-planning executive course when a small team of British Tobacco executives came with instructions to plan for the implementation of this strategy.

Many leaders do keep their corporations on track in a very deliberate way that provides a rigorous test of the Renewed Darwinian Theory of good/moral leadership. They have been succeeding amazingly well in fulfilling all four drives, not only for their employees and their stockholders but also for their other stakeholders and for top management. We are fortunate that the CEO of one such firm has written a crystal-clear exposition of how it all was done. Bill George was CEO of the medical technology company Medtronic from 1991 to 2001. The Medtronic example gives us a chance to examine a top-down application of RD Theory good/moral leadership even as the drilling platform example in Chapter Four gave us a rich example of RD Theory good/moral leadership looking from the bottom up. To provide the full flavor of the Medtronic story, I will quote at some length from Bill George's book, *Authentic Leadership*.[2]

George starts off with a blunt introduction:

> Thank you, Enron and Arthur Andersen. The depth of your misconduct shocked the world and awakened us to the reality that the business world was on the wrong track, worshiping the wrong idols, and headed for self-destruction.... We needed this kind of shock therapy to realize that something is sorely missing in many of our corporations.... I believe deeply that the vast majority of corporate CEOs are honest leaders dedicated to building their companies. Unfortunately, far too many leaders got caught up by the short-term pressures of the stock market and the opportunities it brought for personal wealth. Under these pressures and enmeshed in the quest for personal gain, they wound up sacrificing their values and their stakeholders.[3]

Bill George is insistent that the key to Medtronic's success is the fact that it is "mission-driven." Of course, *mission* is a neutral word; making as much profit as possible can be one's mission. But George clearly had a good/moral mission in mind:

> It is only through a sense of purpose that companies can realize their potential. It is their raison d'être that animates employees and inspires them to turn purpose into reality. The best path to long-term growth in shareholder value comes from having a well-articulated mission that inspires employee commitment.... Employees today are seeking meaning in their work. Since they spend more time at work than anywhere else in their lives, shouldn't they demand meaningful work? In mission-driven companies employee motivation comes from believing in the purpose of the work and being part of creating something worthwhile.[4]

> In my experience, motivating employees with a sense of purpose is the only way to deliver innovative products, superior service and

unsurpassed quality over the long haul. Competitors will eventually copy any innovative idea for a product or service, but an organization of highly motivated people is very hard to duplicate.[5]

George reported on how the focus on mission started:

In 1962, five years after Medtronic founder Earl Bakken invented the pacemaker, the company was losing lots of money and nearing bankruptcy. It was then that Bakken, with the urging of his board of directors, wrote the Medtronic Mission. It gave the company a clear purpose and focus. Within three months the company turned profitable and has been so ever since. The mission of Medtronic is to restore people to full life and health. This is the heart of the company's success. It has led to spectacular results for patients, career opportunities for employees, and a dramatic rise in Medtronic's shareholder value.[6]

The Medtronic Mission is reprinted in Figure 8.1. As in the passages already quoted from George's book, we can see recognition of all four RD theory drives, although George knew nothing of this theory.

FIGURE 8.1. MEDTRONIC MISSION.

- To contribute to human welfare by application of biomedical engineering in the research, design, manufacture and sale of instruments or appliances that alleviate pain, restore health, and extend life.
- To direct our growth in the areas of biomedical engineering where we display maximum strength and ability; to gather people and facilities that tend to augment these areas; to continuously build on these areas through education and knowledge assimilation; to avoid participation in areas where we cannot make unique and worthy contributions.
- To strive without reserve for the greatest possible reliability and quality in our products; to be the unsurpassed standard of comparison and to be recognized as a company of dedication, honesty, integrity and service.
- To make a fair profit on current operations to meet our obligations, sustain our growth, and reach our goals.
- To recognize the personal worth of employees by providing an employment framework that allows personal satisfaction in work accomplished, security, advancement opportunity and means to share in the company's success.
- To maintain good citizenship as a company.

Source: B. George, *Authentic Leadership* (San Francisco: Jossey-Bass, 2003), p. 67.

George explained how the company has been able to make the mission very real in the lives of all its employees:

> One of the most powerful ways of gaining alignment with an organization's values that I have seen is Medtronic's Mission and Medallion ceremony. In this personal meeting with the founder or CEO, new employees hear firsthand about the company's purpose and its values. At the end each new employee is awarded a medallion symbolizing the company's mission.... In 1999, after we had doubled our workforce due to expansion and mergers, I conducted sessions for over eight thousand employees, passing out medallions to each of them.[7]

MEDTRONIC—A VALUES-DRIVEN COMPANY

While there can be no doubt that Medtronic is mission-driven, George emphasizes that it is also a values-driven company. Values for him refer to the *way* the firm pursues its mission.

> Values begin with telling the truth, internally and externally. Integrity must run deep in the fabric of an organization's culture. It guides the everyday actions of employees and is central to its business conduct. Transparency is an integral part of integrity. The truth, both successes and failures, must be shared openly with the outside world. Authentic companies operate in a democratic and collaborative manner. They are inclusive, welcoming talented people from highly diverse backgrounds and recognizing the strength and stability of differing opinions and diverse life experiences. Such organizations are characterized by a spirit of inquiry, the constant desire to understand the issues in their fullest breadth and to challenge people to develop their full potential—and use it on the job, every day. The final value of the authentic company is consistency, the steadiness with which the values of integrity, stewardship, collaboration and inquiry are practiced.[8]

A skeptic could well ask at this point if George really walks this good talk about values. Actually the book is full of concrete examples of the behavior of Medtronic's top executives in this regard. I will cite just one example, involving George:

> To my surprise, I faced a severe values test during my first year with Medtronic. As part of my first reorganization, I appointed a new president of Medtronic Europe, who had previously been president of Medtronic's Dutch pacemaker subsidiary. Shortly after taking over, he proposed the acquisition of the subsidiary's Italian distributor. The price for the business was very high, but he insisted we had to buy it or risk losing the business. During due diligence, Medtronic's auditors uncovered inappropriate accounting for a sham contract for Italian marketing services. When the controller was asked what the account was for, he refused to answer, saying that it was integral to doing business in Italy.
>
> After our General Counsel brought the issue to me, we hired a special legal investigator. His preliminary report indicated that the funds were traced to a secret Swiss bank account set up on behalf of the Italian distributor. There the trail stopped. Although he could not prove it, the investigator believed the funds were being used to pay off Italian physicians. At this point we informed the Medtronic board and asked them to set up a special committee to oversee the investigation.
>
> I called our European president and told him to come to Minneapolis immediately. When asked about the promotion account, he replied, "You don't want to know about that fund." I told him that indeed we did. At this point he got very defensive, even hostile, saying, "That's the trouble with you Americans. You're always trying to impose your values on Europeans. Business is done differently in Europe." Finally, I said, "These are not American values. They are Medtronic values that apply worldwide. You violated them, and you must resign immediately."[9]

MEDTRONIC—A PERFORMANCE-DRIVEN COMPANY

George did not ignore his various stakeholders' drives to acquire. Under his leadership, Medtronic had an explicit focus on performance in terms of productivity gains and innovation. Sometimes this required some tough love. For example, when George arrived at Medtronic, he found that the company's long history of success had led to a "soft underbelly"; targets were being missed, responsibility for performance was diffused, people failed but did not lose their jobs, and there were excuses for all of this. George realized that these aspects of Medtronic's culture had to change if it was going to compete effectively and fulfill its mission of being a global leader in medical technology. "We had no choice but to make the Medtronic culture more performance-oriented if we were going to fulfill our mission. Otherwise, we would lose out to more aggressive competitors and never earn the right to serve those patients."[10]

One step to increasing performance was to reduce what are known as *transaction costs*. The well-established transaction cost theory holds that a relatively unnoticed but significant cost of doing business is the cost of executing exchanges between departments within the firm and between the firm and its suppliers and customers.[11] It has been demonstrated that these costs can be greatly reduced when relationships of hostility and distrust are replaced with relationships of trust and mutual caring. This is what George did. This is one way that Medtronic pulled off the "paradoxical" feat of achieving superior performance for stockholders (over eighteen years, Medtronic has maintained a 19 percent average gain per year in revenues and a 22 percent average gain per year in earnings per share) while emphasizing benefits for customers and employees—an excellent example of multiple-drive success.

As George put it, "One of the greatest challenges of businesses today is creating a culture that is both values-centered and performance-driven. Many business executives believe they must make trade-offs between the two. I don't buy it. But doing both simultaneously requires skillful leadership."[12] Or to put his last sentence into our Renewed Darwinian Theory terms: all four drives can be balanced and satisfied for all of the organization's stakeholders, but only if the organization's leadership group serves as its balancing prefrontal cortex and works hard at finding the all-purpose path forward that fits the relevant circumstances. This is the road, the only road, to sustainable long-term success. This positive set of results is dependent not only on an appropriate governance structure—think of the U.S. Constitution—but also on the appropriate good/moral leadership behavior that George and the other top executives at Medtronic exemplify.

NUCOR: GOOD/MORAL LEADERSHIP IN THE STEEL INDUSTRY

Medtronic is by no means alone in operating with the RD Theory model of good/moral leadership. There are many such examples. To cite just one, Nucor, a Rust Belt steel maker, "gained renown in the late 1980s as an upstart nipping at the heels of the integrated steel giants. Nucor's legendary leader Kenneth Iverson's radical insight: that employees, even hourly clock-punchers, will make an extraordinary effort if you reward them richly, treat them with respect, and give them real power. Nucor is an upstart no more. Under the leadership of CEO Daniel DiMicco it has clung to that core philosophy even as it has grown into the largest steel company in the U.S." "Nucor's 387% return to shareholders over the past five years handily beats almost all other companies in the Standard & Poor's 500-stock index."[13] A list of some of Nucor's "best practices" shows the RD Theory at work even though no one at Nucor could have known about it:

- Executives listen to factory-floor workers' ideas and put them into action, often with success. Here is the familiar combination of dC (better ideas) and dA (efficiency); because humans have evolved to work well in groups, dA and dC are fulfilled together.
- Nucor pushes responsibility (which is also respect and self-respect) down to the lowest-level worker who can fulfill it. For example, workers order parts rather than having to ask their supervisors to do it for them.
- The company takes its corporate culture seriously. For example, cultural compatibility is an important criterion for acquisitions.
- Nucor is willing to try new technologies even when it's not absolutely sure they will work out. Of course, current success and profit are important, but so is continuous learning and a certain amount of excitement (one way of fulfilling dC).
- Every single employee's name goes on the cover of the annual report.

- Bonuses reflect overall corporate success, making it hard to earn a bonus through actions that are ultimately harmful to the company. A plant manager's bonus is based on the entire corporation's return on equity. Workers really do feel the company's success or failure year by year. A typical worker's bonus in 2002 was $58,931, while in 2005 it was $91,293.
- Pay disparities are modest at Nucor. Last year the CEO collected a salary and bonus twenty-three times the compensation of his average steelworker. The ratio for typical CEOs is four hundred times as much.

ENRON: A COUNTEREXAMPLE OF OFF-TRACK LEADERSHIP

There are sound reasons why Enron has become the poster child of bad (as defined by RD Theory) corporate leadership. Several books have appeared to examine the story of Enron's meteoric rise and total collapse. For me, the definitive book is Malcolm Salter's *Innovation Corrupted: The Origins and Legacy of Enron's Collapse.* Salter tells, of course, a very complex story. For our focus on top leadership, however, I will draw on Salter's account of the defining leadership decisions taken by CEO Ken Lay that started the "culture of deceit" which eventually characterized the entire firm. Salter draws particular attention to Lay's response to an oil-trading scam that came to light in a company called Valhalla, which Enron had just acquired.

Valhalla's lead trader, Louis Borget, its treasurer, Thomas Mastroeni, and several others were reporting phony profits from sham transactions carried out by shell companies they had set up in Panama. The huge bonuses they paid themselves, based on these phony profits, were quite real. In January 1987, a New York bank called an Enron auditor to ask about some suspicious cash transfers. Not long after, Ken Lay invited Borget and Mastroeni to a meeting to discuss what was going on. The two men told Lay that their actions were legal and that, having fulfilled their current profit targets, they were trying to reserve profits to meet future targets.

In fact, that kind of manipulation is both unethical and illegal. But Lay did not fire Borget and Mastroeni. He sent them back to work, apparently because he needed the profits they were generating. As Salter puts it, "Lay's failure to deal decisively with this rogue trading behavior became part of Enron's cultural lore.... His behavior set a tone that had enormous adverse consequences for his organization and its stockholders a decade later, when traders and originators were routinely overstating the value of deals to inflate their own bonuses."[14]

So Enron's eventual collapse can accurately be described as a moral failure which started a "culture of deceit," an infection at the top that eventually poisoned the entire organization. It was driven by an excessive drive to acquire (dA) that overrode any concern for the harm that tolerating Borget's lies about profits would eventually cause for stockholders, creditors, customers, and honest employees. Lay's decision to accept Borget's behavior—his lack of moral outrage when he found out about it—makes him a likely person-w/o-conscience. Exclusively concerned with his dA, he tolerated an illegal and deceptive business practice because he apparently thought he could profit from it. His brain seemed to have no way of anticipating how his decision would send a signal to his entire staff that immoral behavior was okay if it was profitable. In his widely reported final speech to his managers about the strengths of the company, even as it was collapsing, Lay also showed that he was an extremely competent liar, another sign of a leader-w/o-conscience.

So far, we have seen notable contemporary examples of both *good/moral* corporate leadership and *bad* corporate leadership. Rather than offer a contemporary example of *misguided* corporate leadership, however, I will offer a contemporary leadership theory that is doing much to misguide corporate leaders. Its name is "agency theory."

Misguided Leadership: The Role of Agency Theory

Agency theory is a branch of neoclassical economics specifically adapted to corporate management. Its primary author is Michael Jensen, with major assists from William Meckling.[15] Its chief axiom, drawn directly from neoclassical economics, is that all humans, in making all their decisions, are motivated to maximize their rational self-interest. In its original and basic form, the theory explicitly defines "self-interest" to be acquiring the very same valued objects that define the RD Theory's drive to acquire (dA). In short, agency theory assumes that all people operate on the single innate drive to acquire.

What are the logical implications of this axiom for corporate leadership? Agency theory focuses on a problem faced by the owners of corporations (stockholders): they must hire agents (top management) to manage their properties, but these agents, according to the theory, will naturally focus on maximizing their own material interests, not those of the owners. The resulting gaps between potential profits for shareholders and the profits they actually earn with self-interested agents in charge are referred to as agency costs. In the mid-1970s, agency costs were judged by agency theorists to be a serious problem, on the basis of evidence that profits and CEO pay did not correlate at all well. What, then, could motivate the agents to maximize the owners' interests and minimize agency costs? Since agency theory does not recognize an innate drive to bond or a moral sense common to all humans, it turned to elaborate financial incentives as the logical remedy. Agency theorists recommended very high monetary rewards for top management (agents) who generate increased profits for shareholders (owners). The tight connection of CEO pay to current profits was called "pay for performance."

Agency theory attracted a great deal of attention in the business press and in business schools and is credited with triggering the so-called "stockholder revolution" of the 1980s and 1990s. This was marked by a wave of stockholder suits, CEO turnover, and hostile takeovers by managers of other corporations who promised more aggressive profit-seeking. Inside the firms, it led to aggressive cost-cutting, "downsizing" (laying off of employees), high managerial turnover, and, in general, a move to "lean and mean" management. CEOs found themselves under intense pressure from stock analysts to make and then meet or exceed ever-higher profit predictions; failure to do so would bring them bad analysts' reports, a significant drop in share price, and therefore a significant drop in pay—if not dismissal. Cutting out the costs of new product development was but one obvious way to play this game, as long as the consequences for future profits were ignored.

CEOs pressed their subordinates to "make their numbers or else"; subordinates usually found some way to do it, even if they would have to restate these earnings a year or two later. Naturally, some crossed the line into such illegal practices as reporting fraudulent numbers, but it all served to reward the investor insiders and top corporate officers. The more aggressive CEOs could use their inflated stock to buy out more prudent—and less-highly-(over)valued—firms.

The stock market did its part by regularly rewarding announcements of layoffs or "restructuring" with a stock-price increase. And since the sudden movement of stock prices was the favored way to test the theory, being "mean" not only rewarded the managers involved with big bonuses but also proved to the agency theorists that their theory was accurate. Business schools often found that agency theory courses were their most popular ones.

In terms of the RD Theory of leadership, agency theory offered a great opportunity for profiteering by leaders-w/o-conscience, and even for copycat misguided leaders, by displacing good/moral leadership. Agency theorists, of course, did not recognize that their model of man was nearly identical with that of Machiavelli and Hobbes, which, in turn, was based on those authors' study of rulers of the Dark Ages. But clever people-w/o-conscience were quick to recognize a terrific opportunity to quickly acquire great personal wealth and power by following a "scientifically legitimated" economic theory which exactly matched their genetic makeup. Doing anything that put money in their pockets and getting rid of anything that didn't was exactly what their three-drive brains told them to do anyway. The trick was to get into the right power position and then time one's exit carefully. Normal leaders, caught in this free-for-all rush to the bottom, were pressed to start looking out for "number one." Some were manipulated into becoming misguided managers (of themselves and of their employees) as a combination of their dA (skillfully manipulated by a leader-w/o-conscience) and their dD (knowing the boss would be quick to replace anyone who was too "soft") overwhelmed their dB (the innate moral code telling one not to cheat other people).

All of this helped create the stock market bubble at the turn of the twenty-first century and its inevitable collapse, epitomized

by Enron, Tyco, and WorldCom. This undoubtedly contributed to
the recession at the time, from which the nation took a long time
to fully recover. Perhaps the deepest, costliest, and most persistent
wound to the country has been the erosion of trust in our
corporations and in our overall economic system. This wound will
take years to heal, even if stricter regulation of financial reports
has stopped many of the corporate abuses of that time. No less
an exemplar of the "maximizing shareholder value" movement
than Jack Welch, former CEO of General Electric, summed up
the mistake in almost–RD Theory terms: "On the face of it,
shareholder value is the dumbest idea in the world. Shareholder
value is a result, not a strategy.... your main constituencies are
your employees, your customers and your products."[16] In other
words, agency theory couldn't be more wrong. Humans are
genetically wired *not* to be maximizers of self-interest; they
are genetically wired to be *satisficers* of their own interests and
other people's interests, not in order to be good scouts but
because that is the very successful survival mechanism which our
species has evolved.

DESIGNING CORPORATE STRUCTURES TO ENCOURAGE GOOD/MORAL CORPORATE BEHAVIOR

While agency theory has been, I argue, misleading corporate
leaders, have there been other theories and structures available to
help managers stay on track?

A book by Robert Simons, *Levers of Organization Design*,
demonstrates explicitly how RD Theory can be applied to the
structural design of corporations to help satisfice all four drives
of employees.[17] Without knowing of the similarity, Simons was
also following the lead of the Framers when they designed checks
and balances into the Constitution. Simons offers the most
sophisticated and advanced model available on how to build
attention to all four innate human drives into the structures and
standard practices of a firm:

- (dA) Design the structures of each working group, using
  incentives and some control of corporate resources, to give

all employees a chance to acquire financial gain, status, and a sense of personal accomplishment. (Think of Nucor.)

- (dD) Provide early-warning systems to alert individuals and groups to threats to the achievement of their goals. Use diagnostic control systems and define each person's and each group's span of accountability. These methods avoid surprises and let individuals and groups make trade-offs and adjustments so that group assets and individual achievements are reasonably secure.
- (dC) Give all employees "an outlet to exercise their innate desire to create, experiment, improve and learn" by appointing them to teams and task forces that cut across organizational lines and charging them with innovating on behalf of the entire organization.
- (dB) Because humans have an innate "drive to bond" (Simons uses that very phrase), successful and sustainable organizations must make it possible for their people to work together cooperatively, sharing not only the sense of belonging in various groups but also "the purpose, history, and culture embodied by the entire organization itself."[18]

I would add one structural feature to Simons's list: minimize the number of hierarchal levels, which will foster the kind of trust associated with face-to-face relations. This will also make it easier to delegate some decisions to every employee, even at the lowest rank, which will in turn require every employee to activate his or her drive to comprehend.

Simons has arranged these design elements so that each element can serve as a check on the other elements in the interest of achieving integration and balance in the entire organization.

One important element of corporate structure that Simons does not address is the design of the very top-level governance system of the chief executives and the board of directors, for which there are two existing models. The conventional model is that of a single office of the CEO/board chairman combined with a board of directors selected by a forced-choice election—only one panel of nominees that are selected by the CEO and the incumbent directors—with the stockholders given one vote per share. This standard design obviously places the entire corporation under the control of the CEO and the large stockholders represented on the board of directors. These are the people who, by law, are expected by the capital market makers (that is, Wall Street) to place top priority on their drive to acquire—on the maximization of profits. This arrangement is certainly not designed to strike a balance among the four drives.

An alternative—the stakeholder model—was well expressed as early as 1945 by John Baker, the number two dean of the Harvard Business School: "The essential concern of corporation directors, particularly in our large corporations, is not today, nor should it ever have been, merely protection of stockholders and their interests. The problem is the reconciliation of private enterprise with the smooth functioning of a democratic society with justice to all groups: stockholders, executives, employees, creditors, customers and the public. Such a broad concept of the functions of directors is frequently overlooked. Nevertheless, this should be the contribution of directors to our national life."[19] (Baker served under Dean Wallace Donham, who consistently stressed the responsibilities of corporations to all stakeholders.)

After World War II, the stakeholder model for top corporate governance was becoming standard doctrine, gaining strength alongside McGregor's widely used Theory Y model of employee motivation.[20] Business leadership groups such as the Business Roundtable endorsed it. The stakeholder principle also went international. Germany, under the postwar occupation, put the stakeholder principle into its corporate laws by requiring corporations to put employee representatives on their boards. In this chapter, we have seen stakeholder theory practiced by George at Medtronic and Iverson of Nucor, and there are others like them. Nevertheless, the theory is not built into the legal structure—the charter—of any U.S. firm. Today, the reigning philosophy in business leadership groups is that of maximizing stockholder value, with no representatives of other stakeholders at the top board level.

Note that leadership under the RD Theory does not mean that everything the leader does must be motivated by some humane concern other than profit. It means that, whatever originally motivates a particular action, that motivation must then be checked and balanced with due consideration for the consequences, plus and minus, for the full set of corporate stakeholders. This is what our prefrontal cortex is doing all day long and, in a sense, all a leader has to do is make sure to have enough information and then let his or her prefrontal cortex do its job. But of course, the decisions are often difficult, it is often impossible to have enough information, and it is easy to make mistakes. While decision making with the "whole brain" is by no means perfect, it is the best game in town, and we are fools to keep it bound and gagged while top-level business is being conducted.

But as long as corporations are legally defined and chartered exclusively to fulfill dA, what will provide the opposing impulses at the top level? (Remember William James's comment that "Cognition, per se, cannot check the impulse of a drive. That can only be done by an impulse the other way.") Although there are times when the public itself can provide the opposing impulse, this is not enough and, in any case, it is often a reaction to an abuse that has already occurred. If we're looking for an external institution that can check and balance dA impulses at the top corporate level before they cause harm (as our drives do for us every day under the supervision of the prefrontal cortex), only the government itself is strong enough. All of which leads us to our next two big and controversial topics: government regulation of corporations and campaign finance reform. By the time we have examined the regulation issue it will become clear why campaign finance reform is key, not only to corporate regulation but to reforming the federal government itself.

THE ROLE OF GOVERNMENTAL REGULATION IN KEEPING CORPORATIONS ON TRACK

As we saw in Chapter Six, effective government regulation of corporations has been a protracted and often unsuccessful struggle. The corporate world has typically regarded regulation as a necessary evil at best, fighting hard and often successfully to avoid, dilute, or pervert it. But does that position make sense? Unrestricted competition may be seen by some as a kind of ultimate, total freedom, but it is a one-dimensional dA freedom. Does anyone feel that removing the prefrontal cortex would be any kind of liberation? Many worthwhile (and even profitable) things cannot be done when one innate human drive out of four always has to win and oneself or one's organization is always at war with the rest of the world.

We saw in Chapter Five how the Framers of the U.S. Constitution created, in effect, a prefrontal cortex for their new national government, while in Chapter Six we saw that no such organ of four-drive self-government has been required of corporations. Earlier in this chapter, we saw that balanced four-drive corporate self-governance can be achieved (Medtronic and Nucor are but two of many examples), but it seems to be dependent on top managers who are dedicated to balanced four-drive good/moral leadership. This type of leadership was reinforced in the past by the dominance of stakeholder theories of top-level governance and by McGregor's theory of employee motivation. The current dominance of agency theory has undermined that influence even as a run of federal deregulation has weakened governmental constraints, inviting new bouts of corporate abuse, most recently in the form of the subprime mortgage financial crisis. Without doubt, there is such a thing as overregulation. But well-designed regulation channels competitive striving into the positive, constructive efforts at which corporations are able to excel.

Normal four-drive CEOs should not be pressured—forced, really—to engage in practices that are violations of their consciences. These business leaders need to start lobbying the government to establish carefully drafted regulations; not so much to constrain themselves—under reasonable circumstances, their own consciences can do that—but to constrain any misguided CEOs or those leaders-w/o-conscience in their industries. Corporations desperately need good regulations that help them steer between the two rocks of no competition (monopoly) and destructive, immoral competition. Tom Wilson, CEO of Allstate Insurance, even published an opinion piece titled "Regulate Me, Please," in which he wrote,

> Unlike banks or investment houses, insurance companies are not regulated by the federal government. Instead, they are regulated by individual states, which lack the expertise to properly oversee rapid innovation or systemic risks. Business leaders must work with the government to create a new regulatory structure.... A good start would be for Congress to eliminate the hodgepodge

of state regulatory systems by establishing a federal regulator for national insurance companies. . . . We must all accept responsibility for our current situation, and *work together to broaden the scope of federal regulation to protect both consumers and financial markets* [my italics].[21]

Corporations, in their own long-term enlightened interest, would be wise to approach Washington with good ideas for rules that would help all firms in their industry stay on track in a four-drive, moral manner. Outlawing the dirty tricks prevalent in one's industry and getting the help of government to enforce the rules would prevent leaders-w/o-conscience from forcing the rest of the CEOs down the path of immorality. Setting up regulatory commissions for each type of industry, along the lines pioneered by the two Roosevelts, seems the sensible way to go. No competitive sport thrives without a carefully-thought-out rulebook, designed around the facts of its particular sport. Why is that not also true of competition between corporations?

The topic of corporate regulation is very closely tied to that of campaign financing. It is generally assumed, and I think accurately, that a good deal of corporate campaign giving is directed at securing regulations favorable to corporate profits. This means, I argue, that we will have to reform campaign financing before we have a prayer of establishing effective corporate regulation.

CORPORATE CORRUPTION OF THE ELECTORAL PROCESS

The U.S. Constitution was devised to keep a dangerously potent arsenal of interests—economic, social, religious, and political—on track. From the very beginning, the Framers of the Constitution worried that particular elements of that arsenal—factions, in their language—might get too much of an upper hand. George Washington himself warned that factions were "likely in the course of time and things, to become potent engines, by which cunning, ambitious, and unprincipled men will be enabled to subvert the Power of the People and to usurp for themselves the reins of

Government." It sounds as if he were worried, very worried, about people-w/o-conscience. In any case, he was right. The influence of corporate factions in U.S. government affairs, largely through the vehicle of large campaign donations, has been so pervasive for so long that it is taken for granted. In fact, a dominant theory in the academic field of political science argues that policy outcomes can best be predicted by the relative power of the special interests involved (not all of which, of course, are corporate; there are the unions, the National Rifle Association, the National Educational Association, the American Medical Association, the Association for the Advancement of Retired People, and many others). This theory does not even factor in the general public interest, presumably because it is so unlikely to influence the outcome.

The current form of corporate influence over government has been building year by year, particularly since 1980. It is a subtle but pervasive and powerful influence. Charles Lewis concludes his book *The Buying of the President 2004* with the following comment: "Despite the many warnings about the vulnerable state of our democracy today . . . most Americans are woefully uninformed or unconcerned about their *decreasing* access to political power and the government decision-making process that affects their daily lives. In every election cycle that process becomes more exclusionary, more expensive, more secretive, and a little less *of the people, by the people, and for the people.* . . . For our democracy, the skies are anything but blue."[22]

The spectacular success of modern corporate influence on government hinges heavily on the following conditions:

- The cost of running successful campaigns in primaries and final elections has been steeply and steadily increasing for many years.
- Corporate donations to election campaigns, while regulated to some extent, are entirely legal and very effective.
- Corporate lobbyists have learned well how to manipulate the natural inclination of all normal four-drive people to reciprocate—to help those who have helped them. (Remember that this is one of the four skill sets for balancing dA and dB which I discussed in Chapter Two.)

HIGH AND RISING COST OF ELECTION CAMPAIGNS

Of course, every year there are more voters, but that's not what has been driving campaign costs through the roof. The really big increases have come with a whole set of essential and expensive campaign tools: radio, air travel, television, opinion polling, and professional campaign managers. Once elected, incumbents— who usually are, after all, the most skillful fundraisers—have an enormous advantage in subsequent elections. Only 19 of 469 candidates for reelection lost in the 2002 House and Senate elections.[23] So incumbent politicians have the most to lose by reforming the existing campaign finance system and making it easier for others to run against them.

LEGALITY AND EFFECTIVENESS OF CORPORATE DONATIONS TO ELECTION CAMPAIGNS

Corporations rightly consider their campaign contributions and lobbying expenses to be business investments, and they can predict the rate of return fairly accurately. While the investments are often large, the rate of return can be spectacular. For example, an organization called Pharmaceutical Research and Manufacturers of America and its member companies spent, over the decade prior to 2003, over $1 billion on campaign contributions and lobbying.[24] But the payoffs have, in all likelihood, more than justified this expense. Consider, for example, the law passed in 2003 requiring Medicare to pay drug companies the full retail "sticker" price for drugs rather than bargaining for quantity discounts. And then there are all the other industries that have received "favorable consideration" by Washington in the last few years, such as the tobacco, credit card, auto, gun, construction, insurance, oil, gas, coal, and defense industries. Arguably the biggest contributor to campaign financing in 2008 was the financial services industry; that is, Wall Street. In 2008 alone, Wall Street financial firms contributed $331 million to Washington campaigns. Is it a coincidence that, leading up to the 2008 election, Wall Street was given significant freedom from regulation, with disastrous results that, as I write, are still beyond calculation?

LOBBYISTS' SKILL AT MANIPULATING dB
OF LEGISLATORS

Clearly it is the drive to acquire that is motivating this escalating exchange between corporations and public officials. Corporations want legislation favorable to their profit-making activities; politicians want enough money to run winning campaigns. Yet, rather surprisingly, it is the drive to bond that seems to get the job done. How can this be? Bullying or arm-twisting by corporate contributors isn't necessary and would, in most cases, be counterproductive. Just plain friendliness will work because any candidate, no matter how committed to the public's welfare, has an innate drive to bond (unless he or she is a person-w/o-conscience) and will experience some sense of gratitude toward any large donor and some impulse to grant that donor's wishes. It is likely that the majority of elected politicians really are "strong on bonding" people, and the very drive to bond that makes them successful campaigners will also make them vulnerable to manipulation by donors. As Bill Brock, former congressman, senator, and chairman of the Republican National Committee, testified during the litigation following the McCain-Feingold campaign finance legislation, "When elected officials solicit contributions . . . [they] become at least psychologically beholden to those who contribute. It is inevitable and unavoidable."[25]

There is a compelling need to get our government working the way the Framers of the Constitution intended, as an impulse/check/balance mechanism for *the general welfare of the entire population*. But until our political process is freed from excessive corporate influence—until the drive to acquire is evenly matched by the other human drives in this domain as it is in our own brains—we will suffer three serious and still-growing problems:

1. Real progress is unlikely on such pressing issues as health care insurance coverage and costs, corporate environmental abuses, foreign energy dependence, the gross size of the military budget, retirement security, or tax reform. These are all issues in which corporations—either in particular industries or as a whole—currently have an influence far beyond their legitimate stake.

2. American voters have become dangerously cynical about the decision process on public policy issues,[26] which, in turn, must have something to do with the fact that roughly half the voting-age population routinely does not vote.
3. The next generation of political leadership is being nipped in the bud. Jim Leach, a former Republican congressman from Iowa, explained this concern: "The most stifling effect of the large amounts of money being played with is not so much one candidate versus another candidate. It's the extraordinary scorching effect on candidacies emerging. People don't want to run for office (a) if they have no money, (b) if they have to raise money, and (c) if they have to put up with the effects of what other people's money says about them.... It puts a pall that is quite chilling on the political process."[27]

REFORMING THE FEDERAL ELECTORAL SYSTEM

I believe that there is a readily available way to free our government from *excessive* corporate influence; that is, to restore the political system's connections to all interest groups and to all four drives, not just the drive to acquire. The solution is to provide for the public funding of all federal elections. Years of pushing for incremental campaign finance reform, by groups such as Common Cause, have not made any real headway. But a new organization, Americans for Campaign Reform (ACR),[28] has surfaced, with a much more practical plan for public financing. ACR has joined with members of Congress from both parties to advance the Fair Elections Now Act for consideration of the 111th Congress. ACR has learned from the experience of other nations with public funding and from the experiences of Arizona and Maine with their state plans and has created a carefully-thought-out plan of which I will give only a few details.

Their bill would establish a *voluntary* system of funding for qualified House and Senate candidates who say "no" to all (not just corporate) large special-interest funding and accept only small donations. Candidates seeking to participate in the Fair Elections program would first need to collect a predetermined number (based on an agreed percentage of eligible voters) of contributions of $5 to $100 each from their supporters. Candidates so qualified would then receive a public match of $4 for every additional $1 raised in the same size range from their constituents up to the primary date. Participating candidates who receive their party's nomination are then eligible to receive a public grant—an amount calculated to make them fully competitive with other candidates—for use in the general election. In return for such public funding, participating candidates agree to accept *only* small additional donations of $100 or less up until the final election.

The secret of the ACR approach is that it does not propose to restrict private campaign financing beyond the current rules, but rather to make enough public financing available to enable publicly funded candidates to compete effectively with privately funded candidates. (In RD Theory terms, it checks one drive with another—the corporations' drive to acquire with the public's drive to bond in the sense of providing for its collective best interests.) While the treasury funds required for all federal Congressional elections are estimated to be $.5 to $1 billion per year, this is only 0.0005 percent of the federal budget. This, ACR argues, is a great bargain for the taxpayers, compared to the price we all pay for the special subsidies, hidden tax breaks, pork-barrel grants, and sweetheart contracts which the current system regularly provides, at our direct or indirect expense, to corporations. The funds needed for public financing would be determined in advance for each election cycle by an independent commission and presented to Congress for an up-or-down vote to ensure adequate funding. Election winners who had opted into the system would then be able to focus on the public's business instead of focusing on fundraising for the next campaign.

Whenever we become accustomed to thinking of a particular group as typically dishonest or difficult to deal with—from used car salesmen to Somali pirates—the RD Theory warns us that most human beings have four-drive brains and therefore it demands that we ask why this particular group seems to act in an unbalanced way. The advantage of the proposed Fair Elections system in comparison to our present system is that it would make it easier, at least, for politicians to behave like four-drive human beings, which all but a few actually are, by altering the mix of pressures that tend to lead even four-drive humans off track.

Once the incumbents who have always used private funding can see that it gives them no advantage over candidates choosing public funding, they can be expected to choose public funding for themselves. After all, the amount of discontent, even disgust, felt by Congressional incumbents with the present arrangements should not be underestimated. Robert Dole commented, "There's something about it that is so demeaning. To get on the phone and say, 'This is Bob Dole—you know, the majority leader? And I know you've been thinking about my campaign, and I know you want to make a good contribution, don't you?' Ah, with the poor guy going yah-yah-yah trying to find out 'what bill do I have pending up there?' [It's] torture."[29] I am also confident that most business leaders would be quietly grateful for such a change. The present arrangements are demeaning to them, too. Without being aware of the RD Theory itself, many of them realize that the present system forces them to shortchange some of their own important values in order to fulfill others.

THE POTENTIAL ROLE OF SCIENCE IN KEEPING CORPORATIONS ON TRACK

Science can help organizations keep on track by further testing the RD Theory good/moral leadership model exemplified at Medtronic and Nucor. I offer these suggestions:

1. Use several different methodologies to test scientifically which model of human motivation—agency theory (based on neoclassical economics) or the Renewed Darwinian Theory four-drive model—is the more accurate. (The remaining suggestions rely on supportive findings from this research.)

2. Develop a model corporate charter, similar to the U.S. Constitution, to implement a check-and-balance system for corporate governance. This would be done, for example, by separating the roles of board chairman and CEO, by having the chief financial officer report to both the chairman and the CEO, and by having a majority of independent directors. Charters based on variations of this theme have been and are being adopted.[30] I would further recommend that an enhanced version of the German corporate governance model be tested and

then extended in the United States. This could be done by designating at least one board seat for representatives of each of the other major stakeholders, in addition to those seats held by representatives of shareholders. The board might include, for example, one seat for representatives of employees, as is done in Germany, but also one for customers and one for a government official representing the wider public. This would create a built-in reinforcement for the stakeholder model used by Medtronic and Nucor and thereby contribute to both the creation and the equitable distribution of value. Informed by all this work, national corporate charters would be required of all companies beyond a "start-up" stage in size.

3. Establish federal regulatory commissions for each major business sector and charge them with developing a code of rules outlawing the major abuses specific to that industry, keeping these rules up-to-date, and enforcing them. These commissions would be expected, in a fully transparent manner, to draw on the advice of their industry's top executives and on representatives of employees, consumers, investors, suppliers, and environmentalists to ensure that the rules are suitable, enforceable, and cost-effective.

4. Reshape business school curricula to do a better job of teaching future executives how to provide good/moral leadership to corporations in a way that helps all stakeholders to satisfice all four drives rather than ignoring or violating any of them. The research findings from suggestion 1 would be very important here.

5. If so indicated by additional research on people-w/o-conscience, develop and implement a governmentally monitored scientific testing procedure to screen and license candidates for corporate positions with significant power over other people and bar positively identified people-w/o-conscience from such roles. This recommendation will be controversial, but the evidence of the harm such people can do provides a compelling case for limiting their access to the more powerful roles in society. This licensing process would also be a crucial step toward the professionalization of leadership, which a scientific theory of leadership now puts within reach.

CHAPTER NINE

A WORLDWIDE SWINDLE
By Banking Leaders-w/o-Conscience?

Never give a sucker an even break.
— ATTRIBUTED TO W. C. FIELDS

The worldwide economic meltdown of 2007–2009 took place as this book was being written and presented an unavoidable challenge: Does the Renewed Darwinian Theory of Human Behavior and Leadership offer a better explanation of this complex event than the available alternatives?

WAS THE MELTDOWN REALLY A BLACK SWAN?

On November 11, 2009, the U.S. government lost the case it had brought against two former Bear Sterns hedge-fund managers for securities fraud. As reported in the *Wall Street Journal,* the two men were accused of lying to investors, "telling them they were optimistic about their funds, while privately worrying they were all but dead."[1] This was the government's first major attempt to assign criminal liability for the meltdown, but the jurors' "not guilty" verdict seemed to support a widespread agreement that the meltdown was a so-called "black swan," an occurrence completely outside the range of what could have been anticipated. To quote the *WSJ* article again, "The acquittals are a setback for the U.S. attorney's office...underscoring the difficulty of assigning criminal liability for Wall Street's mistakes."

Financial writer William Cohan expressed this view in the last sentence of his book on the meltdown: "These things happen.... It was a team effort. We all f—ed up. Government. Rating agencies. Wall Street. Commercial banks. Regulators. Investors. Everybody."[2] So, we are to conclude that there were a lot of serious mistakes made, but nothing really illegal.

It seems we are to believe that the financial leaders who contributed to the crisis were simply misguided by some combination of the following pieces of conventional wisdom:

- Human behavior can be entirely explained by rational self-interest.
- The purpose of corporations is to maximize shareholder value.
- Markets are rational and efficient; they will automatically self-correct.
- No top executive, especially in banking, would deliberately destroy his or her own company or the entire economy, simply to gain more wealth.
- The price of such a clear-cut commodity as housing cannot be artificially pumped up into a bubble and hence cannot collapse like a bubble.

Do these sound reasonable to you? What if we translate them into RD Theory terms and see if they still sound as reasonable?

- Human beings are only driven by dA and dD; the independent drives to bond and comprehend do not exist.
- A corporation need only be concerned with fulfilling its owners' drive to acquire, not the drives of other stakeholders.
- The focus of bankers exclusively on their dA is enough to prevent market disasters—no regulations needed.
- Since there is no innate, independent dB drive, or an innate conscience, "people-w/o-conscience" is a meaningless designation.
- Market bubbles cannot be artificially created and exploited by bankers.

Is it any wonder that an economy being run on so many dubious premises should run into trouble? I acknowledge that a plausible case can be made that the entire subprime mortgage mess could have happened because "misguided" financial leaders behaved consistently with such beliefs and therefore cannot be held personally responsible for any crimes in connection with the massive worldwide pain and damage their actions have created.

In sharp contrast to this explanation, I believe that there is a *much more plausible* case that some very few top-level bankers were people-w/o-conscience who knowingly took advantage of certain social and economic conditions to orchestrate the massive subprime mortgage disaster. They did so to greatly enhance their own personal wealth in accordance with their innate, insatiable dA and with total disregard for the impact of their actions on their own companies or even on the worldwide public, all in perfect accordance with their lack of an innate, independent dB and therefore their lack of a moral sense and a conscience. The dubious beliefs listed above were only a necessary precondition for enlisting the help of an army of innocent contributors to the swindle, but they were not, I argue, a sufficient cause of the swindle.

I hasten to add that I do not have enough evidence to prove my argument beyond reasonable doubt, nor can I say exactly "who did it." I only argue that the RD Theory explanation needs to be taken seriously. An important part of my argument will be the preconditions that made the meltdown possible.

As we saw in Chapters Four through Eight, human institutions work best when they dovetail with the workings of the human brain itself—with its four innate, independent drives managed by the impulse/check/balance decision-making process of the prefrontal cortex. This is why the United States government, based on the U.S. Constitution—for all its specific faults and failings over the years—has been a huge improvement over previous types of government. But its power is now rivaled and sometimes stalemated by the modern corporation, a type of institution that was, by accident of history, chartered to fulfill only the drive to acquire. In many important ways, corporations have become worldwide forces of dA that are not controlled by any external equivalent to the prefrontal cortex. Nor is there any *required* internal equivalent. Rarely does a corporate decision-making process accord the other three drives anything like the decisive quality accorded to dA. As we will see, CEOs such as Merrill Lynch's E. Stanley O'Neal were charged with making as much or more money as their competitors were making, received enormous compensation for doing so, and were forced out only when their schemes began to fail *in purely financial terms.*

It is this freedom from four-drive impulse/check/balance decision making that makes the corporation such a perfect vehicle for a smart person-w/o-conscience. Opportunity is not proof of existence. Nevertheless, I propose that (1) the 2007–2009 meltdown occurred because there were a few brilliant people-w/o-conscience top executives in key financial firms who recognized the near-perfect conditions for a brand-new, high-tech type of Ponzi scheme and that (2) being what they are, these people had no qualms about seizing the opportunity. They did, however, have to put a few preconditions in place before they could get the swindle started.

THE FLEECING MACHINE

These bankers created what I call a "fleecing machine." The sheep were not the poor mortgagees who ended up losing their homes, but the institutional buyers of CDO (collateralized debt obligation) bonds, also in a different variety called CMO (collateralized mortgage obligation bonds—some with government guarantees). Providing mortgages to people who cannot pay them back is *not* a money-making proposition. But selling those mortgages as "bonds" in vast quantities for a great deal more than they are worth can be very lucrative. Institutional bond buyers (or the taxpayers) were always the real target, the real sheep to be fleeced.

The large multinational "Wall Street" banks were the prime movers, the quarterbacks of the swindle. They had the initial equity resources to invest in the mortgage part of their businesses to get the action going. For every dollar of equity, under standard banking rules, banks were allowed to loan ten dollars, their "ten-times multiplier." With this money they offered to buy *extremely* subprime mortgages—at full face value, in tremendous quantity from their "partners," the regional specialist mortgage banks.

This was a very attractive offer to the regional mortgage banks, who could easily supply a vast number of such mortgages simply by dropping their normal standards regarding the ability of mortgagees to repay. Regional mortgage banks knew that, by quickly reselling these very low-quality mortgages to the big banks, they could collect the full face value of the mortgages including any expenses they incurred in securing these mortgages, plus their own fat fees. They could then quickly use this money to write more such mortgages. If the regional banks needed help in writing all these mortgages, they could turn to the smaller *unregulated* local mortgage brokers who could speed up the procurement of these low-value mortgages.

As soon as the big banks secured these mortgages, they cut them up and repackaged them into bonds, had them rated as very safe, and sold them through their worldwide branches and affiliated agents. As the revenue from doing this flowed back to the big banks, they used their ten-times-equity multiplier once again to offer to buy many more such mortgages from the regional banks. In 2006 alone, the ten biggest banks sold $1.5 trillion of these "bonds" to the unsuspecting sheep.[3] This was big business.

We need to remember that these few masterminds needed a lot of ordinary people to do the work. It is estimated that, when this fleecing line was working at top speed, it employed 250,000 people, most of them "earning" much more money than they ever had before. All of this was added to the price of the bonds. And, of course, these "bonds" were backed up, not with the full faith and credit of the issuing banks but only with the bits and pieces of bad mortgages. The issuing banks did not expect to be held accountable for redeeming these bonds when they became due. Does this all qualify as a scam? As I am writing this, at the end of 2009, I have seen no explanation of this scam in these terms. This book will appear in print around the middle of 2010. I hope it will be common knowledge by then.

To advance my analysis, I will now lay out the preconditions that made it possible for the swindle to work. I have sorted them into three categories, shown in Exhibit 9.1

Some of the items in Category B need explanation, not only because some are confusing technical terms but also because these items would not have aided the scam unless they were knowingly exploited for that purpose.

EXHIBIT 9.1. PRECONDITIONS FOR THE FINANCIAL MELTDOWN.

A. Helpful preconditions *but not essential to the scam*
  1. A general awareness of the social benefits of providing poor people with help in owning their own home.
  2. The example of Freddie Mac and Fannie May routinely selling *prime* quality mortgage-backed bonds.
  3. Hedge and private equity funds available to create speculative markets in hard-to-evaluate derivatives, such as subprime mortgage-backed bonds.
  4. A large worldwide pool of investment capital seeking higher returns than available, at the time, in stocks or traditional bonds.
B. Essential preconditions available by chance *but deliberately used to enable the scam*
  1. Misleading assumptions (cited earlier) to rationalize the whole process.
  2. Complex derivative instruments available that can hide their actual values.
  3. The Value at Risk (VaR) formula, which could be "gamed" by traders to hide the high risks they were taking on instruments such as credit default swaps.
  4. Very short-term financial incentives that could reward traders and bond salesmen collaborating in the scam.
  5. A fee system available to hide excessive rewards to fleecing-line collaborators.
C. Essential preconditions *deliberately established in advance*
  1. The recruitment of regional and local mortgage-writing banks and brokers (such as Washington Mutual) into writing large numbers of subprime mortgages.
  2. The recruitment of bond-rating firms (Moody, Fitch, and Standard & Poor's) to rate hard-to-evaluate derivative bonds as if they were conventional bonds.
  3. The recruitment of insurers (such as AIG) to create and sell credit default swaps, term-insurance contracts that hide the risk of mortgage-backed bonds and that interlock the fate of large financial institutions, making them "too big to fail."
  4. The recruitment of large numbers of frontline fleecing-line workers.
  5. The recruitment of the Bush administration to suspend virtually all bank regulation.
  6. The recruitment of the Bush administration to endorse and partially subsidize subprime mortgages.

B1: MISLEADING ASSUMPTIONS

Earlier chapters explained how some of these beliefs arose by way of neoclassical economics and agency theory. Here I only need to explain the assumption about the housing bubble, described earlier. It is historically inaccurate, given the crash of housing prices during the Great Depression and the more recent housing crash in Japan. More important, the recent housing bubble was deliberately created by pumping vast amounts of capital into the housing market via subprime mortgages. Artificially created bubbles of value, even housing value, are certain to burst at some time, as in every Ponzi scheme.

B2: DERIVATIVES

A set of so-called "derivative" instruments had been invented in the early 1970s for bundling up equity stocks for resale, a transparent and harmless transaction. The form was then adapted to many other uses, some of them increasingly opaque regarding real value. By 2000, these instruments were available to help hide the weakness of the collateral behind the collateralized debt obligations (CDO) "bonds." For example, a thousand or so risky subprime mortgages would be cut up into small chunks, called "tranches," and reassembled into bonds so that the risks of any given mortgage would be scattered among many bonds and therefore hard to trace. This was presented as a way of spreading the risk, but when *all* the mortgages were risky, scattering any individual mortgage had nothing to do with reducing the risk of such bonds and everything to do with obscuring it. The rapid sale of such bonds would, in turn, help obscure the leveraging of the ratio of loans to equity of key large multinational banks far above the usual ten-times-equity level.

B3: VALUE AT RISK (VaR)

This widely used overall measure of portfolio risk was invented in the early 1990s at JPMorgan. When banks began to compensate managers not just for making big profits but also for making these profits with low risks—as measured by their VaR score—unscrupulous managers learned to "game" the VaR by loading up on insurance contracts that were very modest in price but high in face value since they insured against the bankruptcy of the big banks themselves and this was *never* expected to happen. (The credit-default swaps issued by AIG were the prime example of such products.) The VaR formula simply *ignored* the remote possibility that these banks might fail. But failure, however unlikely, was possible and, if it did happen, the losses would be huge. (It is highly likely that the failure of Lehman Brothers would have bankrupted AIG without the massive bailout.) The sale of credit default swaps went a long way toward creating the "too-big-to-fail" problem.

B5: CHARGING FEES FOR ALL THE TRANSACTIONS

It was standard Wall Street practice to charge fees for each step of a complex financial transaction. This "fee system" enabled the banks engaged in the subprime mortgage swindle to record the oversized fees paid to the many players along the fleecing line, along with the oversized fees that they gave themselves, as "costs of doing business" rather than as bribes for conducting dubious activities.

While the operators of the subprime mortgage scam serendipitously found all of the items in Category B ready at hand, it did take insight to realize what could be done with them. The preconditions in Category C, however, had to be deliberately put into place by leaders-w/o-conscience; I can see no other reason why they would be there. And without RD Theory, we would not even know of the existence of leaders-w/o-conscience and would have no better explanation for these elements of the swindle than to call them "black swans."

C1: LOCAL AND REGIONAL MORTGAGE BANKS AND BROKERS

According to a report in the *New York Times,* sales agents at Washington Mutual, known as WaMu (then the largest of the regional mortgage banks) were "pressed...to pump out loans while disregarding borrowers' incomes and assets.... The bank set up what insiders described as a system of dubious legality that enabled real estate agents to collect fees of more than $10,000 for bringing in borrowers, sometimes making the agents more beholden to WaMu than they were to their clients. WaMu pressed appraisers to provide inflated property values that made loans appear less risky, enabling Wall Street to bundle them more easily for sale to investors."[4] Who or what was "pressing" these people? "Pressure to keep lending emanated from the top, where executives profited from the swift expansion—not least, Kerry Killinger, who was chief executive of WaMu from 1990 until he was forced out in September [2008]. Between 2001 and 2007, Killinger received compensation of $88 million."[5] Kerry Killinger is definitely on my list of suspect leaders-w/o-conscience involved in the meltdown.

Amazingly, WaMu was not an exception. A report in *Business Week* found that, all through the regional mortgage bank industry, "wholesalers [whose job is to buy loan applications from independent mortgage brokers so that lenders can turn them into loans] . . . offered bribes to fellow employees, fabricated documents, and coached brokers on how to break the rules. . . . Brokers, who work directly with borrowers, altered and shredded documents. Underwriters, the bank employees who actually approve mortgage loans, also skirted boundaries, demanding secret payments from wholesalers to green-light loans they knew to be fraudulent. Some employees who reported misdeeds were harassed or fired."[6]

C2: BOND-RATING FIRMS

None of the three firms rating bonds for investment banks—Moody, Standard & Poor's, and Fitch—was equipped to accurately evaluate complex derivatives. One Standard & Poor's employee testified before Congress that when he complained to his superior that he "simply could not rate the CDO bonds," he was told to stop asking questions and rate the bonds or else. The fees for rating these bonds fueled rapid earnings growth for all three rating agencies. Joseph Stiglitz, a Nobel laureate in economics, noted that the bond rating firms "were the party that performed that alchemy that converted the securities from F-rated to A-rated. The banks could not have done what they did without the complicity of the ratings agencies."[7]

C5: The Elimination of Virtually All Bank and Mortgage Regulations by the Bush Administration

The George W. Bush administration favored financial regulators who believed regulation should be kept to a minimum. His first chairman of the Securities and Exchange Commission offered a "kinder, gentler" agency. Bush's banking regulators posed holding a chain saw over a mound of regulations which they intended to cut. States agencies that tried to apply consumer protection laws to predatory lending practices were blocked on the grounds that states lacked authority over national banks.[8]

As the Bush administration came to an end, the *International Herald Tribune* of December 20, 2008, headlined, "Policing of Stock Fraud Falls in the U.S.: Bush-Era Records Show Major Drop in Prosecutions." According to the article, "At a time when the financial news is dominated by the $50 billion fraud that Bernard Madoff is accused of running, U.S. officials are on pace this year to bring the fewest prosecutions for securities fraud since at least 1991."[9]

C6: Bush Administration's Early Sponsoring of Subprime Mortgages

Lax federal regulation seems not to have been an accident but rather part of a wider plan by the Bush administration to support the subprime mortgage process. "Bush pushed hard to expand home ownership, especially among minority groups, an initiative that dovetailed with both his ambition to expand Republican appeal and the business interests of some of his biggest donors."[10] But as housing prices rose, he had to "use the mighty muscle of the federal government," as he put it, to accomplish this goal. To this end, he proposed tax incentives, pressured Fannie Mae and Freddie Mac to increase low-income lending, pushed for government spending to help first-time buyers with down payments and closing costs and for government-insured no-money-down mortgages for first-time homebuyers, and encouraged mortgage brokers and lenders to find innovative ways to help more people buy homes. As long as easy credit was helping to expand home ownership, "No one wanted to stop that bubble," said Lawrence Lindsay, Bush's first chief economic advisor. "It would have conflicted with the president's own policies."[11]

In the 2004 election cycle, mortgage bankers and brokers poured nearly $847,000 into Bush's reelection campaign, more than triple their contributions in 2000.[12] Among the Republican Party's top ten donors in 2004 was Roland Arnall, founder of Ameriquest, then the largest U.S. lender in the subprime market. In July 2005, the company agreed to set aside $325 million to settle allegations in thirty states that it had preyed on borrowers with hidden fees and ballooning payments. In December 2005, Brian Montgomery, the Federal Housing Administration commissioner, drafted a memo on risky subprime lending practices and brought it to the White House. But more senior aides, such as Karl Rove, Bush's chief political strategist, were wary of *overregulating* an industry that provided such "a valuable service to people who could not otherwise get credit."[13]

All of the preceding preconditions were in place for the potential advantage of a few leaders-w/o-conscience. Although the massive subprime swindle did not require every one of these preconditions to be in place, each one helped. Could so many useful conditions all have been in place by sheer happenstance? Who, for example, were the "big donors with business interests" who pushed Bush to provide early and continuing top-level support for subprime mortgages? How did these bankers expect to make big money by lending to such high-risk mortgagees? Was there really nobody high in the Bush administration who understood that only a massive swindle could make such lending profitable? I don't find it very plausible that so many convenient and otherwise unnecessary conditions were just lying around, waiting to be stumbled onto by experienced, high-level executives who didn't realize they were playing with fire.

To me, it is much more logical to surmise that a few leaders-w/o-conscience, scattered around the top levels of the mega-banks, did recognize the possibilities and made the initial trades to pre-test the fleecing machine. It isn't necessary to postulate a direct conspiracy; they could learn by watching each other, and each could devise a mass-production procedure to transform toxic subprime mortgages into Aaa (or maybe just Aa) bonds, and then send them on their way to the suckers around the world.

And once they got going, who could question them? It all seemed to work like alchemy, turning straw into gold.

The people-w/o-conscience bankers behind the swindle may not have cared about the consequences to others, but they cer-tainly would have cared about the consequences to themselves and would therefore have thought carefully about an endgame strat-egy. These sophisticated bankers must have known that any Ponzi scheme will eventually collapse, even such a complex, high-tech one. They would have known that when the subprime mortgage default rate started to climb, as it did in mid-2007, the "deleverag-ing" could come quickly. This would be the time to cash in their stock options, sell their stock, collect their bonuses and severance pay, and depart. They would come out okay, even if their banks did not. Those who can be shown to have followed this plan are clearly people-w/o-conscience suspects.

A few of the schemers might have figured out that the federal government could not let any really big bank go bankrupt since this could bring down the entire global financial system. A bailout was inevitable, so these people-w/o-conscience might have held out long enough to exit with some of the bailout money in their pockets. I argue that only people-w/o-conscience would be capable of such selfishness.

But nobody can run such large operations alone. Surely some of the four-drive peers and direct reports of these people-w/o-conscience must have known what was going on and silently witnessed it even if they did not take part. I also think that, in a situation with such enormous wealth at stake, some four-drive people—people *with* a conscience—might be able to override their consciences if they did not think too much about the longer-term consequences for others, if it were someone else who had invented the scheme, and if they could rationalize their behavior with the common but dubious beliefs listed at the beginning of the chapter. Charles Prince, the former Citigroup chief executive, famously explained how it worked for him: "As long as the music is playing, you've got to get up and dance." However, I would point out, as explained in Chapter Eight, that bank executives like Prince *could* have taken the better option of going to Washington with other honest bankers to seek government help in getting the cheating stopped and the leaders-w/o-conscience out of the game.

Thousands of people at lower levels were "misguided" in the RD Theory sense that they were encouraged or manipulated to suppress some of their drives as the price for fulfilling dA very successfully. As one report put it, "The mortgage industry was turning ordinary people into millionaires. One of them was Sharman Lane, a high school dropout who, like many other young women during the boom, found her way into an obscure banking job with the clunky title 'mortgage wholesaler.'...Wholesalers work for banks and other lenders. The wholesaler's job is to buy loan applications from independent mortgage brokers so that lenders can turn them into loans. Wholesalers are paid on commission: as the housing bubble inflated, wholesalers...became high-earning superstars. Lane, a manicurist before joining now-defunct subprime lender New Century Mortgage in 1997, says she brought home $1 million in 2002 and $1.2 million in 2003."[14] And remember that the cost of paying all the Sharmans along the fleecing line wound up built into the cost of the bonds.

THE ROLE OF THE BIG MULTINATIONAL BANKS IN THE SUBPRIME MORTGAGE MESS

We have discussed all of the players along the fleecing line except the primary ones—the big multinational banks. Merrill Lynch provides a representative case. In 2005, envious of Lehman Brothers' hugely profitable "mortgage assembly line," Merrill Lynch set to work creating its own, driven by CEO E. Stanley O'Neal. By the end of 2006, Merrill Lynch was the world's largest underwriter of CDOs, profits were huge, and share price was up 40 percent for the year. Risk management, however, had taken a back seat to the rapid development of a fleecing machine. And in

2007, the whole thing collapsed. O'Neal was fired by his board, but with a $161 million golden parachute, not to mention the $70 million he had earned in his four years as CEO. In 2008, Merrill Lynch itself had to merge with Bank of America in order to avoid bankruptcy.[15]

I still need to summarize the whole sequence of the swindle in order to establish the flow of causation. As the scheme got rolling, it pushed up real estate prices just by pushing a lot of fresh money into the home-building market. As economic laws would predict, demand in excess of supply drove prices up. In other words, the housing bubble was deliberately inflated from the beginning. Once the revenue and profits from the sale of CDOs started rolling in, the banks' stock valuations also began to rise. With them went commissions, bonuses, and executive salaries. Copycat banks got into the act as the culture of "greed is good" spread throughout Wall Street. Then came the tipping point. Mortgages began to default. Some of the people-w/o-conscience started to bail out. CDO bond prices fell. Credit froze. The slump hit the stock market and then Main Street. Consumer spending dropped. Assets crashed, businesses failed, and jobs disappeared all around the world. Then came the required TARP bailout and the stimulus package.

Once the emergency rescue effort is completed and credit is flowing again, will the government seek justice for the victims, and especially for the perpetrators of this huge swindle? It will be difficult, but I believe that there must be enough of a paper trail and enough potential state witnesses to prove the guilt or innocence of senior leaders in the finance industry. The senior people in big multinational banks who engineered it—the ones who carefully designed, manufactured, and sold the CDO "bonds"—were in fact selling bonds that could be considered counterfeit. For simplicity they should be called "phony bonds." The taxpayers footing the bailout bill have every right to insist that federal prosecutors move directly against these leaders-w/o-conscience with security fraud charges. The courts have already sent a few small-time operators to prison for their parts in the swindle; perhaps they can lock up some top-level leaders and, while they're at it, "claw back" whatever ill-gotten gains are still recoverable.

Perhaps as many as 98 percent of the participants along the fleecing line were misguided but innocent. As they come to understand the evil in which they were involved, some might even be willing to return their "dirty" money to clear their consciences and clear themselves with the courts.

In any event, sensible regulations are clearly essential to keep this all from happening again. A simple rule such as "Never cheat a customer," which Franklin Roosevelt proposed for Wall Street, would have gone a long way toward preventing the current scam, had such a rule been established and enforced by the top leadership of the top banks and by government regulations. More specifically, an "ingredient specification" rule could require bond sellers to provide rating agencies and prospective customers with a computer listing of information about every mortgage that has been sliced and diced into a particular bond—that is, the name, address, and payment record of every mortgagee and the name of the mortgage writer—as well as the percentage of the bond price going to fees. After all, the banks must have such information readily available to send the mortgage interest collections on as interest earned by the relevant bondholders. With this kind of disclosure, very few, if any, purposefully confusing derivative bonds would be sold. The simple truth would stop it all.

The leveraging of bank equity also needs stricter regulation. The public has every right to expect banks to extend credit as a utility distributes electricity—safely and for a modest return on the invested capital.

Finally, I cannot help wonder what would happen if, sometime in the future, a federal court found that the bank whose name is on the subprime mortgage bonds is guilty of defrauding the buyer and is therefore responsible for redeeming the full face value of the bonds when due?

LACK OF CONTROL, LACK OF SELF-CONTROL

Humans have evolved their four-drive decision-making process so as to be able to fulfill their drives, to a large extent, in groups. And, on the whole, the decision-making process itself works better in groups. We benefit from *external* four-drive control as well as from the internal four-drive self-control of our conscience. As I see it, the modern corporation suffers (and inflicts suffering) for having too little of both.

You may be getting the impression that I am anti-business and all for a lot more government regulation of business. I am not at all anti-business. I spent my career teaching future business leaders and would not for a moment wish away the modern corporation and the enormous constructive power of this great nineteenth-century invention. But my researches leading up to this book have made me aware of the modern corporation's major flaw, its definition as the embodiment of one innate, insatiable drive, not balanced by the other three. I am therefore not so much for more regulation as for more balanced, four-drive regulation. The U.S. Constitution and Bill of Rights, for example, are remarkably sparse.

Lack of External Control: Regulation

To some extent, the failure of regulation to prevent the economic meltdown is about as plain as it could be. A look abroad shows that this big swindle need not have occurred. Yaga Venugopal Reddy, governor of the Reserve Bank of India from 2003 to 2008, thought that Indian bankers might be tempted to adopt a "bubble mentality" and considered it his job to make sure they never got the chance. He restricted the use of securitizations and derivatives and "when he saw U.S. banks setting up off-balance-sheet vehicles to hide debt, [he] essentially banned them in India." The net result of these and other actions was that Indian bankers simply weren't allowed to get themselves into the trouble that American bankers did.[16]

The lack of regulation in the United States was no historical accident, as the failure of the Constitution to address corporations was. Important parts of the financial system were either unregulated or only laxly regulated as a matter of George W. Bush administration policy.

I believe that, in this relatively unregulated condition and under the influence of a few high-powered leaders-w/o-conscience, all the many varied participants in the fleecing machine were willing to jump into line like iron filings in the presence of a magnet. Of course, the promise of making a lot of money would exercise a magnetic pull on almost anyone, but most of us feel other pulls as well that we need to listen to and not squelch. A corporation, of course, is not a sentient being and has no drives. It is, however, set up to simulate a person with an innate, insatiable dA but with no dB of equal power and no impulse/check/balance prefrontal cortex to take other drives seriously and insist on trying to satisfice them all.

And in that regard, nothing has changed. In December 2008, when the Associated Press asked twenty-one banks that had received at least $1 billion to provide details on how the money had been used, it received a number of refusals such as the Bank of New York's statement, "We're choosing not to disclose that." An outraged editorialist for the *Boston Globe* wrote, "They get to choose?" But the banks—chastened or not—are still corporations, designed exclusively to fulfill the dA of their owners. Other considerations don't hold a candle to that one, any more than they did before the meltdown. They are still fighting to hang onto their bonuses (even if they have to use bailout money to pay them) and still lobbying to prevent regulation of the very activities that brought on the meltdown.[17] Will they never learn? Or more to the point, will the rest of us ever learn that people-w/o-conscience will never change—they *cannot* change—as long as they can get away with their schemes? Any appeal to their conscience would be a waste of breath. RD Theory predicts that people-w/o-conscience bankers will pay attention to well-drafted regulations that are enforced with tough penalties that match the magnitude of their crimes.

CONCLUSION

In an odd way, the Renewed Darwinian Theory demands that we look at the corporate institutions involved in the economic meltdown of 2007–2009 with pity as well as anger. Lacking any equivalent to the human being's prefrontal cortex with its impulse/check/balance decision-making process, these organizations seem helpless to protect themselves from their own worst impulses. I can't help but think of those poor chimpanzees in

Chapter Two, compulsively grabbing for the bigger dish of candy and always ending up with the smaller one. I keep coming back to William James's observation that the only thing that can counteract an impulse is another impulse pushing in the opposite direction. The corporation as presently chartered is denied any other impulse strong enough to counteract dA, even when the dA impulse is going to prove suicidal to the corporation and enormously damaging to others.

Nor are corporations sufficiently able to protect themselves from leaders-w/o-conscience, as long as those leaders are presiding over growth and profits (or, as at Enron, the convincing appearance of growth and profits). Leaders of Merrill Lynch, for example, were dismissed, but only, it seems, once it became clear that their companies were losing money or market valuation rather than gaining them. But the most important point is that, as long as corporations, including banks, are left defenseless against their own worst impulses and their own worst leaders, so are we.

This chapter started by stating that the current consensus seems to be that the financial meltdown was caused by a whole bevy of misguided contributors. The book we quoted on the subject, *House of Cards: A Tale of Hubris and Wretched Excess on Wall Street* by William Cohan, offers a host of details about the ways the managers of Bear Stearns contributed to the disaster.[18] It reveals, for example, that Bear Sterns managers at times let their leverage of loans to equity run up to around a hundred times, even as they depended *every morning* on borrowing the cash they needed to cover their obligations that same day. What a "house of cards"! The book provides detail about the behavior of the two Bear Stearns hedge fund managers who were acquitted of security fraud as described in the *WSJ* article cited at the start of this chapter. This raises the big question, Why did the U.S. prosecutors choose these managers as the first ones to indict? They were only trading in subprime mortgage bonds. When the price of the phony bonds collapsed they got burned along with their customers. At the same time the top leaders of Bear Stearns were boasting in their 2006 annual report that they were number one in manufacturing and selling these toxic bonds. Why prosecute the traders and leave the perpetrators alone? I can think of only two plausible reasons: either prosecutors were afraid that the entire financial system is still vulnerable to being tipped into collapse, or they still simply *could not* believe that any top managers of Wall Street firms could be so utterly selfish. So the story of the great financial meltdown is still unfolding. The emperors are still strutting on Wall Street without clothes. Can we not see that?

To repeat, the *House of Cards* book ends by saying, "These things happen.... It was a team effort. We all f—ed up. Government. Rating agencies. Wall Street. Commercial banks. Regulators. Investors. Everybody." Please note that this summary joins the current consensus in offering no insightful explanations, no suspects of illegal behavior, and no clear actionable recommendations. While the subtitle of this chapter ends with an appropriate question mark, it at least offers a plausible and testable explanation, some prime suspects of illegal activity, and suggestions for remedial action.

In his book *Bad Money*, Kevin Phillips offers on page 31 a figure titled "The Rise of Financial Services and the Decline of Manufacturing."[19] It shows that manufacturing's share of U.S. GDP fell from 29.3 percent in 1950 to 12 percent in 2005. This is compared with financial services, whose share rose from 10.9 percent in 1950 to 20.4 percent in 2005. Corporate profits are shown as an even more extreme reversal. Manufacturing profits fell from 55 percent to 5 percent, while profits for the financial services sector rose from 9 percent to 45 percent over these same years. Readers should note that all the financial transactions discussed in this chapter count as part of the GDP. Readers should also note how much the profits have switched from feeding "Main Street" to feeding "Wall Street." The financial services sector seems to have been making out like bandits—and given their 2009 record of bonuses and profits, they still are. The term *service* in their name now seems like a very bad joke.

I will end this chapter with a personal story. As a young research assistant at Harvard Business School I attended my first Christmas faculty party, at which our president, James Conant, made an informal challenge to the assembly. He simply wished that the eminent minds in the room would focus on finding a scientific explanation of the periodic depressions that have plagued humans throughout history. Based on my own experience with the Great Depression, I shared his wish. But as a student of human behavior and leadership, it never occurred to me that I had anything to do with explaining depressions. Now, in my advanced years, I believe I have more or less stumbled on a better explanation than has been available before. It is now my wish that the experts on depressions, and recessions, run the idea past their vast data set and test my simple idea that depressions have been primarily caused by people-w/o-conscience.

CHAPTER TEN

KEEPING A GLOBAL ECONOMY AND A GLOBAL COMMUNITY ON TRACK

Human history is a nightmare from which all of us are trying to awake.
— GENERALIZING JAMES JOYCE'S INSIGHT IN *Ulysses*

In Chapter Three, we saw the expansion of the drive to bond from the immediate family to the tribe. Over time, the drive to bond has been extended to much larger collectives—states and nations, ethnic groups, political parties, and religious collectives such as Christendom and its Muslim equivalent, *Ummah*. In 1860, Robert E. Lee was asked by Lincoln to command the Union forces and at the same time by Jefferson Davis to command the Confederate forces. It was a painful decision for him, whether his most basic patriotic loyalty lay with his home state of Virginia or with the United States, which he had served with distinction throughout his military career. Today it would be hard to find many Americans for whom this would be a difficult choice.

This chapter will look at leadership in regard to problems that must be addressed at the world level: (1) the abuses of multinational corporations, run at times by international criminal organizations, and the possible harmful effects of globalization (keeping in mind that globalization is not inherently harmful)

and (2) the devastation caused by war and state-sponsored genocide. These are problems which call for some kind of world-level
leadership and control and, as well, for an expansion of the drive
to bond to the world level. Can this possibly be done?

Of course, there are numerous international bodies that
exercise some limited power over multinational organizations
and even over the member countries themselves. But for the
most part, nations have ceded very little sovereignty to such
international entities. Even willing governments can only go so far
if the people themselves do not feel sufficiently bonded to people
all over the world. When a problem is global but most people's
dB does not extend beyond the nation, dB will consistently carry
less weight than dA and dD at the global level, and it will remain
impossible to solve such problems, including those described in
this chapter, in any fair, reasonable, and nonviolent—that is,
four-drive—way.

THE GLOBAL ECONOMY AS A CHALLENGE TO THE DRIVE TO BOND

It's easy to name some of the uglier aspects of the global
economy—the sweatshop workers in poor countries producing
cheap goods for customers who are fabulously wealthy by comparison; the dumping of toxic wastes in countries with little or no
regulation or at least, due to corruption, little or no enforcement;
the trafficking—including the kidnapping or entrapment—of
prostitutes and sex slaves. The pirates operating off Somalia are
part of the global economy; they sell a service—releasing captured
ships and crews—to a worldwide clientele of shipping companies
and national governments. An international set of criminal firms
has been peddling fake drugs, carefully designed to look exactly
like the real thing but containing little or none of the active
ingredients.[1] For example, a drug for malaria is being sold in
such a diluted form that it is worse than no drug at all; the recip-
ients are mainly poor children in Africa. One expert estimates
between one-half and one million deaths per year due to this
scam alone.

But that's not the whole story. It seems that some major drug companies, themselves multinationals, knew their products were being faked but hoped to stamp out the problem without involving the authorities, in order to avoid publicity that could harm their reputations. Since they didn't succeed, withholding the information has resulted in even more victims.

A recent book by Raymond Baker, *Capitalism's Achilles Heel: Dirty Money and How to Renew the Free-Market System*, points up a different and largely unrecognized problem, the huge drain of what he calls "dirty money" from the poorer to the richer nations. Baker calculates that the dirty money flow amounts to $500 billion per year—ten times the amount of all types of aid flowing in the other direction—and that this illicit transfer of funds accounts for much of the fact that people in the richer countries have thirty-one times more income per capita than people in poorer countries.[2]

This enormous flow of illicit funds is entirely off the books of organizations concerned with international record keeping, such as the World Bank and the IMF. The techniques are various: the stripping of commodities (such as diamonds, gold, oil, and scarce minerals) from the poorer producing countries and the invoicing of those assets to richer countries at far below world market prices; the plundering of the public treasuries of poor states by despotic heads-of-state; the overstatement, by top executives of otherwise legitimate corporations, of the value of their corporations' exports to subsidiaries in poor countries so that these executives can later deposit the excess payments into their private accounts; the illegal trade in drugs, sex slaves, weapons, and so on; the distorted transfer prices used by legitimate multinationals as they move their profits into low-tax states to cheat the governments of the weak states in which the money was made. The rewards of such illicit transactions are huge profits that can be "laundered" and securely hidden away in solid banks and other financial institutions in the developed world.

Baker accuses those banks and financial institutions of quietly colluding with this traffic for the fat fees they earn. These institutions even send salespeople to the less-developed world to solicit such deposits. We can call it a case of misguided leadership because they do not even think of it as what it is—robbing the poor to enrich the rich.

Keeping a Global Economy on Track

I said at the end of Chapter One that my conclusions about leadership might seem too obvious or simplistic to take seriously without knowing that they are rooted in the workings of the human brain itself. I hope by this time I have made clear that following the Golden Rule is not only a very nice thing to do—something with which almost all of us feel comfortable without much thought—but that, with awareness of our four drives, following it is actually the way to make the most of the particular decision-making process our species has evolved. I hope that I have also shown that this is true for world-level collectives as well as for individuals, although, given the existence of people-w/o-conscience, it is a difficult thing to accomplish collectively.

My suggestions for keeping a global economy on track are therefore not simply what I think or feel would be nicest and most fair, but what the Renewed Darwinian Theory tells me would lead to four-drive fulfillment for as many people as possible. (And this, of course, is what most people will experience as being nicest and most fair.) Keep in mind that, while our four-drive brains are constantly making trade-offs between the drives, there is no *permanent* trade-off. The long-term or permanent subordination of one drive to the others or the long-term or permanent domination by one drive of the others would be unhealthy and unpleasant. It is just the same on a larger scale. Even in what appear to be purely economic decisions, the long-term or permanent domination of dA over the other drives will lead to unfair, unhealthy, and ultimately intolerable results.

Let's see what RD Theory can contribute to the daunting task of leading the way to keeping a global economy on track—satisficing the drive to acquire for people all over the world while enlisting rather than frustrating their drives to bond, to comprehend, and to defend themselves.

UNDERSTANDING THE MULTIPLE FORMS OF GLOBALIZATION

To deal with the much-discussed but still poorly understood complex of economic affairs known as globalization, we must examine its several forms from an RD Theory point of view. Some can have positive effects for all parties while others inherently benefit the rich and strong at the expense of the poor and weak. Furthermore, some can be beneficial but also lend themselves to abuse, especially by people-w/o-conscience, and therefore call for some kind of world-level impulse/check/balance control.

The *classic* trading system of exchange is identified with David Ricardo, the early nineteenth-century economist who first analytically clarified it. Imagine that tribe A is good at both hunting and fishing, but more efficient at hunting. Tribe B is not as efficient as tribe A at either hunting or fishing, but is more efficient at fishing than at hunting. Ricardo pointed out that both tribes would eat somewhat better if tribe A sold game to tribe B in exchange for fish. Both parties would win; most notably, the poorer one. Ricardo's theory is the basis of the very strong support that most economists now give to the overall benefits of globalization.

As practiced today, Ricardo's classic system results in win-win exchanges when both trading partners are either (1) industrialized nations with modern impulse/check/balance governments, no excessive unemployment, and reasonably effective control of corporate abuses or (2) less-developed nations roughly equal in power and with some control of corporate abuses. Unfortunately, much of today's international trade does not meet these conditions.

Under the *colonial* system, powerful industrialized countries gain political control (typically based on military control) of less-developed countries and exploit their workers and natural resources. This form of globalization is clearly a win-lose system in terms of all four drives. And while political colonialism is practically dead, economic colonialism is still alive and well in many extractive industries, including timber, oil, gold, silver, and titanium. (Later in this chapter, the story of Leopold of Belgium will offer an extreme version of the colonial system.)

A good example is the South African diamond industry, which has been operating virtually unchanged since Cecil Rhodes consolidated the South African mines around 1890. Rhodes took advantage of the fact that the mines were in an undeveloped country whose government the British colonists quickly came to dominate. His mining company was then able to minimize its mining costs by exploiting the native workforce with low wages, poor working conditions, and cheap dormitory housing far from the miners' families. The semi-processed stones were shipped and invoiced to Europe at near-cost "transfer" prices. The big markups to largely controlled market prices were collected in Europe. At the end of the day, the Africans were left with the disastrous social and medical consequences of abusive labor practices, while the wealth created was enjoyed almost exclusively in Europe—not only the direct profits but also the resultant tax revenues and the trickle-down effects of all that wealth.

Under the widely practiced *international sales* system, a corporation in a developed nation sells finished goods to a consumer in a less-developed nation; this is McDonald's selling a hamburger in El Salvador. This system is not inherently abusive; the citizens of the developed country are winners and the citizens of the undeveloped country may be getting a better or cheaper product. But when regulation is weak or nonexistent, this system can lend itself to severe abuse, as in the sale of fake drugs described earlier.

Transnational outsourcing, as when a U.S. auto company builds a parts plant in Mexico, has come into prominence only in the past few decades. Cutting costs is fair enough, *unless* it is done by paying less-than-living wages, creating unsafe working conditions, or causing environmental damage which would be prohibited in the United States. But because most American corporations are currently designed and mandated to fulfill dA exclusively, both top management and shareholders might object to incurring any costs in Mexico beyond those that are legally required, so transnational outsourcing is frequently a win-lose exchange between nations which are unequal either in their power or their willingness to enforce basic standards of human rights, worker safety, and environmental impact. Another golden opportunity for people-w/o-conscience.

Japan and China have updated the old-fashioned *mercantilist* model of government-managed trade. Japan's version of mercantilism primarily used its own banking system, as well as export revenues themselves, to generate the needed capital (in contrast to making heavy use of foreign investments) and used its own well-educated and well-motivated (with decent pay and job security) workforce to supply the manpower with which to create sophisticated products. The export of these well-designed and efficiently produced goods was actively supported by the government in many ways while domestic consumption was constrained by progressive taxation. This type of mercantilist system was, with a short time lag, a winner for all Japanese citizens, who were all able to raise their living standards; the income gap between the upper and lower quintiles was actually reduced to only 3.4 percent, the lowest among all the economically developed countries. Japan's trading partners were also winners, receiving excellent value in the goods they imported from Japan. Other nations, such as South Korea, Taiwan, and Singapore, as well as Hong Kong, have followed Japan's example with excellent results. The Japanese model of mercantile globalization scores high on all four drives for all of the stakeholders involved.

In contrast, China primarily finances its rapid industrialization by attracting large amounts of foreign investment capital. Domestic consumption is constrained only among the poorer working masses, while there is rapid growth of wealth among the party and governmental elite and among a new class of entrepreneurs. Surprisingly, Chinese mercantilism is also widening the income gap in Western trading partners. For example, Wal-Mart, the largest and fastest-growing trader with China, is famous for cutting off purchases from U.S. manufacturers and switching to Chinese firms. Wal-Mart has even hired the owners or managers of its abandoned U.S. suppliers to teach their efficient methods to the Chinese. As a result, many Americans have lost their manufacturing jobs and often have been forced into lower-paying service jobs—a net loss for lower-income families. Meanwhile, the resulting profits add to the wealth of the Walton family and their fellow stockholders—a net gain for higher-income families. If one considers only dA, this profit gain could well be more than the wage losses and thus create a net gain in America's gross domestic product. But from a four-drive point of view, this is a serious loss for American society.

The economist Benjamin Friedman has found evidence that a steadily rising standard of living provides not only material benefits but also moral and political benefits. People whose standard of living is rising are happier, more tolerant, and more willing to settle disputes peacefully and democratically. Stagnating or declining economic growth is associated with intolerance, ethnic strife, and dictatorship. But here Friedman adds an important conditional factor. The social benefits of economic growth will arise only if people at *all* socioeconomic levels are gaining from that growth. If, for example, the richer classes are gaining while the poorer and middle classes are stagnant or declining, the *moral* benefits go into reverse, resulting in frustration, intolerance, and social conflict. And even in pure dA terms, these are not good conditions for economic growth. Friedman concludes, "Broadly distributed economic growth creates the private attitudes and public institutions that foster, not undermine, a society's moral qualities.... Any nation, even one with incomes as high as America's, will find the basic character of its society at risk if it allows its citizens' living standards to stagnate.... At the outset of the twenty-first century, America's problem is not unemployment. It is the slow pace of advance in the living standards of the majority of the nation's citizens."[3]

The positive and negative consequences of the various kinds of globalization and of economic growth versus economic stagnation are consistent with the Renewed Darwinian Theory's proposition that one's sense of dA fulfillment is relative to that of other people to whom one compares oneself. The innate insatiable drive to acquire cannot be fulfilled, even by a steady increase in wealth, if one is steadily falling behind others. This may be illogical—a Porsche is a Porsche, no matter what's parked in the driveway next door—but it is the way our minds have evolved to work.

It is disturbing, then, that in both the United States and China the rewards of globalization are flowing disproportionately to an elite few. A 2003 Congressional Budget Office report found that the share of income going to the wealthiest 1 percent of American households was more than the amount going to the bottom 40 percent. In contrast, as recently as 1979, the top 1 percent had less than half the income of the bottom 40 percent.[4] When *Business Week* writers commented on what was to blame for this increasing gap, their answer was the same as mine: "Certainly globalization has taken its toll."[5] In China, as in many developing countries, it is estimated that only 1 percent of China's population now controls 60 percent of its wealth.[6] Sure enough, the Chinese government itself has recently reported that there have been thousands of bloody clashes between police and the farmers who are being displaced by industrial expansion.[7]

Globalization need not work this way. Its benefits can be steered to all nations and to all levels in each nation in a more equitable manner. But a free-market, laissez-faire process will not do this automatically. It will require governmental regulatory action with guidelines and incentives that can best be established at the world level.

GLOBAL ECONOMIC REGULATION

We saw in Chapter Six that, when American corporations expanded across state lines in the nineteenth century, they outgrew the ability of individual states to control abusive corporate practices. Such practices could only be checked by a national government which was ill-prepared for this responsibility. Today, virtually all large corporations are multinational and have similarly outgrown the ability of national governments to control abusive corporate practices. Government at the world level must now "walk like men," as Henry Demarest Lloyd put it in 1884, and take some responsibility for keeping the global economy in line.

Baker claims, for example, that the kind of "dirty money" flow he has studied cannot be controlled by existing legal systems. U.S. law, he notes, covers sixty-five kinds of money laundering committed entirely inside the country but only thirteen kinds from outside the country. "Going global" is clearly the way to go if one expects to squirrel away profits from immoral acts that exploit the weak and poor.[8] Public health officials have responded to the fake drug scam by calling for international legislation to require drug companies to make public all reports of fake drugs and require government authorities to investigate such reports and issue public warnings. This would give those companies a way to deal with the rogues of their industry without having to commit corporate hari-kari one by one. But there is no world body with the authority to draw up and enforce such rules.[9] For lack of it, the drug companies missed their chance to do the right thing and many more innocent people almost certainly have been hurt or killed.

As I said in Chapter Six, a pure laissez-faire economy is not really total freedom, but rather thralldom to one of our four drives—the drive to acquire. It is as if an athlete were to take performance-enhancing drugs which gave him a hugely strong right arm while paralyzing his left arm and both legs. Today's global economy could benefit from a regulatory liberation from the tyranny of the most unscrupulous. Until such abuses are stopped, much of the world will be unable to realize the vast potential benefits of Ricardo-style globalization.[10]

The lack of global economic regulation may also hinder companies from taking full advantage of a potentially huge new market, the so-called "bottom of the pyramid." C. K. Prahalad and Allen Hammond have argued that, while the 80 percent of the world's people who are classified as poor and who are largely disconnected from the global economy have little disposable income individually, they have quite a lot of it collectively.[11] Not only is there a lot of money to be made at the bottom of the pyramid, but according to industrial designer Gianfranco Zaccai, there are also a lot of great ideas, innovations, products, and materials that could be of enormous economic value to the rest of the world. Striking all that water from the stone of poverty will be done most successfully by people taking a balanced four-drive approach to the individual and organizational stakeholders at both ends of the pyramid.[12] Furthermore, should the bottom of the pyramid prove to be a big growth segment, it will invite abuse of its particularly vulnerable population and will certainly need the protection of global regulation.

The same can be said for the promising new microcredit movement, pioneered by Muhammad Yunus of Bangladesh. It involves making very small loans to very poor people—often women—so that they can start or expand a small business such as making bamboo stools or selling the milk and cheese from a dairy cow.

These are not gifts; they are loans that have to be paid back with interest—and the default rates have been extremely low. Since Yunus's original success, about a dozen other significant microfinance firms have entered the field. In addition, several well-known entrepreneurs and their foundations have started to contribute to the effort, including Pierre Omidyar, one of the founders of eBay; Michael Dell, founder and CEO/chairman of Dell; Google; and most recently Bill and Melinda Gates with the further backing of Warren Buffett. With such support, the microcredit movement could, over time, significantly reduce the income gap between the have and have-not worlds, especially if it is accompanied by the regulation of dirty money. But there are already indications that a few people-w/o-conscience entrepreneurs are moving in as well, charging interest rates that border on loan sharking. One hopes that carefully designed world-level regulation can ensure that the promise of microcredit is not lost. After all, the essence of Yunus's brilliant idea, in terms of the RD Theory, is that, from the lender's point of view, dA (profits) and dB (relieving poverty) can both be satisfied (rather than either being maximized) simultaneously; setting out to maximize profits would defeat the purpose.

WAR AND GENOCIDE AS CHALLENGES TO THE DRIVE TO BOND

Intra-family or domestic violence must always have been around, usually instigated by infidelity, but local government has long since minimized it. The same is true of violent feuds between families. Inter-tribal warfare, however, has a long and bloody record that has only been "cured" by escalating it into inter-nation warfare. Wars between nations and internal, state-sponsored genocide are the persistent problems that have taken humanity furthest off track. The harm done far exceeds the immediate loss of life and property. Many of the survivors carry the gross physical and psychological damage to their graves. And the hatred and thirst for revenge can survive for many generations. It was the massive wars and genocide between 1914 and 1945 that historian Norman Davies referred to as "the era when Europe took leave of its senses" and "threw away its position of world *leadership*."[13]

Many feel that such violence is an inevitable result of immutable human nature. The Renewed Darwinian Theory of good/moral leadership offers both a more comprehensive explanation and a somewhat hopeful remedial proposal. But the proposal requires good/moral leadership at the worldwide level, which simply isn't possible without reforming the global institutions we have today.

AN RD THEORY VIEW OF THE CAUSES OF WAR AND GENOCIDE

All four of our innate drives have a dark side that can contribute to mass violence. The drive to acquire (dA), insatiable because it is relative to the acquisitions of others, is an obvious case. Ancient wars have been described as cattle raids or, in some cases, raids for wives and slaves. Since then, the collective dA of nations—and the resulting "raids"—have often focused on such resources as gold, silver, diamonds, timber, oil, and, of course, land and access to ports. The United States, still the richest and most powerful country on earth by far, is nevertheless much discomfited by the relative rise in wealth and power of other countries, particularly China.

Our brains are built to check and balance this drive on an individual level, and one of the primary functions of nations and their laws is to constrain the acquisitive competition between individuals and between collectives to fair and nonviolent means. But these constraints are never foolproof at the individual or the national level. Nations can be misguided by both their leaders' and citizens' drives to acquire more than other nations.

What can constrain this collective dA to fair and nonviolent means such as Ricardo-style trading? The constraint has generally been the threat of violent retaliation, but maintaining that threat is a vast drain on resources, not to mention a temptation for all kinds of abuse, especially by leaders-w/o-conscience, who tend to be good at inciting people to fight.

The dark side of the drive to bond (dB) is genocide, an extreme expression of the human tendency to bond with "us" as distinct from "them." In the twentieth century, genocide has usually been a state-sponsored assault on one of a country's own ethnic or racial minorities, such as Jews in Nazi Germany and in Inquisition-era Spain or Muslim Bosnians and Albanians in Milosevic's Serbia.

The dark side of the drive to comprehend (dC) is the human susceptibility to believing in seriously incomplete ideologies. When these ideologies are adopted by local religious sects or by academic schools of thought, there may be a war of words but rarely any violence. When such an ideology is adopted as a national creed, however, and is found to conflict with the ideological creed of another nation, real war all too frequently results. This has been the nature of the many religious wars, it was a major source of the tension in the Cold War, and it is a major element of the persistent Arab-Israeli conflict. Making such wars less likely has been an underlying reason for the modern movement to separate church and state.

The drive to defend (dD) has an obvious potential for generating wars that are primarily to defend one's own life and the lives of fellow citizens, to defend land and possessions, to defend bonded relationships (for example, to the inhabitants of a country's "lost territories"), and to defend religious or political beliefs that give meaning to people's lives. This underlying cause of violence has regularly been manipulated by fear-mongering national leaders-w/o-conscience who themselves have an exclusive focus on their own dA goals. Hermann Goering, Hitler's right-hand man, put it bluntly: "Naturally the common people don't want war; neither in Russia, nor in England, nor in America, nor in Germany. That is understood. But... the people can always be brought to the bidding of the leaders. That is easy. All you have to do is to tell them they are being attacked, and denounce the pacifists for lack of patriotism and exposing the country to danger. It works the same in any country."

People-w/o-conscience introduce a very special factor into the vast human problem of war and genocide. The RD Theory proposes, somewhat counterintuitively in an era shaped by Freud, that the people whom Darwin characterized as "monsters"—the Pol Pots and the Richard Specks—are made so not by the workings of an unconscious drive (aggression), but by the *absence* of a drive, the drive to bond in long-term caring relationships. The drive to bond has done more than anything else to restrain our insatiable drive to acquire wealth and power, and the lack of it may well have done the most damage. In Chapter Five, we saw how the tiny minority of people-w/o-conscience (estimated at 1 percent to 4 percent) could dominate political structures during the Dark Ages at enormous human cost. We would like to think that those awful conditions have been left behind by our modern civilized life. We would like to think that the grossest crimes against humanity—those of Hitler and Stalin, for example—are freak events. (It's too late to hope they never happen again, as they already have.) But to think of them that way is to put ourselves in the greatest danger of repeating them, because these "monsters" spring from a cause—a genetic defect—which has not gone away.

For a clear-cut and fairly modern example of the full scope of the evil that can be done by a head of state who is a person-w/o-conscience, one can hardly do better than King Leopold II of Belgium. This will come, I venture, as news to most readers. Leopold's case is surely the best-hidden modern example of large-scale, state-sponsored genocide. It is estimated that Leopold's victims number more than ten million human beings; he thus joins the ranks of Hitler, Stalin, and Mao. Anyone who wants to understand in full depth the behavior possible in a person-w/o-conscience who attains a position of great power must read *King Leopold's Ghost: A Story of Greed, Terror, and Heroism in Colonial Africa* by Adam Hochschild.[14] It might be the most complete and detailed record available of the life of such a person from birth to death.

Leopold's first step toward power was simply to be born; he was heir to the throne of Belgium. But Belgium was only a small monarchy and a constitutional one at that. How Leopold parlayed this limited power base into a personally owned and dictatorially controlled territory, seventy-six times larger than Belgium itself, seems miraculous. Only an exceedingly cunning person, driven by an intense passion for wealth and power and without a shred of constraining conscience, could have pulled it off. But this is the kind of man Leopold was, as the historical record demonstrates. His story offers us the ultimate warning of the magnitude of the hazard we face as long as such truly weird people have the power to exploit other people.

In brief, Leopold, with the key help of the famous explorer Henry Stanley, conned some 450 chiefs in the Congo River basin to sign over their land to him for almost nothing. He then managed to recruit—basically enslave—his own private army of Congo natives to forcibly confiscate elephant tusks throughout the area. When this source of wealth became depleted, he switched to forcing the natives into the jungle to collect raw rubber, a deadly process. This went on for thirty years until international exposure of his crimes forced Leopold to cede his Congo property rights to the Belgian government. Leopold himself died unpunished and unrepentant. There was nothing for him to repent; lacking a drive to bond, he couldn't have seen that he had done anything wrong.[15]

To demonstrate that people-w/o-conscience were still in business as heads of state, at least of small states, in more recent times, I will briefly recount my own brush with such a person. In 1964, along with three faculty colleagues in an executive education program, I traveled to the small princely state of Swat, set in a remote valley in Pakistan and surrounded by the Himalayas (roughly where Osama bin Laden is reportedly hiding out today). We were invited to dinner by the heir apparent of the state, the eldest son of the reigning elderly prince.

Our host told the story of how his father, who had once been only one of several minor chiefs in the region, came to be the single prince of the entire area. It seems that his father had invited all the chiefs of the region to a great feast. After dinner he explained that he had a special treat for them. He had hired a fine photographer to take a picture of the entire group and each would receive a framed print as a memento of the occasion. He led them into his garden and onto an ornamental bridge to pose for the picture. The "photographer" was facing the bridge with his "camera" covered by the usual black hood. As his father moved to one side, the photographer removed the hood to reveal a machine gun and quickly killed all the men on the bridge.

Our host finished his story by sorrowfully saying that, after that day, his father had never been able to leave his house without heavily armed bodyguards. Nor could our host himself. I doubt that the old prince had needed to read Machiavelli to come up with his deadly plan. He was simply doing what comes naturally to people-w/o-conscience. In his pursuit of wealth and power, he felt no moral constraints. He did what he could get away with—and he apparently succeeded.

I have dwelt much on people-w/o-conscience in this book. Their existence was an unpleasant surprise to me, discovered in the course of my research for this book, and I know others will find it hard to believe, as I did myself. In this regard, one pattern needs to be remembered. People-w/o-conscience seem especially able to worm their way into powerful positions during periods of social disruption, which are themselves sometimes the legacies of earlier people-w/o-conscience.

The social turmoil in Africa, dating back to the slave trade and colonization, continues to provide opportunities for people-w/o-conscience to secure top power positions in an appalling number of the "freed" nations. The roster of such states is certainly not limited to Africa. And we can now add the leaders of stateless groups such as Osama bin Laden.

Nonviolent Resistance

One response to the rule of leaders-w/o-conscience or of seriously misguided four-drive leaders is nonviolent resistance. Political scientist Gene Sharp, who has studied nonviolent resistance for fifty years, points out that despots rely on their ability to terrorize their subjects into obedience and has developed, from historical cases, some practical guidelines for successful nonviolent struggle against despotism.[16] We need much more research of this kind. We still know too little about how to deal with person-w/o-conscience heads of state, support internal reform groups and help them exploit the vulnerabilities of tyrants without being crushed themselves, apply effective sanctions, focus world attention on abuses and mobilize world opinion, deploy internationally sponsored armed peacekeepers without spilling blood, and build the international consensus and the resources that will support all of these efforts. At the least, it should be clear from the current situation in Iraq that there must be better ways to displace grossly abusive dictators than an all-out war that is likely to spawn and proliferate at least as many problems as it solves. The world, after all, has no shortage of people-w/o-conscience who will be looking for their chance to step into any vacated power position in the midst of the disruption of war.

KEEPING A GLOBAL COMMUNITY ON TRACK

Given the vast amount of violent death and suffering that humans have experienced throughout history from genocide and inter-nation warfare, it is not surprising that much human thought and effort has gone into searching for less painful ways to resolve the underlying conflicts between large collectives. But, by and large, this search has failed. Many have argued that this failure will continue indefinitely, that war and genocide are inevitable. Perhaps so—but perhaps much can be learned by reviewing the well-known attempts of the past in the light of the Renewed Darwinian Theory view of human behavior and leadership.

According to traditional social contract theory, it is a basic func-tion of the state to protect the lives and possessions of its citizens. Locke focused on the state's role in protecting private property, but it is not hard to extend this principal to the defense of lives (dB) and beliefs (dC). When states neglect their obligation to maintain law and order and protect these valuable "possessions"—both the tangible and the intangible—individuals can be expected to seek retribution and revenge and to take the law into their own hands. Intra-nation disputes can usually be handled with-out violence when effective state institutions are in place, such as police and courts; generally obeyed social norms of nonvio-lence are also essential. But when the threat to citizens' lives and their material, social, and spiritual possessions comes from outside—from other nation-states and from stateless networks of terrorists (not to mention polluted air and water, accidental releases of radiation, or laxly controlled diseases)—where can the attacked nation and its citizens look for defense? What are the options other than violent defense, counterattack, or even preemptive attack?

Probably the oldest and most persistent attempt to control violence between nations has been, paradoxically, by conquest. Alexander the Great had a vision of unifying the world with his armies leading the way. The Roman legions fought to pacify the "uncivilized" tribes. But history shows that putting tribes and nations together by armed force eventually fails, and modern empires have failed much more quickly than did the ancient ones. World War I saw the breakup of the Austrian-Hungarian Empire, the Ottoman Empire, and the more limited German empire. After World War II, the empires of two of the victors, Britain and France, collapsed. And as the Cold War wound down, so did the Soviet empire. These empires had been built on conquest and experienced much briefer successes than the Roman and Byzantine Empires. Fighting wars to end all wars has not worked, as Wilson's effort in World War I should have taught us all. The recent wars in Iraq and Afghanistan were supposedly intended to prevent future violence from terrorist organizations based there, but so far the costs seem to outweigh the benefits.

The peaceful federation of nations into larger regional unions has a better record than conquest, but is extremely difficult to accomplish. Perhaps the medieval attempt to unite the former Roman colonies in Europe under the banner of Christianity as the Holy Roman Empire was an early attempt at federation, but the amount of violence associated with this effort makes it a dubious exemplar. Switzerland is a successful small-scale federation; the United States is a successful large-scale example. Yet even the United States was not truly united until after the Civil War.

The gradual evolution of the European Union is a very promising model. It began in the aftermath of World War II with a modest iron and steel agreement between France and Germany. Step by step, for about sixty years, it has moved ahead to address issues on which joint agreements were advantageous to the nations involved: freer trade, environmental protection, farm price supports, freer movement of people, economic development, and many others. Direct public elections of representatives to Brussels are now routine, and the single currency issue is nearly resolved. Joint security and foreign policies are gradually coming into place. Careful choices are being made to clarify which decisions can best be retained at the traditional national and local levels even as more decisions are moved to Brussels. Now the term *United States of Europe* is beginning to appear in the press and even in the speeches of a few political leaders.

Signs of a backlash against the move toward European unification are also present. Fears of the "loss of sovereignty" are being voiced. This is largely a problem of conceptualization. If sovereignty were conceived as a single, indivisible entity, then it might at some point jump from the national level to the EU level. But would it not be more accurate to conceive of sovereignty as covering a range of issues that can be resolved at different levels of government? The rule of thumb would be to leave each decision at the lowest level that can handle it effectively. This consideration is at the heart of the next approach to addressing inter-nation conflicts without violence: international law.

International law may have begun with the informal but powerful code of chivalry and honorable behavior, even between combatants, that arose during the wars of the Middle Ages. Today it is evolving through a network of treaties. The process moves slowly but it does keep moving. Today the range of issues covered by international agreements is impressive: chemical and biological warfare, fishing in international waters, international trade, Antarctica, ocean-going ships, outer space, prisoners of war, nuclear proliferation, airspace, air pollution, the airwaves, war crimes, land mines, and many more. Some, but clearly not all, of these international laws are backed up by judicial institutions and by sanctions. They are all designed to resolve inter-nation conflicts without violence. Many of these bodies of international law deal with the classic "tragedy of the commons" problem.[17] The length and diversity of the list above demonstrates how creative people have been in recent years in resolving these age-old issues.

The further extension and strengthening of such multilateral agreements is one clear and useful way to address the lack of effective institutions to resolve inter-nation conflicts without violence. Some would argue that a fully developed set of these agreements would be the functional equivalent of world government. But at this stage of world history, no treaties have been able to effectively outlaw war and genocide. That is probably beyond the power of any treaty to achieve. What, then, of the attempts to establish world-level governmental institutions? Remember that a "world government" does not "rule" the world; it is meant to serve as a prefrontal cortex, checking and balancing the independent and conflicting—but often equally legitimate—drives of nations and their people regarding a limited set of issues that can only be addressed effectively at the world level.

The first major attempt at world government was the League of Nations, established after World War I and primarily the brain-child of Woodrow Wilson. He was forced to back away from some of his basic conditions for establishing a just and lasting peace in order to get the other allies to establish the League. The U.S. Senate then failed to ratify the treaty because the requirement that all League members pledge to comply with League votes calling for military action to stop any aggressor nation from attacking League members was considered an unacceptable reduction of U.S. sovereign rights. Without the United States, the League was doomed to ineffectiveness in controlling inter-nation wars.

The United Nations, established by the Allies after World War II, is the most recent effort to establish world government. It is too soon to say whether the UN can evolve into an effective deterrent to war and genocide. The Korean War was fought under the UN flag, which may have kept that war from expanding, yet the UN was almost totally on the sidelines during the Vietnam War and has had only limited success in terminating the smaller wars of the past fifty years and even less in stopping genocide. As a global prefrontal cortex, the UN has been unable to reliably check the violent dA impulses of its members with equally powerful dB impulses. The UN may well deserve some credit for the fact that no worldwide war has occurred since its founding, but it has done little to reduce the greatest threat to world-scale destruction, the constant possibility of nuclear conflict.[18]

I believe most observers would agree that the UN must be changed before nations and individual citizens can count on it to deter military aggression and genocide initiated by nations or, these days, by stateless terrorist networks; that is, before citizens of member nations feel bonded enough (dB) to the UN and to the people of other nations to entrust it and them with their own safety (dD). Only one nation, Costa Rica, has disarmed and taken the path of reliance on the United Nations for defense against foreign aggression. At the moment, it seems nearly impossible to see how the nations of the world will find a path to mutual defense in place of self-defense. Yet the thirteen colonial states of America found such a path and even now it is happening in Europe. In a world still full of nuclear weapons and—in all likelihood—people-w/o-conscience in powerful political positions, it is hard to see how our species can stay on track without finding some path toward effective world-level institutions that can not only outlaw wars, genocide, and comparable world threats but actually stop or prevent them. The Framers were convinced that people need the help of effective national governments to stay on track, and their insight is just as true at the world level. I will explore in the following what the Renewed Darwinian Theory suggests about the path toward such a world-level institution, but first I must be more specific about the nature of the crisis we face.

FACING UP TO THE COMING CRISIS AT THE WORLD LEVEL

I believe that the human species is facing a massive three-headed crisis that, without a major change of course, will lead to a catastrophic population collapse—possibly even extinction— sometime in the twenty-first or twenty-second centuries. The three heads of the crisis are

1. The exhaustion or degradation of environmental resources to the point that the world's human population can no longer be sustained. The most obvious and pressing issues in this regard are global warming and the loss of biodiversity.
2. The proliferation of weapons of mass destruction to the point that their use in a war simply awaits the inevitable spark.
3. The existence of people-w/o-conscience in our midst, able to attain top positions in governments and large corporations and willing to instigate large-scale violence and global economic chaos.

Any one of these three problems has the potential to collapse human civilization as we know it. The first one to reach a crisis point will probably trigger the other two, a point well illustrated by Jared Diamond's case histories of collapsing societies such as that of Easter Island.[19]

I argued in Chapter Three that the hominid line probably faced such survival crises in the past and survived by a combination of genetic change and cultural inventions. When the survival of *Homo habilis* was threatened, the combination of a cultural invention (controlling fire for cooking), sex selection, and pair-bonding produced the new species *Homo erectus,* keeping the hominid line on track even as the species *H. habilis* died out. The evidence for the next crisis is not nearly as clear but does suggest that, around 200,000 years ago, the survival of *Homo erectus* was threatened and the hominid line was saved by the emergence of early *Homo sapiens,* with a modified brain that extended dB to the tribal level and established dC as an independent drive. Then, around 60,000 years ago, modern *Homo sapiens* emerged from 30,000 years of intense environmental pressure with an even more sophisticated brain, capable of language and possessing a moral sense—a conscience. None of these survival-ensuring changes resulted in hominids who were stronger, faster, or fiercer. They resulted in hominids who were more willing and able to work together for their mutual survival and who were quicker and more versatile at solving problems.

I believe this is the trajectory on which we need to continue. But we can no longer expect the slow process of genetic change through natural, sexual, and group selection to help us avoid collapse and stay on track. We must feel, think, plan, and act our way through any modern crisis, and we must make *full* use of the four-drive impulse/check/balance decision-making capability our species evolved during its passage through previous crises. Over the past five centuries or so, science, in particular, has made us more able than ever to solve many kinds of problems. And over the past two-and-a-quarter centuries, we have become somewhat better at working together for mutual survival in larger and larger groups. But, as I pointed out in Chapter One, this dB-driven progress has been much more gradual and has suffered many more setbacks than our dC-driven scientific and technical progress.

I believe we have to look to science as the institution that must lead the way. Having a unified and tested theory of human behavior would clearly be an enormously helpful starting point. To restate a message that runs through this book: I believe the first big step toward such a theory is not only more research but also much more focused research. The set of hypotheses offered by this book—what I call the Renewed Darwinian Theory of human behavior and good/moral leadership—needs to be rigorously tested for accuracy and then either accepted (with improvements) or rejected. I hope that all the scientific disciplines that bear on human behavior will be involved, each using its own refined research methods to frame the hypotheses in testable forms and conduct the empirical tests. (Some of this needed scientific work bearing on corporations was spelled out at the end of Chapter Eight.)

While such research is sorely needed, we cannot afford to wait idly until it is completed. We need to use what we already know about the three-headed monster threatening us. Humans never have *all* the information needed—there is always a risk of making a wrong decision. But our mental process of satisfying all four innate drives does an amazingly good job of devising solutions even with incomplete information; we should and can make much better use of it:

- *Environmental disaster.* We already know enough about global warming and the pace of its advance that we must respond now. It will be too late by the time we can be 100 percent sure about it.
- *Threat of nuclear war.* Again, we need not and cannot wait until we are 100 percent sure who has what weapons and what intentions. We need to start the complicated work of establishing world-level institutions to adequately address this issue.
- *People-w/o-conscience.* I believe we should move now to establish check-and-balance structures in all major institutions as a guard against people-w/o-conscience and move later to explicitly forbid or remove them from power positions, if and when we have reliable, DNA-based diagnostic methods.

It is therefore with a sense of urgency that I offer a few suggestions about possible responses to the major threats at the world level.

INSTITUTIONAL SUGGESTIONS AT THE WORLD LEVEL

I believe that humanity must establish a world governance system if we are to cope successfully with the three-headed crisis we face as a species. It must be carefully designed and strong, but strictly limited—as the U.S. government is strictly limited by the Bill of Rights. Nothing short of such a world-level institution will work.

I am fully aware of the arguments against it. I am fully aware of the strength of the fear, especially among Americans, of losing our sense of sovereignty and independence. "Don't fence me in" has been one of the most powerful themes throughout American history. But it is pure hubris to think that Americans are the exceptions who can get along as free-standing rugged individuals and even as a free-standing rugged nation. The Framers knew better. It was Hamilton who said, "Have we not already seen enough of the fallacy and extravagance of those idle theories which have amused us with promises of an exemption from the imperfections, weaknesses and evils incident to society in every shape? Is it not time to awake from the deceitful dream of a golden age, and to adopt as a practical maxim for the direction of our political conduct, that we, as well as other inhabitants of the globe, are yet remote from the happy empire of perfect wisdom and perfect virtue?"[20] Hamilton was sensing that America had its share of the world's power-seeking people-w/o-conscience.

I believe that the scale of the wars and genocides of the past century provide more than ample justification for a world-level governance institution capable of dealing with all three of the looming crises. Further justification is provided by the little-known close calls we have had with nuclear war, brought on not by leaders of rogue states but by top American officials. Recently released records include a harrowing scene in 1957 in which

Curtis LeMay, commander of the Strategic Air Command bombers and a man whose entire military record identifies him as a possible person-w/o-conscience, told a presidential advisory committee that if he identified signs of preparation of a large Soviet bomber launch, he would initiate a first strike with the SAC nuclear bombers under his command. "If I see that the Russians are massing their planes for an attack," he said, "I'm going to knock the shit out of them before they take off from the ground." When he was reminded that this was not national policy, he responded, "I don't care. It's my policy. That's what I'm going to do."[21] On three occasions, President Nixon ordered B-52 bombers into full wartime alert, flying an Arctic route that bordered Soviet airspace. If the Soviets had ordered such a high alert, which they never did, the United States would have considered it an act of war.[22]

Today, we need to be smart enough to realize that all nations, including America, need some degree of "fencing in," some carefully constructed powers and constraints at the world level. Harry Truman made this point in 1945 in anticipation of the conference that brought the United Nations into being: "We all have to recognize, no matter how great our strength, that we must deny ourselves the license to always do as we please." Think again of those chimpanzees. With nothing in their brains to inhibit them from grabbing the biggest dish of candy, they indeed had the license to do always as they pleased. They were not fenced in. Yet they never got what they wanted.

America still needs to be a leader, but it cannot police the world alone. Humanity must manage its global issues through a global institution. We need to move the insights of the Framers to the world stage and establish the kind of world institution without which our very survival as a species will be at too great a risk. Each of our three life-or-death challenges can be met with an effective world-level institution. It is unlikely that any of them can be met without such an institution. It is really that simple, and we can be grateful for the example set by the Framers.

The kind of institution I envision could be created by a few major changes to the United Nations charter. These changes would be patterned after the U.S. Constitution and undertaken by a special UN constitutional convention. Franklin Roosevelt anticipated such changes when he told Congress that the initial UN Charter would need to be revised many times to keep up with new problems. What follows is only a preliminary sketch of the same basic elements that brought success to the U.S. experiment, somewhat modified for the world stage:

1. *Provide checks and balances at the top of the UN system* by retaining the familiar tripartite system of legislative, executive, and judicial branches, with a few critical changes:
   - The Security Council's representatives would be selected by the national governments of *an expanded set of major nations with a few rotating seats for smaller nations.*
   - The Security Council would make decisions by majority vote, except for supermajority votes on the most critical issues, but with *no more single-nation vetoes.*
   - The General Assembly's representatives would be *selected by direct popular voting in each member nation.*
   - Rules for *conducting worldwide elections* would be specified.
   - The executive branch would continue to be headed by a secretary general selected by the Security Council.
   - There would be an *independent consolidated judiciary,* encompassing the World Court and other international judiciary bodies, with judges nominated by the secretary general and ratified by the Security Council.
2. *Establish the limited agenda of worldwide issues* that the reorganized UN would be expected to address, leaving all other issues to be resolved at the national level or below. This list would include such issues as inter-nation wars; genocide; major human rights violations; worldwide environmental abuses; pandemics; governance of the open oceans, international air space, outer space, and arctic regions; and the chartering and regulation of multinational corporations over a specified size. The importance of this last function justifies the establishment of a special office, discussed in the next paragraph.
3. *Provide for an office to charter and regulate large multinational corporations.* Charters would specify a top-level impulse/check/balance governance structure with stakeholder representatives. Regulation would be carried out by a set of commissions, one

for each major industrial group, which would establish rules to constrain the major abusive practices associated with each industry and provide for the enforcement of those rules. A commission on financial institutions would be a good place to start. (See Chapter Nine, on the 2007–2009 financial meltdown.)

4. *Provide for the right of direct taxation,* probably by taxing the profits of UN-chartered multinational corporations or by putting a very small tax on international transactions, starting with currency transactions.

5. *Provide for a permanent armed force* of UN police and peacekeepers.

6. *Provide for the right to suspend,* with no voting or other rights within the UN, any member nation that commits major violations of the human rights of its citizens or acts of aggression against other nations. Such suspension would be initiated by executive order of the secretary general and ratified by supermajority vote of the Security Council. The executive order would specify the grounds for suspension. The UN suspension could, if necessary, escalate to economic sanctions and to armed peacekeeper intervention for protracted serious violations. This essential suspension rule would be meaningless without the "no veto" rule for Security Council members.

7. *Provide a Bill of Rights* that enumerates the minimal basic rights both of member nations and of individual citizens.

8. If and when definitive diagnostic procedures are available, *exclude positively identified people-w/o-conscience* from all elective and senior appointive offices in the UN.

9. *Establish a UN goal of controlling and eventually eliminating all weapons of mass destruction.*

10. *Establish a UN goal of having every member nation adopt a constitutional impulse/check/balance form of government.*

As humans, we need to acknowledge that our continued on-track progress is by no means inevitable; humanity, as a species, can wander into a dead end. But neither is collapse inevitable; we are in charge of our future. Staying on track means maintaining our balance while moving forward. That's not easy, but, as I have said throughout this book, evolution has formed us into creatures that can solve just this sort of problem. As individuals, staying on track is the only way to have fulfilling, joyful, and meaningful lives, yet we also need governance institutions as a backup system to help us stay on track and to protect us from people-w/o-conscience. Government can act as a collective prefrontal cortex for us all—at various levels including the world level—but governance institutions themselves need to be carefully designed if they are to be consistently positive in this regard. As Madison observed, "In framing a government which is to be administered by men over men, the great difficulty lies in this: you must first enable the government to control the governed; and in the next place oblige it to control itself."[23]

The Renewed Darwinian Theory shows us what being on track means, suggests what will contribute to it, and helps us recognize the most helpful institutional examples (such as the U.S. Constitution) for what they are. We need these institutions to help us awaken from the nightmare aspects of human history.

Darwin, appropriately, has the last word and leaves us with the same challenge: "As man advances in civilization, and small tribes are united into larger communities, the simplest reason would tell each individual that he ought to extend his social instincts and sympathies to all the members of the same nation, though personally unknown to him. This point being once reached, there is only an artificial barrier to prevent his sympathies extending to the men of all nations and races. If, indeed, such men are separated from him by great differences in appearance or habits, experience unfortunately shows us how long it is, before we look at them as our fellow-creatures."[24] Will we get there in time?

CHAPTER ELEVEN

KEEPING ON TRACK BY PRACTICING GOOD/MORAL LEADERSHIP

> *Even when we are quite alone, how often do we think*
> *with pleasure or pain of what others think of us—of*
> *their imagined approbation or disapprobation; and*
> *this all follows from sympathy, a fundamental*
> *element of the social instincts [dB]. A man who*
> *possessed no trace of such instincts would be an*
> *unnatural monster.*
> — CHARLES DARWIN[1]

LEADING ONESELF

Up to now, I have concentrated on leadership of groups, particularly the largest and most powerful—and therefore the most potentially constructive and the most potentially damaging—groups in the modern world: national governments and corporations. Although we often speak of groups as if they had drives, wishes, intentions, feelings, or neuroses, I have pointed out that groups do not have brains and therefore do not have any of these characteristics; only the individual members of a group do. However distinctive so-called "group behavior" may be in comparison to "individual behavior," there really is no such thing as group behavior. There is only the behavior of individuals when they are acting as members of groups, which is a lot of the time. After all, as we have seen, humans are genetically designed to work in groups because doing so has proven to be essential for our survival. This is the way, as Darwin said, that we have become the most adaptive and most dominant of species, and the process of adapting oneself to one's environment is the same thing as leading oneself.

I stress this point again because the theory of leadership I have been discussing is an application of the Renewed Darwinian Theory of Human Behavior and Leadership. Whatever I have said that corporations and the United States government and the world need to do is only what we all need to do, writ large. And while some of our most powerful institutions are not well designed to achieve four-drive moral balance, each of us as an individual (except the people-w/o-conscience) *is* well designed by the evolution of our species to do so. Harnessing this capability at the individual level is the essential first step toward providing the good/moral leadership needed to solve the large-scale problems we all face.

Of course, we can go astray as individuals. What RD Theory does is tell us what balance we should aim for and why it really is the best state for us to be in. With that in mind, we can see what's missing or what is exaggerated in our own lives. RD Theory is hardly refined enough to tell everyone precisely what to do, but it can help you sort through the avalanche of "personal improvement" advice to see which makes sense. (In other words, RD Theory cannot take the role that the Dr. Phils of the world claim to perform, but it might save you from wasting your time with quite a lot of their advice.)

Consider this story, told in Dr. Jerome Groopman's poignant book, *The Measure of Our Days*.[2] Dr. Groopman had a patient named Kirk, a hard-charging and very successful high-stakes investor who found himself, at age fifty-four, riddled with cancer and facing the worst possible prognosis. Determined not to be defeated by death, Kirk insisted on an extreme course of chemotherapy: four complete courses of interleukin-2 and vinblastine with progesterone. He gradually regained his health—a complete remission. It seemed a miracle. But when Kirk and his wife, Cathy, were about to move back to New York after two months of recuperation, he responded to the question of whether he was ready to return to real life with an unconvincing "I guess so." Two weeks later, Cathy was on the phone to Groopman: "He won't read the newspapers. He used to devour them." Kirk added, "I don't think I am depressed, Jerry. It's just that the information in the papers doesn't seem important anymore."

And what had seemed so important before his illness? Kirk backed startup ventures, but it wasn't the ventures that interested him—it was simply winning a contest against other smart, hard-charging people like himself. "In your world," he told Groopman, "what matters is new knowledge that can lead to curing a disease. For me, the product means nothing. It can be oil or platinum or software or widgets. For me, it's the delicious pleasure of seeing where to go before the crowd does; the challenge of making fast decisions; the fun of everyone trying to outsmart everyone else. It's all a shell game played for big money."

Some months later, during a routine exam, Kirk reported a persistent pain in his back. Testing revealed that the cancer was back in a hopeless way. Groopman tells the story:

> I sat by the bedside and for a long time we were silent. I felt we were speaking telepathically, acknowledging to each other that we knew that we had tried and tried hard but now the end had come.
>
> "I'm sorry that magic didn't work longer," I finally offered.
>
> "It did more than anyone expected, Jerry. But you shouldn't feel sorry. There was no reason to live anyway. When I went into remission, I couldn't read the papers because my deals and trades seemed pointless. The remission meant nothing because it was too late to relive my life. I once asked for hell. Maybe God made this miracle to have me know what it will feel like."
>
> "Have you thought about telling Cathy and the children what you've told me?" I gently suggested.
>
> "Why? So they can hear what they already know? That I was a self-absorbed uncaring s—? That's really going to be a comforting deathbed interchange."[3]

What can we say about Kirk's tragedy? To start with, I do not believe he was a person-w/o-conscience. He certainly seemed to feel guilty about his treatment of his family, as no person-w/o-conscience would. I size him up as an unfortunate four-drive

244 DRIVEN TO LEAD

person who became addicted to his drive to acquire, with additional rewards coming from fulfilling his drive to comprehend. He brought a strong cognitive capacity to his competitive game of outsmarting others. This was rewarding to him, but he got his biggest kicks out of fulfilling his selfish greed. With these skills in play, he probably did not have to worry too much about defending himself. The tragic point is that he let his addiction lead him to neglect his drive to bond with others. With his life hanging by a thread, he seems to have been able to establish a fairly intimate relationship with Dr. Groopman—someone who had a slim chance of saving him. But we'll have to take his own word that he had not fulfilled his drive to bond in his ordinary life. And because all four bonds are independent and insatiable, fulfilling three out of four—even spectacularly well—isn't good enough. In the end, he paid a terrible price for his failure to lead his own life in a balanced way.

Kirk's life story makes the important point that if one wishes to become a leader who is good/moral (leading others to satisfice all four of their drives, though not necessarily all at once all the time) and thereby effective (with highly motivated followers), one must first be able to lead oneself with a balanced attention to all four drives. Can a person who is not satisficing all four of his or her own drives nevertheless help others do so? I would say: in given instances, yes, but over the long run, no. The drive to bond, in particular, as I pointed out in Chapter Two, can only be fulfilled with other people. I also don't see how one could help other people satisfice their drive to comprehend without also satisficing it for oneself. And a person deficient in dA or dD is unlikely to be effective enough in the world to make much of a leader. Even a leader such as Gandhi, thought of as utterly unmaterialistic, had a drive to acquire the resources he needed to carry out his program.

Maintaining a four-drive balance in one's life is not easy. (And for this reason alone, leadership will never be easy.) The world is full of rewarding temptations that might develop into obsessions or addictions. Looking beyond the usual suspects—alcohol, tobacco, drugs, and so on—it is possible to become addicted to an unbalanced life in terms of any of the four drives. I expect that most of us arrive in this world with latent talents that predispose us to favor one drive or another. We are advised to plan our careers around these strengths and that is fine, as long as one does not become as unbalanced as Kirk. This is a hard temptation to avoid; one's special talents are the very things that others notice and reward. This is where we may need the help of a spouse or intimate friend to warn us when we are getting off track. I know I could easily have become an unbalanced intellectual workaholic, more unbearable than I am, if not for the steady help of my wife.

INTERNALIZING THE RD THEORY CONCEPT OF GOOD/MORAL LEADERSHIP

I believe that, to become a good/moral four-drive leader, one must be convinced by one's own experience, observation, and reflection that the RD Theory concept of good/moral leadership is an accurate model of why we do what we do. We are often exposed to other people's theories, whether presented formally in classrooms and books or informally, as when someone says, "You know, there are two kinds of people..." We have all developed our own theories about human behavior, whether we are aware of having done so or not. Any time you find yourself asking, "Who on earth would do *that*?" or saying, "Nah, she'd never do something like *that*" or "I'll bet *I'd* do the same thing in his shoes," you are applying some theory of human behavior that predicts for you what is or is not possible. Is your theory, or any other theory which you have encountered, more accurate and useful than the RD Theory? Take some thinking time and put it to the test. When you are surprised by some aspect of human behavior, would the RD Theory make it less surprising? When you can't figure out why you have done something or failed to do something, can the RD Theory make sense of it for you? Talk it out with others. Try the Ultimatum Game and see whether you can explain the results in any other way.

I am confident that you will need to own these ideas as your own guide to your own behavior, as well as your guide to the behavior of other people, before you can put them into action with consistency and integrity as a leader.

LEARNING AND PRACTICING GOOD/MORAL LEADERSHIP

Four-drive moral leadership is both a theory and a skill. Therefore, for most people, it will require both understanding and practice. (I am granting that a few people have a natural grasp of the theory and a natural gift for putting it into action.) Part of the skill involves getting used to what the theory does and does not tell you. It does not tell you the particular technical means of solving a particular problem. In that sense, mastery of the RD Theory is necessary but not sufficient for good leadership. Each leader must also have the particular skills, knowledge, and experience appropriate to the task at hand. Abraham Lincoln was a great four-drive moral leader of the United States, but that doesn't mean he would have been a great leader of the Manhattan Project or the Metropolitan Opera.

The RD Theory does help you, as a leader, figure out how to listen deeply to the various stakeholders and understand how different people feel and think and how they express their four ultimate motives—their four drives. This, in turn, will help you discover how to talk with different stakeholders and what to talk about. When they see that you understand them and appreciate their four-drive stories, they will be better able to see how their motives fit in with the motives of others, including your motives as a leader. If all this listening and understanding and articulating sounds like the job description of a professional negotiator, that may be because, as a leader, you are acting as a sort of prefrontal cortex for the four drives of many individuals at once. And as we saw in Chapter Two, the prefrontal cortex, with its impulse/check/balance process, is quite a negotiator.

To a large extent, RD leadership skill can and must be developed through on-the-job experience. But my long experience as a classroom instructor at Harvard Business School, where case studies are the primary mode of instruction, convinces me that it can also be developed and improved by a rehearsal process in the classroom. Imagine a class in which all the students have been exposed to RD Theory and have had time to thoroughly discuss it and to run through some experiential exercises to see whether the model is confirmed by their own behavior. At this point, the class is ready for leadership practice, one case at a time. The students are presented with a series of cases involving complex and unique real-life situations with the same query for each case: As a leader, how could you best respond to this situation, while always having the same goal of satisficing the four drives of all the parties involved, including yourself? For each case, many solutions can be proposed and none will be perfect, but the class will judge each one by the criterion of four-drive fulfillment all around. A very tough challenge, no doubt about it, but it's just the challenge our brains have been designed to meet. A year or two of practice like this in a school of business or government would, I believe, turn out some leaders refreshingly unlike the ones we've been reading too much about lately.

SIZING UP THE LEADERSHIP ROLE

For much of his career, the literary critic and biographer Walter Jackson Bate had an ambition to write a definitive biography of Samuel Johnson. But he felt he had to prepare himself for such a task. Among his earlier books were a short biography of a very complex subject, Samuel Taylor Coleridge, and a much more substantial biography of John Keats, which won both a Pulitzer Prize and a National Book Award. Finally he felt ready to take on Johnson, and he was proven right when his biography again won a Pulitzer Prize and a National Book Award and was, indeed, considered a masterpiece. Bate's attitude is just the right one for leaders. Successful leaders need to have some sense of the "size"—however qualitatively measured—of a given leadership role in comparison to the size of the leadership role they are actually prepared to fulfill. While it's true that, every so often, "some have greatness thrust upon them,"[4] this is hardly a viable way to conduct most of the world's business.

The RD Theory suggests that a practical way for aspiring leaders to assess leadership roles is to size up the gaps between the assumptions and worldviews of each of the relevant stakeholders and the balanced four-drive solution toward which the leader would like to lead them. How much difference and conflict has to be overcome? If the task is to lead a small group of close associates toward an agreed-upon goal, many of us would feel up to the job. At the other extreme is the leadership task facing President Obama: many complex problems and drastic differences in how the stakeholders would like to solve them. Can they really let go of their current ideas and come to see a different policy solution as more satisfying to them in regard to all four drives? What RD Theory promises is that leaders can at least count on all the stakeholders having all the same innate four drives in their brains (except for people-w/o-conscience) and the same built-in impulse/check/balance mechanism for satisficing them all. When the leader *knows* that he or she can count on this as a fact, the search for a consensus solution will be easier.

An aspiring leader must therefore expect to hone his or her skills over a lifetime and must be careful not to reach for too high a step before proving himself or herself on each lower step. The fall could be exceedingly painful, and not just for oneself.

SUMMARIZING WHAT LEADERS NEED TO KNOW ABOUT GROUPS

Since this chapter focuses on the practice of leading groups, we now need a straightforward framework to help leaders think about groups. A group of any size, from a married couple to the Family of Man, can best be characterized by (1) the quality and clarity of the group's collective purpose, (2) the match between the competencies needed to fulfill the group's purpose and the competencies the group's members possess, (3) the members' trust in each other, and (4) the members' motivation to put energy into achieving the group's collective purpose. Leaders can significantly affect all four characteristics and can thereby significantly affect the group's performance and survival.

Many fine articles and books have been written about each of these four characteristics. Here I will discuss aspects of these four characteristics which tie in with the RD Theory of human behavior and leadership—which I am glad to say they do very well.

GROUP PURPOSE

Groups will, obviously, perform better when their collective purpose is clear and can be linked to the fulfillment of all four drives of all the group's stakeholders. Leadership involves searching for a workable connection and balance between the "greater good for all," an "honorable purpose," and the narrower self-interests of each subgroup and each individual member.

GROUP COMPETENCIES

Any group with a purpose needs members with the right mix of necessary skills (for example, accounting or salesmanship), personality traits (such as decisiveness or friendliness), and resources (for example, physical endurance or well-placed connections). Leadership involves identifying and recruiting people with these characteristics. It may also involve helping people develop requisite skills (personality traits generally cannot be developed very reliably). It is well established that, as the complexity and uncertainty of the group's purpose increases, securing the appropriate skill mix will create differences amongst group members which will, in turn, make it harder for the leader to achieve the cooperation and integration needed for high performance.[5] That's when the two remaining group characteristics, trust and motivation, will make all the difference.

GROUP TRUST-BUILDING

We have talked about trust in a limited way so far but now, with our focus on the practice of leadership, trust becomes a key concept. The degree of trust is a good way to characterize the range between a relationship that is truly bonded and one that is the opposite, truly hostile. Scholars studying groups and leadership are showing more and more interest in trust.[6] The reasons are not hard to find; recent polls show that Americans distrust the media and unions by a margin of nearly three (distrust) to one (trust) and distrust politicians and big corporations by four to one. Think what has happened in the last year to the public's trust in banks. If distrust were a disease, we'd call it an epidemic.

For both business and government, distrustful relationships are expensive. Transactions become slower, more complicated, and far more fragmented. It is estimated that distrust of other stakeholders adds at least thirty cents to every dollar of health care cost. Naturally, distrust will inhibit, if not prevent, collaborative innovation, teamwork, and rapid decision making. In other words, for business, distrust is a major competitive disadvantage; nothing in a legal contract can entirely substitute for trust. Building trust throughout an organization is therefore a vital leadership skill.

Yet trust is too often taken for granted; our civilization has been surprisingly deficient in studying the practices and methods of building trust. Many people profess a simplistic view: either I trust someone or I don't. Yet it is obvious that we trust an endless stream of complete strangers with our lives when we drive but certainly would not trust them with our credit cards or house keys. We do not have a solid approach to increasing trust, to restoring trust when it's broken, or to "designing" trust so that we can reach new heights in our relationships while protecting ourselves from those who should not be trusted, such as people-w/o-conscience.

The minimum requirement for trust is a level of safety in the relationship; one must believe that one will not be worse off for having had a particular interaction. A lack of trust therefore indicates *fear;* in particular, fear of being taken advantage of or of being emotionally or physically hurt. It is possible to mistrust a perfect stranger walking down the street, but not a baby going by in a baby carriage. The adult stranger is at least capable of harm; the baby is not. RD Theory has shown us that, for humans, the functional opposite of fear is a bonded relationship of mutual caring. (Fellow creatures who look into the whites of each other's eyes to understand and help each other, not to trick and defeat each other.) Our society's widespread distrust must therefore involve a shortfall in the number of bonded long-term relationships of mutual caring in organizations and in society in general.

The conceptual framework of Figure 11.1 helps us think about trust and the RD Theory. The slanted line displays the ladder of trust from the extreme of distrustful relationships, across the horizontal line of neural transactions, and on to the ultimate in trustful relationships. This representation makes the important point that trust is not binary; it comes in gradations. Of course, the division into specific gradations is subjective and arbitrary, but the fact that trust and mistrust can take different forms with different consequences is not. For example, we can easily associate the different labels on the distrust end of the spectrum with different gaming tactics that people have invented either to protect themselves or to counterattack. We can also associate the labels on the trust end of the spectrum with a variety of potential payoffs, benefits, and blessings. What I have gained from my trusting relationship with my dentist has been valuable indeed, but not to be compared with what I have gained from my trusting relationship with my wife.

I submit that this conceptual framework offers a powerful guide for coaching would-be leaders on how to break up a negative cycle of mistrust by calling attention to trust-busting behaviors and how to strengthen trusting relationships, one step at a time, amongst one's group members.

The four compass points of RD Theory's four drives indicate the strong connection of the trust issue to the theory. The SW quadrant is the world of the two pre-human drives, dA and dD. This

FIGURE 11.1.   TRUST AND RD THEORY.

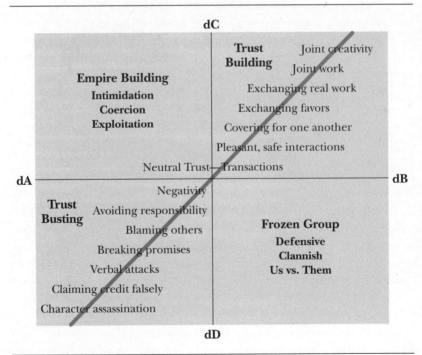

is the world the chimpanzees are trapped in, the world in which they can never get the hidden food because they can never trust the hints given by the human experimenters. The SE quadrant is the world of frozen groups, stuck in a clannish, defensive, "us versus them" mode. This would seem to be the world of *H. erectus*. The whole world to the west of the vertical centerline—the world of dA, dD, and dC—is the world that people-w/o-conscience live in. This is a world in which it is possible to get a great abundance of material goods that one wants if one is clever enough, but still a world devoid of caring relationships and therefore devoid of trust—other than confidence that others over whom one has absolute power will do as one wishes.

The NE quadrant, dominated by the two uniquely human drives, dB and dC, is the world of trust or at least the possibility of trust. This suggests that leaders who wish to build trust in their corporations and other organizations need to be able to activate and satisfice the drive to bond and the drive to comprehend (as well as the other two drives, of course) for all the stakeholders of the enterprise. This is a vital issue that needs to be discussed and rehearsed much more seriously, rigorously, and thoroughly in leadership classrooms. The transformation of the culture of two oil rigs, discussed at length in Chapter Four, shows that leadership that is both good/moral in the RD Theory sense and technically skilled in the ordinary sense can build high levels of trust even where there had been very high levels of mistrust and backstabbing.

GROUP MOTIVATION

RD Theory declares the four independent, insatiable drives to be the "ultimate" human motives and, earlier in this chapter, we saw the importance of balancing these drives in one's own life, exemplified by Kirk's failure to do so. Recently, Paul Herr has taken a practical step on the road from the original four-drive theory presented in *Driven* to the everyday practice of leading groups. In his 2009 book, *Primal Management: Unraveling the Secrets of Human Nature to Drive High Performance,* he points to a crisis in employee motivation.[7] A 2005 Gallup survey of American workers found only 31 percent "engaged" with their work, 52 percent "disengaged," and 17 percent "actively disengaged," a polite way of referring to people so alienated from their work that they look for opportunities to sabotage it.[8] Herr concludes, "If the Gallup survey were a college exam, what grade would we give corporate America for employee motivation? ... I'd give traditional hierarchical bureaucratic management a solid 'F.'" The cost of this failure is huge; the actively disengaged workers alone may directly account for $370 billion in lost productivity annually in the United States.[9]

Herr proposes an approach to this lack of engagement that is based on periodic employee feedback to management of employees' motivational feelings, to be measured by an anonymous seven-question survey. In RD Theory terms, his survey measures whether employees are satisficing their innate four drives at work, although he refers to the drives as "appetites" and adds a fifth—an appetite for self-esteem—to our familiar four. Like RD Theory, Herr predicts that the most effective employee motivation will be that which helps employees satisfice all their "appetites" in a balanced manner. Herr's suggestions on how management can improve the readings on this index would be familiar to readers of this book.

So far, Herr's testing of his feedback method has been encouraging but very limited. While I am eager for much more testing, I think Herr has gotten off to a good start in wringing practical management techniques out of the RD Theory of human behavior and leadership.

GROUP PURPOSE REVISITED

I believe that, as we move on into the twenty-first century, almost all groups, whatever their specific, more limited purposes, will also have a purpose in common—the survival of our species and its earthly environment. Leaders need to raise this question—Where does our group stand on the global sustainability issue?—and search for good answers with all their stakeholders. There are three excellent reasons for doing this: (1) No group in the twenty-first century can be fully motivated to pursue its group purpose if this larger question is neglected, (2) our survival as a species may actually depend on it, and (3) one's inner voice of conscience tells one that it is the right thing to do. We probably need not worry which reason dominates in any particular group, as long as the question is seriously addressed.

PRACTICING GOOD/MORAL LEADERSHIP

This section of Chapter Eleven needs one more paragraph about *practicing* good/moral leadership, using the term in a different sense. Malcolm Gladwell is an excellent science writer. His book *The Outliers: The Story of Success*[10] highlights a uniformity of highly successful people that is often overlooked. He documents the fact that our most gifted leaders in many walks of life—think of such contrasting people as Wolfgang Mozart and Bill Gates—share an early personal history of dedicated, compulsive *practicing* of the skill that made them famous. I have heard complaints from a few of the readers of a draft of this book that it makes an excessive use of the four drives as a part of explaining good leadership. They find it repetitive, even boring. I make no apology for this and I have, obviously, not acted on this advice for three reasons. First, good/moral leadership is a complex skill, and, while our brain is designed to help us do it, it is still harder, I argue, to do skillfully than piano playing and computer programming. Why shouldn't we expect to take a significant amount of repetitive practicing to become a master of it? Second, like any complex skill, practicing it involves learning to execute it in *various contexts,* over and over again. This is why we are discussing leadership in the context of the various basic human institutions that need good leadership. Finally, the four drives, I argue, just happen to be the criteria that humans have evolved in their brains that made it possible for them to survive. It could have been just one, or twenty-five. The RD Theory, based on Darwin's own insights about *human* behavior, asserts that four is the accurate number. Would-be leaders, if they are to improve their skill, must practice using all of their own four-drive, survival-oriented brains to get the best results. So the teacher in me feels like saying to the complainers, stop groaning and start practicing, or, of course, find your own better theory.

ACTION IMPLICATIONS OF THE RD THEORY AT THE INSTITUTIONAL LEVEL

For those who do improve their good/moral leadership abilities step by step, there is much to do. What follows is a summary of the most critical reforms needed to put our most important political and economic institutions more firmly on a long-term *sustainable* track toward a better life for all people. These were all discussed in earlier chapters; I review them here to emphasize that they are not simply a collection of my political grievances and opinions. In each case, both my definition of what constitutes a major problem and my suggestions for solving it follow directly from the RD Theory concept of good/moral leadership. They are presented here in the order of how long I imagine they would take to accomplish.

REFORM OF CONSTITUTIONAL GOVERNMENT: CAMPAIGN FINANCING

In Chapter Eight, I made the case that the United States is considerably off track as a republic because our legislative and executive processes are badly distorted by financial contributions, primarily from corporations, to candidates for federal elective office, followed up by lobbying efforts paid for by the same donors. This private funding process is the single largest impediment to the federal government's performance of its intended purpose to serve the general public's interests. Any practice that regularly defeats this purpose raises a moral issue of the greatest magnitude and cries out for *good/moral leadership*—"moral" as defined by the RD Theory, not simply in the eyes of a particular leader and his or her followers.

Chapter Eight also described a promising effort to reform campaign funding. A new book, Robert Kaiser's *So Damn Much Money: The Triumph of Lobbying and the Corrosion of American Government,* strongly reinforces my view of the scale of the problem.[11] Should the proposed Fair Elections Now Act come to a vote in Congress, the members of Congress will essentially be asked, one by one, whether they prefer to be beholden to corporate and other special interests or beholden to the public interest. If they can take a four-drive view of the matter, trying to sat-isfice *their own* four drives as well as those of their constituents and countrymen, it should be an easy decision. Here, after all, is their chance to be free of the endless and demeaning money-grubbing which Bob Dole evoked so vividly and to do work of which they can be proud and for which they can reasonably expect public approval and reward.

REFORM IN THE CHARTERING OF CORPORATIONS

In Chapters Six and Eight, I described how corporations came to be relatively free of four-drive control (either self-control or outside regulation); the resulting and unsurprising history of corporate abuses; and the spotty record of governments, at all levels, in controlling those abuses.

Proper chartering of corporations is the first step toward effec-tive control of corporate abuses. It is, after all, the corporate charter that mandates the top governance structure of corpo-rations. Today these charters are specified and offered by state governments, and they vary greatly. The states offering the fewest restrictions for the owners are winning the popularity contest. I recommend that all corporate charters be issued by the federal government and have a standardized format. This in itself would go a long way toward reforming corporate abuses. Federal charter-ing would enable government to specify which stakeholders will be represented on the board of directors and how the representatives will be selected.

The current system is traditional and clearly it works, but only up to a point. Highly autocratic and undemocratic, this system has at least two serious flaws from an RD Theory perspective. First, the system makes it relatively easy for leaders-w/o-conscience to gain control of corporations. Second, the system makes it seem perfectly appropriate that corporations should maximize the returns to owners and, therefore, minimize the returns to all other contributors to the enterprise. Owners get to establish the rules of the game even though they are only one of several essential contributors to the game. This arrangement does not meet any elementary test of fairness, and we should not be surprised if other contributors try to minimize their efforts on behalf of the enterprise. (As I heard people say in Soviet factories: "They pretend to pay us and we pretend to work.")

Remember that the earliest economic organization in human history was the hunting party. The best hunters could, in all fairness, expect to receive a larger share of the choice meat than the novices, but not *all* the good meat. This was the way Hauser explained the moral standard of fairness he found around the world (described in Chapter Three); it always provided for significant merit adjustments to any equality rule. Such fair distribution standards were one key to the successes of Medtronic and Nucor (described in Chapter Eight). So far, the available evidence indicates that corporate charters with representation for other major stakeholders (rather than just the owners) work better for all, even for the owners. It is the best-known way to ensure structurally that corporate leaders will address all four drives of all stakeholders and will minimize the opportunities for people-w/o-conscience to work their harm.

In this regard, a new book by Steven Greenhouse, *The Big Squeeze: Tough Times for the American Worker,* offers an up-to-date and alarming picture of the many ways that many corporate leaders are failing to satisfice the most basic needs of American workers in order to enhance their own short-term payouts—their own dA drives.[12] Greenhouse's book underscores the need for both the reform of corporate charters and for our next topic, corporate regulation.

Reform of Corporate Regulation

In Chapter Eight, I recommended that the federal regulation of business be accomplished through commissions established to provide appropriate regulation for specific industries. Congress should be limited to stating only some general moral principles that would apply to any industry, such as "Never cheat any stakeholder," "Distribute the rewards of enterprise in a fair manner with adjustments for merit," and "Discharge only for cause." Such rules can be general because, as I argue in Chapter Three, they are a part of the conscience of all normal humans. I have also argued, with evidence, that everybody is better off if corporations can focus their amazing powers on striving for excellence within a fair framework. A framework in which the suppliers of the essential capital get to set all the rules is no such framework. Of course capital is essential, but so are labor, ideas, managerial skill, a supply chain, and so on. And so are customers and so is a healthy society. Recruiting representatives of the many honest people involved in each industry to do most of the drafting of industry rules will greatly improve the quality of those rules and speed up their implementation.

I am aware that all this may sound terribly complex. But it is not all that complex if one sees it as following our universal sense of conscience in the context of a highly complex society.

RELIGION: SEARCH AFRESH FOR HUMAN MEANING

In Chapter Seven, I argued that the principal function of religious institutions is a quest for the true meaning of the human story, a reflection of the basic human drive to comprehend. I therefore suggest that the leaders of all religious traditions clarify their thinking about this quest and renew their efforts to achieve it. This would entail a review of their faiths' historic beliefs in the light of newer understandings of the human story. I believe religion would become a stronger and healthier institution were it to focus on the meaning of the human story and help find the track toward a sustainable better world for all, without having to divert energy into preserving historical features which no longer serve their original purpose.

For example, I suggest that scholars within the varied forms of Christianity might profit from studying the recovered texts of the Gnostics (discussed in Chapter Seven) to see what new light they throw on the received teachings of their Christian faith. Perhaps such historic study can help Christians refine and enhance their search for the true meaning, more broadly defined, that is embedded in the Christian story. Other major religious traditions might be renewed by their own version of this process.

When the Dalai Lama visited the Boston area in April 2009, he stressed some interesting points that, I believe, could help set a constructive tone for the kind of inquiries just suggested. In one of his addresses he talked about "the path to peace and happiness."

He spoke of "shared dreams and desires." "Emotionally, mentally, physically we are the same. Everyone has the same right to achieve a happy life." These comments are similar to those of the RD Theory. Finally he emphasized his openness to seeing how all faiths can have the potential to guide followers in their individual searches for true meaning. He spoke of the importance of valuing all faiths in the "supermarket of religion." "For example," he said, "I am Buddhist. I studied Buddhism, I practiced Buddhism, and through practice I got some sort of little experience.... Very low is still better than zero. Buddhism is best for my case. That doesn't mean Buddhism is best religion to everyone, certainly not."[13]

Reform of the United Nations

This topic is discussed in Chapter Ten. For many reasons, the world needs a global equivalent of the prefrontal cortex to balance and satisfice the competing drives expressing themselves on a global scale in the form of national governments and multinational corporations. Aside from the many obvious political obstacles to such reform, a key obstacle is the failure to understand the existence, nature, and deadliness of people-w/o-conscience. Without such an understanding, the United Nations cannot overcome the old arguments about the "sacred" importance of "national sovereignty," which is often just a fig leaf for a leader-w/o-conscience, a psychopath masquerading as an entire country.

My list of reforms is a tall order, I know. But I have hope because there has been so much progress already, which I see not as good fortune but as a natural (though not inevitable) consequence of the evolution and skilled use of our amazing four-drive, impulse/check/balance brains.

Overview of the People-w/o-Conscience Issue

It is no accident that I have saved the worst for last—the issue of people-w/o-conscience. I am reasonably confident that this issue remains the one that readers are finding it hardest to accept, in spite of the evidence. The nature and actions of

such people have long resisted comprehension—and even their
existence has seemed unbelievable—for at leastxs two reasons.

We are hard-wired not to believe in people-w/o-conscience. In Chapter
Two, I noted that human beings are one of the very few primates
with whites to their eyes. It has been speculated that this is because
humans are the only primates hard-wired to trust, rather than
distrust, each other—the only primates with a drive to bond that
is independent of the drives to acquire and defend. Chimpanzees,
for example, instinctively distrust each other and distrust human
experimenters who try to help them get hold of some food.
Just as the chimps cannot imagine our human unselfishness, we
find it exceedingly difficult to believe another human can be as
utterly selfish as people-w/o-conscience are. It takes a great mental
effort for us to recategorize people-w/o-conscience from the
unbelievable (Darwin's "unnatural monsters") to the believable.

*We are misled by the causes and ideologies used by people-
w/o-conscience.* Going back over this book's examples of
leaders-w/o-conscience made it clear to me that the particular
ideology each one picked to help him ride to power was incidental,
only an opportunistic choice, a historic accident. With Constantine it was the rise of Christianity. There is no evidence of sincerity
in his "conversion"; it was strictly an opportunistic choice. With
Napoleon it was the mystery of monarchy and empire, the "divine
right of kings." Napoleon himself expressed his opportunism
perfectly: "I saw a crown in the dust, picked it up with my
sword, and put it on my head." For Leopold it was the ideology
of colonialism, "helping the downtrodden heathens." For
Hitler it was the rising tide of socialism; his opportunism
became clear when, in his final grab for power, he abandoned
his socialist supporters for more useful elite allies in the
German military and big business. Osama bin Laden selected
fundamentalist Islamism as his convenient ideology. Lenin,
Stalin, and Mao all opportunistically selected the very popular
doctrine of communism to help them gain power. Most of the
top corporate leaders who I suspect are leaders-w/o-conscience
have adopted some version of laissez-faire capitalism as their
convenient ideology for grabbing power. It seems to me that
historians have been too fascinated by the content of these
various doctrines—and the undeniable meaning they have

for many of these leaders' followers—to recognize these doctrines' role simply as convenient vehicles for power grabs by leaders-w/o-conscience.

But while the general failure to grasp the nature of people-w/o-conscience is understandable for the reasons just stated, it is also too deadly to tolerate much longer. We need to do scientific research on this issue and make up for lost time. I see no way to stop the wheel-spinning of the world's efforts to outlaw war and genocide without coming to terms scientifically with people-w/o-conscience. Of course, this work will be scientifically and morally challenging. Even if we can make a definitive diagnosis of its genetic roots, it will be hard to decide how to act on that information without violating the humane values we hope to protect. In the next few pages I will try again to help the remaining skeptics make this switch, without leading them to make the enormous mistake of becoming suspicious of the vast majority of normal fellow humans. Let me proceed by presenting yet another tyrant with all the earmarks of a leader-w/o-conscience. I like this story because it presents so compactly—beginning with the name "Bloodthirsty"—the defining characteristics of a person-w/o-conscience. I recently discovered it in an online encyclopedia.

> *Moulay Ismail the Bloodthirsty (1675–1727)* was a Moroccan ruler. The Alaouite sultan is said to have sired 888 children (548 sons and 340 daughters) through a harem of 500 women during his life. Meknes, the capital city he built, is sometimes called the "Versailles of Morocco" because of its extravagance.... At its peak, Ismail's empire spread from present day Algeria to Mauritania.

> The success of his empire was not without cost. Ismail is noted as one of the greatest figures in Moroccan history, well known for his legendary cruelty. In order to intimidate rival tribes, Ismail ordered that his city walls be adorned with 10,000 heads of slain enemies. Legends of the ease with which Ismail could behead or torture laborers or servants he thought to be lazy are numerous....

> Moulay Ismail enlisted over 25,000 Christian prisoners and 30,000 common criminals as laborers in the construction of his great city. Over 16,000 slaves from sub-Saharan Africa were captured to serve

in his elite Black Guard. By the time of Ismail's death, the guard
had grown tenfold, the largest in Moroccan history... Ismail's
grand mausoleum is open even to non-Muslims as a testament to
the greatness of this effective but barbaric ruler.[14]

I would only ask the author of this brief biography, In what
terms was Ismail "successful" and "effective" beyond terrorizing
and killing thousands upon thousands and making so many "look-
alike" babies? In this book, we have seen a similar pattern of
behavior from tyrants throughout history. In Chapter Five, I cited
David Geary on a very consistent pattern of behavior among the
leaders in all the most ancient empires in the world. This cannot
be a coincidence.

How long must the vast majority of *humane* citizens of this
world put up with such leaders? We must start calling them out
for what they really are, *evil* leaders-w/o-conscience.

For a final example of what a leader-w/o-conscience can do
with a good opportunity, I will turn again to ancient history, as told
in an op-ed piece in the *International Herald Tribune* by historian
Robert Harris.

The "War on Terror" That Ruined Rome

In the autumn of 68 B.C. the world's only military superpower was
dealt a profound psychological blow by a daring terrorist attack on
its very heart. Rome's port of Ostia was set on fire, the consular
war fleet destroyed, and two prominent senators, together with
their bodyguards and staff, kidnapped.

The incident, dramatic though it was, has not attracted much
attention from modern historians. But an event that was merely a
footnote five years ago has now, in our post 9/11 world, assumed
a fresh and ominous significance. For in the panicky aftermath
of the attack, the Roman people made decisions that set them
on the path to the destruction of their constitution, their democracy and their liberty. One cannot help wondering if history is
repeating itself.

Consider the parallels. The perpetrators of this spectacular
assault were not in the pay of any foreign power. No nation
would have dared to attack Rome so provocatively. Like Al

Qaeda, these pirates were loosely organized, but able to spread a disproportionate amount of fear among citizens who had believed themselves immune from attack.

What was to be done? Over the preceding centuries, the constitution of ancient Rome had developed an intricate series of checks and balances intended to prevent the concentration of power in the hands of a single individual. The consulship, elected annually, was jointly held by two men. Ordinary citizens were accustomed to a remarkable degree of liberty: the cry of "Civis Romanus sum"—"I am a Roman citizen"—was a guarantee of safety throughout the world.

But such was the panic that ensued after Ostia that the people were willing to compromise these rights. The greatest soldier in Rome, the thirty-eight-year-old Gnaeus Pompeius Magnus (better known to posterity as Pompey the Great) arranged for a lieutenant of his, the tribune Aulus Gabinius, to rise in the Roman Forum and propose an astonishing new law, the Lex Gabinia.

"Pompey was to be given not only the supreme naval command but what amounted in fact to an absolute authority and uncontrolled power over everyone," the Greek historian Plutarch wrote. "There were not many places in the Roman world that were not included within these limits."

Pompey eventually received almost the entire contents of the Roman Treasury to pay for his "war on terror," which included building a fleet of 500 ships and raising an army of 120,000 infantry and 5,000 cavalry. Such an accumulation of power was unprecedented.

Once Pompey put to sea, it took less than three months to sweep the pirates from the entire Mediterranean. Even allowing for Pompey's genius as a military strategist, the suspicion arises that if the pirates could be defeated so swiftly, they could hardly have been such a grievous threat in the first place.

But it was too late to raise such questions. By the oldest trick in the political book—the whipping up of a panic, in which any dissenting voice could be dismissed as "soft" or even "traitorous"—the powers had been ceded by the people that would never be returned. Pompey stayed in the Middle East for six years, establishing puppet regimes throughout the region, and turning himself into the richest man in the empire....

An intelligent, skeptical American would no doubt scoff at the thought that what had happened since 9/11 could presage the destruction of a centuries-old constitution; but then, I suppose, any intelligent, skeptical Roman in 68 B.C. might well have done the same.

It may be that the Roman republic was doomed in any case. But the disproportionate reaction to the raid on Ostia unquestionably hastened the process, weakening the restraints on military adventurism and corrupting the political process. It was to be more than 1,800 years before anything remotely comparable to Rome's democracy—imperfect though it was—rose again.[15]

Harris was clearly worried about what might happen to the American republic in the post-9/11 years. Now the Bush administration has gone, but the United States is still dealing with the longer-term consequences of its response to the shock of 9/11. Only future historians can tell us how close it came to the fate of the Roman republic.

ENDING THE NIGHTMARE

This book has told the story of many people-w/o-conscience who had a massive negative impact on human history. Naming them chronologically can help keep them in mind. From Pompey, the most ancient, we moved to Constantine, who, I argue, threw the Catholic Church off track for many years until the corrupt indulgence system for fleecing the sheep of the Middle Ages sparked Luther into leading the reformation of the Church. We jumped forward to Napoleon, whose leader-w/o-conscience ways created an all-Europe war for nearly two decades and whose evil impact was felt long afterward. We identified Gould and Vanderbilt as likely leaders-w/o-conscience among the early "robber barons" of American industrialism. The next impactful leader-w/o-conscience we analyzed was the low-profile Leopold, who did such lasting harm to the continent of Africa.

Then we examined the stock market crash of 1929, which triggered the Great Depression. Our story here points to the master stock manipulators of the 1920s as the men who may well have precipitated this all-time depression; we suspect them of being people-w/o-conscience. Coping with this mess fell to Franklin Roosevelt, and it is noteworthy that, when asked what would be the central theme of his administration, Roosevelt responded that Americans needed *moral* leadership.

Nearing the present, we examined the collapse of Enron, led to disaster by a CEO who showed signs of being a leader-w/o-conscience. We have touched on Osama bin Laden, one of our prototype leaders-w/o-conscience, and dwelt at length on the subprime mortgage meltdown of the Bush years, which I argue was the work of business leaders-w/o-conscience, although it is too soon to be able to name names. The common denominator of all these massive—often worldwide—troubles was the leader-w/o-conscience. I invite the reader to examine the extensive list of major problems that President Obama faces. Even I was surprised that so many of them, foreign and domestic, have people-w/o-conscience as root causes.

Current research is moving quickly to test those elements of the Renewed Darwinian Theory of Human Behavior and Leadership which were built on the insights of Darwin. But I am pleading for research—as quickly as possible—on the one part of my theory which is only alluded to as a hypothetical question in Darwin's work—the existence and nature of people-w/o-conscience. Some help has been provided by a recent book, *Evil Genes: Why Rome Fell, Hitler Rose, Enron Failed, and My Sister Stole My Mother's Boyfriend,* by Barbara Oakley.[16] This book strongly reinforces the existence of psychopaths in top power positions, documents the case that Mao was an especially deadly head-of-state person-w/o-conscience, and comes to the same conclusions I have regarding Rome, Hitler, and Enron. But its title is seriously confusing since it proposes, in a rather figurative way only, that there are "evil" genes behind psychopathy. I, of course, hypothesize that the absence of the genes for bonding is the explanation of psychopathy. I worry that it will be impossible to find the genes causing psychopathy if the search is for "evil" genes.

I began this chapter by quoting Darwin: "A man who possessed no trace of such instincts [social instincts—dB] would be an unnatural monster." The only excuse I have for having taken so many words to express so simple a thought is that so very few have paid any attention to Darwin's more concise statement. Even the contemporary expert on psychopathy, Robert Hare, does not tie his essential work to an absolute lack ("no trace") of human social instincts (dB). We might take some limited comfort in the recent tentative findings that, with rigorous training, people-w/o-conscience might be able to learn what their brains are missing and what very unpleasant things will happen to them if they cross the moral line.[17] In the longer term, the new technology of gene therapy might even develop a way of transforming psychopaths into normal humane people by providing them with normal human dB genes.[18] Another promising lead toward finding the DNA footprint for psychopathy is based on the identification of the gene that seems to explain the difference between prairie voles, which are monogamous, and their close relative montane voles that are totally polygamous.[19]

But for now, the nightmare can end only when normal people catch on to it and, armed with this knowledge, find humane ways to keep people-w/o-conscience out of positions of power. Of course, the people-w/o-conscience will fight back, but for the rest of us, using violence in this struggle will almost always be counter-productive. Humane four-drive people will have to use humane methods—based on scientific research—with persistence and unity to win the struggle. We can be thankful that evolution has given us brains that are up to the task.

This continuing struggle in itself puts great meaning and drama into the human story. Once the struggle is won, there will be "a new birth of freedom"—freedom in the old-fashioned sense, freedom from tyrants, from people-w/o-conscience. Exploring the possibilities of this true freedom will keep meaning and drama in the human story for all the imaginable future.

CHAPTER TWELVE

RENEWING THE STORY OF HUMAN PROGRESS WITH DARWIN'S HELP

*I fully subscribe to those writers who maintain that of
all the differences between man and the lower
animals, the moral sense of conscience is by far the
most important.*
— CHARLES DARWIN[1]

To close this book I will return to its central theme of building
on Darwin's work. This year, people around the world are celebrating Darwin's two-hundredth birthday. This fact is in itself
wondrous. Many Darwin stories are being told. I have found two
that stand out from the crowd. Instead of just relating familiar facts
and rehashing old arguments, they significantly move forward the
discussion of Darwin's work.

Nicholas Wade caught my attention with an article bearing
the intriguing subtitle: "Even Biologists Now Agree [Darwin] Was
Right."[2] Is that really something new? It is when it comes to
Darwin's concept of group-level selection, which is crucial to the
Renewed Darwinian Theory. Wade explains,

> Darwin's theory of evolution has become the bedrock of modern
> biology. But for most of the theory's existence since 1859, even
> biologists have ignored or rigorously opposed it, in whole or in
> part.... [In addition to the concepts of natural selection and
> sexual selection, Darwin] also presented a form of group-level

selection that was long dismissed, but now has leading advocates like the biologists E. O. Wilson and David Sloan Wilson.... Darwin proposed group selection to account for castes in ant societies and morality in people. Darwin believed there was continuity between humans and other species, which led him to think of human morality as related to the sympathy seen among social animals. This long-disputed idea was resurrected only recently by researchers like the primatologist Frans de Waal. Darwin "never felt that morality was our own invention, but was a product of evolution, a position we are now seeing grow in popularity under the influence of what we know about animal behavior," De Waal says. "In fact, we've now returned to the original Darwinian position."

So Wade provides strong support for a controversial point made both in *Driven* and this book, that it was by group-level selection that humans evolved an independent drive to bond with others in long-term caring relationships and, in turn, evolved an innate moral sense and conscience.

Another major unresolved issue about Darwin was directly addressed in the second "birthday" article in *The Economist*, titled "Unfinished Business."[3] The article questions the persistent and widespread interpretation of Darwin's work that argues that his theory of evolution infers that there is no direction, no general sense of purpose behind evolution.

To understand *human behavior* [italics added] properly, the world needs Darwin. Some have said it is the best idea that anyone ever had. If it isn't, it certainly comes close. Despite so much evidence, evolution remains difficult to accept because it implies everything living is largely accidental. Stephen Jay Gould, an American evolutionary biologist, who died in 2002, argued that misunderstandings about Darwinism were rife not because the theory is difficult to understand but because people actively avoid trying to understand it. He thought a misunderstanding about *progress* [italics added] was the problem. People are comforted by the idea of a designed and harmonious natural world, with themselves at the top. It is hard to accept that such harmony has arisen as an accidental consequence of a brutal system with no principles beside the one that every individual is striving for reproductive success. It is depressing to think that life is purposeless and that evolution has no higher destination....

It is a commonly held view that evolution implies progress; even among those who believe in natural selection. Most biologists disagree. They argue, along with Gould, that evolution has no fixed direction. A creature can become fitter by getting more complex. But it can also become fitter by getting simpler. It all depends on the circumstances.... That view is being questioned. For example, in a study published last year in the *Proceedings of the National Academy of Sciences* a group of researchers looked at crustaceans (crabs, shrimps, woodlice and so on) over the past 550 m[illion] years and found far more examples of groups of species evolving towards complexity than in the other direction.... Simon Conway-Morris, a paleontologist at Cambridge University in England, is the champion of this new interpretation of evolution—one that challenges the view that it is largely governed by the accident of circumstances. Unlike Gould, he thinks that if evolution were replayed from the beginning, a lot of things would turn out the same.... His argument is that, given the nature of physics and chemistry there may be only a limited number of ways in which things can work. Evolution will be channeled into these successful paths, and thus does have trends. Two of these, he thinks, are towards complexity and intelligence. He adds that things "don't just happen in chemistry. They happen because of preexisting causes.... Evolution is a mechanism, and it works within rules."

In some ways, though, it does not matter whether humanity's evolution was entirely random or was predictable in its general form. For people do, now, have a united evolutionary common purpose: to halt natural selection in its tracks. The species has evolved to the point where it understands itself, and can seek to escape the brutal handcuffs of nature and end the struggle for existence. The beginning of that understanding was provided by Darwin, and the application of Darwinism will be an important part of the process. That gives people every reason to celebrate his 200th birthday.

I know that Darwin himself saw progress in the human story. *The Descent of Man* presents a struggle—by no means over—by humans from the brutish world of nothing but dA and dD toward "a potentially harmonious world with themselves at the top." The quote at the beginning of this chapter says it all in Darwin's concise way: "I fully subscribe to those writers who maintain that of all the differences between man and the *lower* [italics added] animals, the moral sense of conscience is by far the most important." This one sentence puts progress and profound meaning into the human story.

These two articles give me even greater confidence that this book, building upon Darwin's insights all the way, can help people "escape the brutal handcuffs of nature and end the struggle for existence." Darwin has cautioned us that we will still have to cross the hurdles of distance and difference for people around the globe to recognize that we are all the same kind of creatures, that we all have the same four drives to keep us moving together, wholeheartedly and whole-mindedly, on a sustainable track forward. We will need many good/moral leaders to help us keep on track at all levels. Fortunately, almost all of us have brains designed to let us be good/moral leaders at some level. We will also probably need a few exceptionally good/moral leaders who, following the RD Theory formula, can help us span the enormous gaps between nations, religions, and cultures and who can show us how to humanely keep the people-w/o-conscience from ever leading us into economic chaos, genocide, and wars again.

But if we can understand our own past and our innate nature, the human story can become glorious. Darwin ended *On the Origin of Species* with a sentence that captured his sense of wonder at this prospect:

> There is grandeur in this view of life; with its several powers having been originally breathed by the Creator into a few forms or into one; and that, whilst this planet has gone cycling on according to the fixed law of gravity, from so simple a beginning endless forms most wonderful and most beautiful have been, and are being evolved.[4]

DARWIN MISUNDERSTOOD

Serious confusions and controversies still plague Darwin's theories in scientific as well as in lay circles. While I do not propose to examine all the ins and outs of this prolonged debate, I hope to foster an open-minded consideration of the Darwinian-based propositions in this book by addressing the major points.

RELIGION

It is generally well known that the first major attack, and the most persistent attack, on Darwin's theories came from organized religion with its millions of adherents. The response of the religious establishment at the time of the publication of Darwin's *On the Origin of Species* can best be summarized as horrified. The debate was energetically engaged not only by the most distinguished prelates of England but also by many of the most famous naturalists, also on religious grounds. The theory seemed to undermine the most basic of religious beliefs, the very existence of God. Over the years the debate quieted down somewhat, but recently it has heated up again. It is clearly not resolved. A recent poll indicated that a significant majority of Americans favor creationist theories on the origin of all living things over Darwin's theory of evolution. This is true even though many major religious leaders, including the late Pope John Paul II, accepted the general idea of Darwin's evolutionary theory as an explanation of how God created living species.

SOCIAL DARWINISM

The second wave of controversy and confusion over Darwin's theories has been attributed to Herbert Spencer with his ideas on Social Darwinism. These ideas were and still are a major obstacle to the understanding of Darwinism. It was Spencer, not Darwin, who coined the vivid but misleading phrase "survival of the fittest." Darwin might have agreed on the condition that "fit" was understood to mean "adaptable" (as in "fit in"). Darwin said, "It is not the strongest of the species that survive, nor the most intelligent. It is the one most adaptable to change." But in fact, the phrase is almost universally understood to mean "survival of the toughest and most ruthless." As applied to humans, this is very clearly not at all what Darwin meant, yet it has come to summarize, for most of the public, what Darwinism is all about. I have yet to find a single use of the term *Darwinian* in contemporary print that did not reference this distorted version of Darwin's ideas. Given such a massive basic misunderstanding of Darwin, is it any wonder that a majority of the American public resists his ideas?

THE RESPONSE OF MAINSTREAM BIOLOGISTS

The next source of misunderstanding about Darwin has come, rather surprisingly, from the evolutionary biologists themselves. As a prime example, consider Richard Dawkins, whose widely read and respected writings, especially *The Selfish Gene,* have inadvertently served to reinforce the erroneous "most ruthless" interpretation of Darwin. So has some of the popular work of Stephen Jay Gould. This has all happened over the years in a rather complex way that has been clearly explained by Ernst Mayr, a key contributor to the modern synthesis of Darwin's theories with the theories of genetics. In his book *One Long Argument,*[1] Mayr explains how confusion arose among biologists; I will be drawing heavily on Mayr's analysis in the following paragraph.

Darwin's theory of the "common descent" of all organisms from a primordial ancestor was quite quickly accepted by biologists. After Darwin's death, however, his theory of "natural selection" remained controversial among biologists for several decades. This controversy, while eventually resolved in the confirmation of Darwin, had led biologists to focus on the natural selection mechanism as if it were the one and only mechanism that Darwin used to explain the process of evolution. While natural selection was the most prominent evolutionary mechanism for Darwin, it was by no means the only one. Darwin emphasized the mechanism of "sexual selection" as a crucial mechanism in explaining evolution. Sexual selection is the focus of his second major book on evolution, *The Descent of Man,* which also is, of course, the book that offers almost everything that Darwin had to say about humans. Yet sexual selection is still treated as a relatively minor mechanism by many biologists, who often subsume it as one aspect of natural selection. In addition, Darwin's extensive discussion in *Descent* of "morality" as being derived from "social instincts" has also been almost totally ignored by subsequent biologists. And it is probably fair to say that most biologists still reject Darwin's idea of "group selection" as a valid selection mechanism. Another of his ideas was that biological variations were subject to the "use it or lose it" principle. For years, biologists who otherwise embrace Darwin's theories have cited this as one of his mistakes. Now we know that this is exactly the way that the brain works. The brains of young children contain many more synapses then will ever be used, and they are pruned by disuse. Darwin at times also referred to variations being established by "habit." If this is taken literally, it is clearly a Lamarckian mistake. But, as Baldwin (a contemporary of Darwin) pointed out, acquired habits (read *culture*) could change the context of human life and hence change the selection pressures in ways that could, by natural selection, change the gene pool. For example, if humans acquired the cultural "habit" of wearing fur clothing and, partly as a result of that, moved to colder climes, the change in climate would generate natural selection pressure for fair skin and blue eyes, which is probably what happened. Also, any widespread "habit" will have been established in society by Darwin's variety/selection/retention process, even though it will have been spread by culture, not by genes.

Determinism—or even fatalism—is the other idea that some mainstream evolutionary biologists have reinforced and, by inference, attributed to Darwin, creating a massive obstacle to the acceptance of his ideas. Determinism clearly suggests that humans have no possible way to improve the condition of their lives. As Dawkins wrote in the preface to his book, *The Selfish Gene,* "We are survival machines—robot vehicles blindly programmed to preserve the selfish molecules known as genes. This is a truth which still fills me with astonishment."[2] Such a view flies in the face of all common sense and of the historical record of humankind. It creates only despair about the human condition. When Darwin's most widely recognized spokesperson of our times makes such statements, would it be any wonder that such "Darwinian" ideas were to meet resistance? Yet Darwin himself said no such thing. He recognized the fact of human choice and the resulting possibilities for human improvement.

THE RESPONSE OF THE SOCIAL SCIENCES

A fourth source of massive misunderstanding of Darwin has come from the social sciences. Ever since Darwin's work became available, social scientists have essentially given it the silent treatment. They have, of course, accepted that Darwin was right about the evolution of our bodily parts, but they have almost entirely denied that his theory can in any way explain human *behavior.* This is what has become known as the "blank slate" assumption. The idea is that the brain is a passive (blank) organ at birth that gradually fills up over our lives with things learned from our cultures and other aspects of our environment. This is also known as the social construction of reality. There is little doubt that this early and persistent rejection of Darwinism was triggered by Social Darwinism with its tooth-and-claw determinism, a broad worldview about the human condition that horrified and revolted the social scientists for totally understandable reasons. It clearly could be used to advance racist and sexist agendas—and it was in Hitler's Germany. Social Darwinism was totally at odds with the view of social scientists that humans are flawed but have a capacity for compassion and cooperation and are always striving to improve their condition. If Darwinism denied all of this, social scientists wanted no part of it; this aspect of Darwinism struck very deeply into the essence of their professional outlook, triggering a visceral reaction that persists in many circles today. This was the response to Darwinism that created the "blank slate" doctrine, and these ideas are still mainstream among social scientists, even though they are currently under vigorous attack from evolutionary psychologists (see Pinker's *Blank Slate*[3]) and from a few behavioral economists.

The psychologists who highlighted Social Darwinian ideas about human behavior were Watson and later Skinner. They argued that all human behavior could be explained as responses to environmental conditioning by a reward-and-punishment process. This is ironic since Watson's ideas were built upon those of McDougal, the extreme instinctivist disciple of James. It is even more ironic that, in sociology, the blank slate tradition was established by Durkheim, and yet Durkheim himself conducted the empirical study that presented the most compelling evidence of the essential role of bonding to human survival itself. Durkheim studied the rates of suicide in a wide variety of collectives across Europe. He found a consistent pattern. The people who had the fewest number of bonded relationships with others had the highest suicide rates. For instance, he found that among religious communities, Protestants with the "least degree of integration" had more suicides than Catholics and that Jews, with the densest network of social bonds, had the fewest suicides. He found the same pattern among families. People living alone were most likely to kill themselves, married couples less likely, and married couples living with children, still less likely. This research offers powerful proof of the existence of Darwin's social instincts by demonstrating the extreme cost of human isolation.[4]

THE RESPONSE OF THE PHYSICAL SCIENCES

While the physicists and chemists of Darwin's time did not notably attack Darwin's ideas and have not done so since his time, the fact is that many of the well-established scientific ground rules for pursuing knowledge about physical phenomena could not be applied directly and consistently to biological phenomena. To develop his ideas, Darwin was forced to invent his own ground rules and methods, tailored to the emerging study of biological phenomena. This caused problems and confusions concerning appropriate scientific methods, which greatly delayed the acceptance of Darwin's ideas in some scientific circles. Mayr has only recently clarified this complex issue in *What Makes Biology Unique?* His chapter "On the Autonomy of Biology" spells out the problems that have been caused by the misapplication of the scientific methods of physics and chemistry to biology and to all its branches in the social sciences.

As Mayr reports, "Darwin's ideas were particularly important in the discovery that a number of basic concepts of the physical sciences are not applicable to biology."[5] Mayr went on to specify a number of very important differences:

The Absence of Universal Natural Laws in Biology. Owing to the probabilistic nature of most generalizations in evolutionary biology, it is impossible to apply Popper's method of falsification for theory testing because a particular case of a seeming refutation of a certain law may not be anything but an exception, as are common in biology. Most theories in biology are based not on laws but on concepts. Examples of such concepts are, for instance, selection, speciation, phylogeny, competition, population, imprinting, adaptedness, biodiversity, development, ecosystem and function.[6]

The Complexity of Living Systems. There are no inanimate systems in the mesocosmos that are even anywhere near as complex as the biological systems of the macromolecules and cells. These systems are rich in emergent properties because forever new groups of properties emerge at every level of integration.... Owing to their complexity, biological systems are richly endowed with capacities such as reproduction, metabolism, replication, regulation, adaptedness, growth, and hierarchical organization. Nothing of the sort exists in the inanimate world.[7]

Dual Causation. All biological processes differ in one respect fundamentally from all processes in the inanimate world; they are subject to *dual causation.* In contrast to purely physical processes, these biological ones are controlled not only by natural laws but also by *genetic programs.* This duality fully provides a clear demarcation between inanimate and living processes.[8]

Evolutionary Biology Is a Historical Science. It is very different from the exact sciences in its conceptual framework and methodology. It deals, to a large extent, with unique phenomena, such as the extinction of the dinosaurs, the origin of humans, the origin of evolutionary novelties, the explanation of evolutionary trends and rates, and the explanation of organic diversity. There is no way to explain these phenomena by laws.... We cannot experiment about the extinction of the dinosaurs or the origin of mankind. With the experiment unavailable for research in historical biology, a remarkable new heuristic method has been introduced, that of *historical narratives*. Just as in much of theory formation, the scientist starts with a conjecture and thoroughly tests it for its validity, so in evolutionary biology the scientist constructs a historical narrative, which is then tested for its explanatory value.[9]

Chance. The natural laws usually effect a rather deterministic outcome in the physical sciences. Neither natural nor sexual selection guarantees such determinism. Indeed, the outcome of an evolutionary process is usually the result of an interaction of numerous incidental factors. Chance with respect to functional and adaptive outcome is rampant in the production of variation. Curiously, it was this chance aspect of natural selection for which this theory was most often criticized. Some of Darwin's contemporaries, for instance, the geologist Adam Sedgwick, declared that invoking chance in any explanation was unscientific. Actually, it is precisely the chanciness of variation that is so characteristic of Darwinian evolution.[10]

Holistic Thinking. Reductionism is the declared philosophy of the physicalists. Reduce everything to the smallest parts, determine the properties of these parts, and you have explained the whole system. However, in a biological system there are so many interactions among the parts, that a complete knowledge of the properties of the smallest parts gives necessarily only a partial explanation.... How the smaller units are organized into larger units is critically important for the particular properties of the larger units. This aspect of organization and the resulting emergent properties are what the reductionists had neglected.[11]

Observation and Comparison. These are highly important methods [not only in biology but] also in the humanities, and therefore biology functions as an important bridge between the physicalist sciences and the humanities. The foundation of a philosophy of biology is particularly important for the explanation of mind and consciousness. Evolutionary biology has revealed that in such explanations there is no fundamental difference between humans and animals. Evolutionary thinking and the recognition of the role of chance and of uniqueness are now also appreciated in the humanities.[12]

All the branches of human biology are still suffering to some extent from the effects of "physics envy." This ailment condemns its victims to trying futilely to practice their science by the rules and methods of the physical sciences instead of by the rules and methods relevant to the life sciences that Mayr has so helpfully articulated. Not the least of Mayr's contributions is to elevate historical analysis to a totally legitimate scientific method that is essential to the full range of life sciences. It is in this spirit that Darwin and his followers have applied historic analysis to the hominid line.

Despite so many sources of confusion, Darwin's ideas have stood the test of time and won the day. After a careful study of what Darwin actually said, I find myself in awe of his accomplishments. His insights are especially amazing when one realizes that he made them without the benefit of knowing many things that we know today. He worked without any knowledge about how genes function. He had practically no information about hominid fossils, very limited and, at times, erroneous facts about the behavior of primates in the wild, no systematic anthropological information except from his amateur recruits, and essentially no direct knowledge of the inner workings of the brain. In spite of all of these limitations, he got so much right that we are only now developing more complete maps of the virgin terrain that he first pioneered and surveyed.

His brain must have had a particularly powerful drive to comprehend. He spent his entire life pondering the meaning of the observations he made as a young naturalist on the *Beagle*. He knew very well that his theories would challenge the most basic assumptions of the society of which he was an elite member. Before publishing his ideas, he refined and reflected on them for more than two decades in order to make them as accurate and clear as possible. He will always be a preeminent example of a person who acted with courage and persistence on his convictions.

In Chapter Three, I presented a Renewed Darwinian Theory of how hominids evolved into humans, drawing on Darwin's original insights and updating them with the recent work of scholars from many relevant disciplines. I have presented the Renewed Darwinian Theory as the final piece of the puzzle of the *H. erectus* transition and the Upper Paleolithic Transition to *H. sapiens*. In so doing, I hope to have helped to resolve the controversies and confusions associated with Social Darwinism and determinism, while helping to restore and advance Darwin's neglected or misunderstood ideas regarding sexual and group selection, social instincts, conscience, morality, and human choice. I addressed the religion issue in Chapter Seven.

In the Introduction I asserted that Darwin's ideas about human behavior had been neglected by biologists and social scientists. I have not been surprised that some have questioned this as an accurate statement. Is it really true that Darwin's comments on human behavior have been neglected? In this regard I have now reflected on nearly all of Darwin's insights about human behavior that I have cited in this book. All but one of these quotes have come from *The Descent of Man* (the sole exception is my quote of Darwin's last sentence in *Origins*). I cannot recall a single one of these Darwin quotes in any of the publications of biologists or social scientists that I have read. Of course, I have read only a sample of these publications, and my memory is not infallible. As one way of checking out my assertion I reexamined Pinker's classic book, *How the Mind Works*.[13] Pinker is, of course, a staunch supporter of Darwin, and Darwin is the most frequently cited author in this book. Yet even Pinker, a widely acknowledged expert on both the human brain and Darwin, does not cite one of these quotes or any others from *Descent*. I find it very difficult to account for this strange fact. Could it be just a historical accident? Could these scholars have learned all they know about Darwin from *Origins* and were simply never exposed to *The Descent of Man*? Was I simply the fortunate one who became fascinated with Darwin's insights about *human* behavior in *Descent*? This seems highly unlikely. For me, this neglect of Darwin's *Descent* insights about humans remains a mystery.

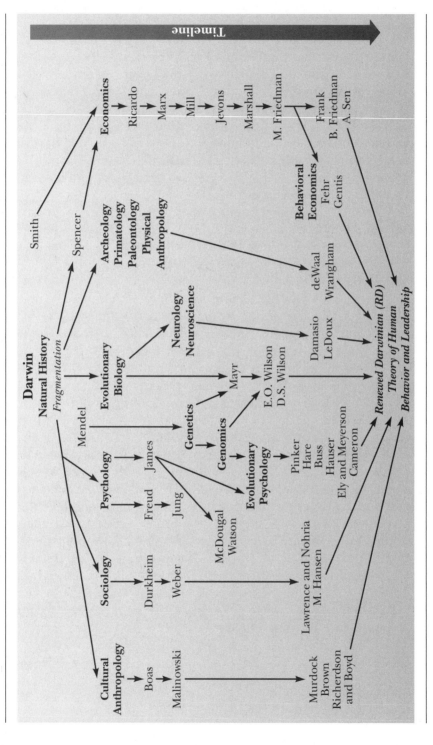

FIGURE A.I. SCHEMATIC OF THEORY FLOW REGARDING HUMAN BEHAVIOR SINCE DARWIN.

Figure I.1 in the Introduction repeated the question "only" in reference to each discipline's approach to its explanation of human behavior. These "only" limitations are, as indicated in Figure A.1, now disappearing in every discipline. Figure A.1 names a sample of the scholars, some of whom I have cited in this book, who are leading the way toward an integrated, tested Renewed Darwinian Theory of Human Behavior and Leadership.

NOTES

INTRODUCTION

1. N. Davies, *Europe: A History* (New York: Oxford University Press, 1996), pp. 897–899. His remarks are in contrast to his previous chapter on Europe's political and cultural dominance in the nineteenth century.
2. P. R. Lawrence and N. Nohria, *Driven: How Human Nature Shapes Our Choices* (San Francisco: Jossey-Bass, 2002).

CHAPTER ONE

1. Often attributed to Charles Darwin. See C. Darwin, *The Descent of Man* (Amherst, MA: Prometheus Books, 1998 [1871]).
2. John Donne, "Sermon Preached at St. Paul's, upon Easter-day, 1627." "There is nothing that God hath established in a constant course of nature, and which therefore is done every day, but would seem a Miracle, and exercise our admiration, if it were done but once."
3. R. Ely and D. Meyerson, *The Organizational Reconstruction of Men's Identity*, unpublished manuscript, n.d.

CHAPTER TWO

1. C. Darwin, *The Descent of Man* (Amherst, MA: Prometheus Books, 1998 [1871]), p. 65.
2. In 1998, my colleague Nitin Nohria and I decided to try to identify the basic, universal motivators of all human beings of all ages at all times in all places. We emerged from our efforts with a set of four drives, which we presented in *Driven: How Human Nature Shapes Our Choices* (San Francisco: Jossey-Bass, 2002). Since then, I have continued to gather evidence for these four drives in a variety of scientific studies of the workings of the human brain. It is with even greater confidence now that I present these four drives, not as a

description of human behavior observed from the outside, but as a description of what is actually happening inside our brains, causing us to behave as we do.

3. The fact that our behavior is governed by a survival mechanism is obscured by the fact that we have long been capable of so much more than survival. After all, what survival drive could be responsible for playing tennis, eating ice cream, keeping a scrapbook, or having a pen pal in Ghana? But that "overcapacity" has come relatively recently by evolutionary standards.

4. Stevie Smith (1902–1971), English poet. These lines are from her most famous poem, "Was He Married?"

5. R. N. Becerra, H. Beriter, W. Roky, R. Kgonzalez, and D. Borsook, "Circuitry Activation by Noxious Thermal Stimuli," *Neuron* 323 (2001): 927–946.

6. G. S. Becker, *The Economic Approach to Human Behavior* (Chicago: University of Chicago Press, 1976). Also note M. C. Jensen and W. H. Meckling, "The Nature of Man," *Journal of Applied Corporate Finance* 7, no. 2 (Summer 1994): 4–19.

7. R. Carter, *Mapping the Mind* (Berkeley, CA: University of California Press, 1998), pp. 90–91.

8. Darwin, *Descent of Man*, p. 112.

9. Using a similar logic, banks reward you for opening a savings account right now, even though the benefit to them comes later. Imagine the survival rate of a chain of banks which offered you a toaster a year after you opened an account with them; that would soon be an endangered species.

10. This research by Jorge Moll and Jordan Grafman, neuroscientists at NIH, was reported by Shankar Vedantum, "If It Feels Good to Do Good, It Might Be Only Natural," *Washington Post,* May 28, 2007, Health and Science section.

11. J. LeDoux, *The Emotional Brain* (New York: Simon & Schuster, 1996).

12. H. Tajfel, *Human Groups and Social Categories* (Cambridge, UK: Cambridge University Press, 1982).

13. F. Warneken and M. Tomasello, "Altruistic Helping in Human Infants and Young Chimpanzees," *Science* 311 no. 3 (March 2006): 1301.

14. Warneken and Tomasello, "Altruistic Helping in Human Infants," p. 1301.

15. B. Hare, M. Brown, C. Williamson, and M. Tomasello, "The Domestication of Social Cognition in Dogs" *Science* 298, no. 22 (November 2002): pp. 1634–1636.

16. Darwin, *Descent of Man*, p. 97.

17. A. Maslow, "A Theory of Human Motivation," *Psychological Review* 50, no. 4 (1943): pp. 370–390.

18. I. Biederman and E. A. Vessel, "Perceptual Pleasure and the Brain," *American Scientist* 94 (May-June 2006): pp. 249–255; available at http://geon.usc.edu/%7Ebiederman/publications/Biederman_Vessel_2006.pdf.

19. See C. Argyris and D. Schon, *Organizational Learning* (Reading, MA: Addison-Wesley, 1978). Also see P. M. Senge, *The Fifth Discipline: The Art and Practice of the Learning Organization* (New York: Doubleday, 1990).

20. A. Damasio, *Descartes' Error: Emotion, Reason and the Human Brain* (New York: G.P. Putnam's Sons, 1994), pp. xi–xii.

21. Blaise Pascal, *Penseés and The Provincial Letters* (New York: Modern Library, 1941), p. 95.

22. You don't need to memorize the anatomy of the brain in order to profit from this book. I specify the various parts of the brain—a very complex organ—in order to be accurate but also to reinforce the central point that good leadership is a natural function of the human brain, that the brain has parts and functions that have evolved specifically for good leadership because our species has evolved to survive largely through deliberate (rather than instinctive) cooperation.

23. E. Goldberg, *The Executive Brain: Frontal Lobes and the Civilized Mind* (New York: Oxford University Press, 2001), pp. 2–3.

24. The process of finding out where in the brain different mental functions are performed currently is done mostly by different kinds of brain scanning by tracking electrical impulses and blood flows. Earlier work of this kind was carried out by doing brain autopsies on people with mental disorders.

25. The term *satisfice*, coined by the economist, psychologist, and political scientist Herbert Simon (1916–2001), is a combination of *satisfy* and *suffice*. Simon proposed that, in many circumstances, an optimal solution is either too difficult or too costly to determine, typically because there are too many competing criteria, in which case the goal should be a solution that meets certain thresholds for all criteria and is therefore "good enough." This concept is essential for understanding how the brain works.

26. G. Marcus, S. Vijkayan, S. Bandi Rao, and P. Vishton, "Rule Learning by Seven-Month-Old Infants," *Science* (1999). (German edition originally published 1900).

27. S. Pinker, *The Language Instinct* (New York: HarperPerennial, 1994), p. 420.

28. S. Pinker, *How the Mind Works* (New York: Norton, 1997), p. 301.

29. Pinker points out that the existence of these skill sets should in no way undermine our conventional belief that humans are very skilled in learning new things throughout life. These innate skill sets simply provide a startup kit for learning certain things that have proven to be important for survival.

30. Carter, *Mapping the Mind,* p. 182.

31. J. LeDoux, *Synaptic Self: How Our Brains Became Who We Are* (New York: Viking, 2002).

32. LeDoux, *Synaptic Self,* p. 73.

33. K. Stein, *The Genius Engine: Where Memory, Reason, Passion, Violence and Creativity Interact in the Human Brain* (Hoboken, NJ: John Wiley & Sons, 2007).

34. Damasio, *Descartes' Error,* pp. 212–214.

35. S. Boysen, G. Berntson, and K. Mukobi, "Size Matters: Impact of Item Size and Quantity on Array Choice by Chimpanzees," *Journal of Comparative Psychology* 115, no. 1 (2001): 106–110.

36. J. B. Peterson, *Maps of Meaning: The Architecture of Belief* (New York: Routledge, 1999).

37. Peterson, *Maps of Meaning,* p. 19.

38. A. Fiske, *Structure of Social Life: The Four Elementary Forms of Human Relations* (New York: Free Press, 1991).

39. Fiske, *Structure of Social Life,* p. 408.

40. B. Bower, "A Fair Share of the Pie," *Science News* 161, no. 7 (February 16, 2002).

41. There were two exceptions involving tribal groups from New Guinea. As the researchers report, "Among these groups, like many in New Guinea, accepting gifts, even unsolicited ones, commits one to reciprocate at some future time to be determined by the giver. Receipt of large gifts also establishes one in a subordinate position. Consequently, excessively large gifts, especially unsolicited ones, will frequently be refused because of the anxiety about the unspecific strings attached."

CHAPTER THREE

1. C. Darwin, *The Descent of Man* (Amherst, MA: Prometheus Books, 1998 [1871]), p. 621.

2. Darwin, *Descent of Man,* p. 108.

3. Darwin, *Descent of Man,* p. 101.

4. See especially N. Boaz and K. Ciochon, *Dragon Bone Hill* (New York: Oxford University Press, 2004).

5. R. Wrangham, *Catching Fire: How Cooking Made Us Human* (New York: Basic Books, 2009).

6. See S. Hrdy, *Mothers and Others: The Evolutionary Origins of Mutual Understanding* (Cambridge, MA: Harvard University Press, 2009).

7. See D. Buss, *Evolutionary Psychology: The New Science of the Mind* (Boston: Allyn and Bacon, 1999).

8. R. Frank, *Luxury Fever* (New York: Free Press, 1999).

9. L. Trut, "Early Canid Domestication: The Farm Fox Experiment," *American Scientist* 87, p. 160.

10. Unpublished papers and personal conversation with the author.

11. S. Harrell, *Human Families* (Boulder, CO: Westview, 1997), pp. 26–30.

12. A. Kuper, *The Chosen Primate: Human Nature and Cultural Diversity* (Cambridge, MA: Harvard University Press, 1994), p. 174.

13. Darwin himself understood that female mate selection might have been critical to the rapid evolutionary changes that produced the modern human mind. In fact, he understood that human evolution could well have stopped being a blind, mindless process and could have begun to be guided by purposeful minds. And he got all of this in one sentence on page 621 of *The Descent of Man*: "Preference on the part of the women, steadily acting in any one direction, would ultimately affect the character of the tribe; for the women would generally choose not merely the handsomest men, according to their standard of taste, but those who were at the same time best able to defend and support them."

14. Readers of *Driven* will note that this "two transition" story of human evolution is different from that in the earlier book. There we conflated the two steps into one. The story presented here is based on more recent information. Such changes in the particulars of our understanding of these steps and their timing will undoubtedly continue as new evidence becomes available.

15. S. Pinker, *How the Mind Works* (New York: Norton, 1997), p. 202–203.

16. J. Diamond, *The Third Chimpanzee: The Evolution and Future of the Human Animal* (New York: HarperCollins, 1992).

17. T. W. Deacon, *The Symbolic Species: The Co-Evolution of Language and the Brain* (New York: W. W. Norton, 1997).

18. In his book *Art and the Evolution of Man* (London: Freedom Press, 1951), Sir Herbert Read argues that such drawings were the start of art and were an essential step toward the development of symbolic language in humans.

19. See especially M. Hauser, *The Evolution of Communication* (New York: HarperCollins, 1997).

20. S. Mithen, *The Prehistory of the Mind: The Cognitive Origins of Art, Religion and Science* (New York: Thames and Hudson, 1996).

21. However, Buss also found that men, unlike women, also showed evidence of employing at times what he termed a "short-term" mating strategy—with sheer sexual accessibility being the criterion of choice. This short-term strategy could better be termed the "ancient" strategy since it mirrors that of male chimpanzees.

22. Darwin, *Descent of Man*, p. 187.

23. See D. S. Wilson and E. O. Wilson, "Rethinking the Theoretical Foundation of Sociobiology," *The Quarterly Review of Biology* 82, no. 4 (December 2007): p. 328.

24. Wilson and Wilson, "Rethinking the Theoretical Foundation of Sociobiology," pp. 327–344.

25. Wrangham, *Catching Fire.*

26. E. Schultz and M. Tougiasw, *King Philip's War* (Woodstock, VT: The Countryman Press, 1999).

27. E. O. Wilson, "One Giant Leap: How Insects Achieved Altruism and Colonial Life," *Bioscience* 58, no. 1 (January 2008): 17–25.

28. S. J. Gould, *Rock of Ages: Science and Religion in the Fullness of Life* (New York: Ballantine, 1999).

29. Darwin, *Descent of Man*, p. 100.

30. Darwin, *Descent of Man*, p. 101.

31. F. de Waal, *Good Natured: The Origin of Right and Wrong in Humans and Other Animals* (Cambridge, MA: Harvard University Press, 1996), p. 87.

32. Wilson, E. O., *Consilience: The Unity of Knowledge* (New York: Alfred A. Knopf, 1998), p. 179.

33. It is interesting that Darwin added a footnote to his thoughts about morals, on page 101, that takes unusually strong exception to the position of John Stuart Mill, the dominant economist of the day and one of the founding fathers of modern economics. The footnote follows: "Mr. J. S. Mill speaks, in his celebrated work, 'Utilitarianism,' (1864, pp. 45, 46) of the social feelings as a 'powerful natural sentiment,' [in our terms an innate drive to bond].... He [Mill] also remarks, 'if, as in my own belief, the moral feelings are not innate, but acquired, they are not for that reason less natural.' It is with hesitation that I venture to differ at all from so profound a thinker, but [since] it can hardly be disputed that the social feelings are instinctive or innate, [Mill's belief] that the moral sense is acquired by each individual during his lifetime is at least extremely improbable. The ignoring of all transmitted mental qualities will, as it seems to me, be hereafter judged as a most serious blemish

in the works of Mr. Mill." The discipline of economics might have unfolded in a different way if Darwin had convinced Mill of this point.

34. M. Shermer, *The Science of Good & Evil* (New York: Times Books, 2004), pp. 25–26. Darwin made this point about the Golden Rule in *Descent of Man*, p. 136.
35. Lawrence, "The Biological Basis of Morality," *Business, Science, and Ethics*, The Ruffin Series No. 4, A Publication of the Society for Business Ethics (2004): p. 63.
36. M. Hauser, *Moral Minds: How Nature Designed Our Universal Sense of Right and Wrong* (New York: HarperCollins, 2006).
37. Darwin, *Descent of Man*, pp. 112–113.
38. J. Haidt, "The Emotional Dog and Its Rational Tail: A Social Intuitionist Approach to Moral Judgment," *Psychological Review* 108, no. 4 (2001), pp. 814–834.
39. Darwin, *Descent of Man*, p. 112.
40. R. Hare, *Without Conscience: The Disturbing World of the Psychopaths Among Us* (New York: The Guildford Press, 1999), p. xi.
41. Hare, *Without Conscience*, p. 218.
42. Hare, *Without Conscience*, p. 6.
43. S. Williamson, T. Harpur, and R. Hare, "Abnormal Processing of Affective Words by Psychopaths," *Psychophysiology* 28: 260–273. Cited in Hare, *Without Conscience*, pp. 129–131.
44. Hare, *Without Conscience*, p. 132.
45. Hare, *Without Conscience*, p. 145.
46. Hare, *Without Conscience*, p. 157.
47. Hare, *Without Conscience*, p. 165.
48. Hare, *Without Conscience*, p. 170.
49. Hare, *Without Conscience*, p. 215.
50. Hare, *Without Conscience*, pp. 173–174.
51. R. Hare, *Psychopathy: Theory and Research* (Hoboken, NJ: John Wiley & Sons, 1970), p. 110. Cited in Hare, *Without Conscience*, p. 193.
52. Hare, *Without Conscience*, p. 195.
53. Hare, *Without Conscience*, p. 219.
54. Hare, *Without Conscience*, p. 219.
55. P. Babiak and R. Hare, *Snakes in Suits* (New York: HarperCollins, 2005), p. 24.
56. K. Kiehl, A. Smith, R. Hare, A. Mendrek, B. Forster, J. Brink, and P. Liddle, "Limbic Abnormalities in Affective Processing by Criminal Psychopaths as Revealed by Functional Magnetic Resonance Imaging," *Biological Psychiatry* 50, (2001): 677–684.
57. Hare, *Without Conscience*, pp. 1–2.

CHAPTER FOUR

1. C. Darwin, *The Descent of Man* (Amherst, MA: Prometheus Books, 1998 [1871]), p. 136.
2. J. Lorsch, *A Contingency Theory of Leadership,* presented at "Leadership: Advancing an Intellectual Discipline," Harvard Business School, June 2008.
3. A. Chatman and J. A. Kennedy, *Psychological Perspectives on Leadership,* presented at "Leadership: Advancing an Intellectual Discipline," Harvard Business School, June 2008.
4. A. Schom, *Napoleon Bonaparte* (New York: HarperCollins, 1997).
5. Schom, *Napoleon Bonaparte,* p. 175.
6. Schom, *Napoleon Bonaparte,* p. 179.
7. Schom, *Napoleon Bonaparte,* p. 179.
8. Schom, *Napoleon Bonaparte,* p. 188.
9. R. Ely and D. Meyerson, *The Organizational Reconstruction of Men's Identity,* unpublished manuscript, n.d.
10. S. J. Spear, *Chasing the Rabbit: How Market Leaders Outdistance the Competition and How Great Companies Can Catch Up and Win* (New York: McGraw-Hill, 2008). Chapter Four describes a safety initiative at Alcoa.
11. N. Nohria, B. Groysberg, and L. Lee, "Employee Motivation: A Powerful New Model," *Harvard Business Review* (July-August 2008): 78–84.
12. K. Cameron, "Paradox in Positive Organizational Change," *The Journal of Applied Behavioral Science* 44, no. 1 (March 2008): 7–24.

CHAPTER FIVE

1. P. Bondanella and M. Musa (Eds. and Trans.), *The Portable Machiavelli* (New York: Viking Penguin, 1979), Chapter XV.
2. Stanley Milgram of Yale ran a series of famous experiments in 1961 that demonstrated that a significant number of a random set of people would follow the instructions of a "white-coated authority figure" and administer what they thought were electric shocks to innocent subjects.
3. D. Geary, *The Origin of Mind: Evolution of Brain, Cognition, and General Intelligence* (Washington, DC: American Psychological Association, 2005), pp. 74–75. Geary cites as his source for these historical comments L. L. Betzig, *Despotism and Differential Reproduction* (New York: Aldine, 1986); and L. Betzig, "Sex, Succession and Stratification

in the First Six Civilizations," in I. Ellis (Ed.), *Social Stratification and Socioeconomic Inequality,* Vol. 1, *A Comparative Biosocial Analysis* (Westport, CT: Prager, 1993), pp. 37–74.

4. Henry Osborn Taylor starts his classic work *The Mediaeval Mind* (Cambridge, MA: Harvard University Press, 1949) by saying, "The antique civilization of the Roman Empire was followed by that depression of decadence and barbarization which separates antiquity from the Middle Ages. Out of the confusion of this intervening period emerged the mediaeval peoples of western Europe." He dates this transition around 1000 A.D.

5. J. J. Norwich, *A Short History of Byzantium* (New York: Vintage, 1997).

6. Norwich, *A Short History of Byzantium,* p. 9.

7. There is a significant literature on the Gnostics. The key book that revealed their history and theology is E. Pagels, *The Gnostic Gospels* (New York: Random House, 1979).

8. Norwich, *A Short History of Byzantium,* p. 12.

9. Norwich, *A Short History of Byzantium,* p. 13.

10. Augustus may have been the first Roman Emperor to identify himself as a Divine person. See the myths about his birth that Augustus spread as reported by Robin Lorsch Wildfang in her article "The Propaganda of Omens: Six Dreams Involving Augustus," in R. Wildfang and J. Isager (Eds.), *Divination and Portents in the Roman World* (Denmark: Odense University Press, 2000), p. 43.

11. Bondanella and Musa, *Portable Machiavelli,* p. 25.

12. Bondanella and Musa, *Portable Machiavelli,* Chapter XVIII.

13. Bondanella and Musa, *Portable Machiavelli,* Chapter XVII.

14. Bondanella and Musa, *Portable Machiavelli,* Chapter VIII.

15. S. Baldwin, *The Debate on the Constitution: Federalist and Antifederalist Speeches, Articles and Letters During the Struggle Over Ratification, Part Two: January to August 1788,* Bernard Bailyn, ed. (New York: Library of America, 1993), pp. 520–521.

16. *The Federalist Papers* is a collection of articles supporting the ratification of the Constitution. Written by Alexander Hamilton, James Madison, and John Jay, they were published, in newspapers and then as a book, between 1787 and 1788.

17. J. Jay, *Federalist Paper* No. 2, in A. Hamilton, J. Madison, and J. Jay, *The Federalist Papers* (New York: Bantam Books, 1982).

18. A. Hamilton, *The Federalist Papers,* 1982, No. 6.

19. A. Hamilton, *Federalist Paper* No. 34.

20. J. Madison, *Federalist Paper* No. 57.

21. J. Madison, *Federalist Paper* No. 10, p. 43.

22. J. Madison, *Federalist Paper* No. 19, p. 44.

23. D. K. Goodwin, *A Team of Rivals: The Political Genius of Abraham Lincoln* (New York: Simon and Schuster, 2005). Much of the following account of Lincoln is drawn from this book.
24. J. C. Tonme, "Let Us Africans Do the Talking," *International Herald Tribune,* May 16, 2005, p. 5.

CHAPTER SIX

1. M. Friedman, "The Social Responsibility of Business Is to Increase Its Profits," *New York Times Magazine,* September 13, 1970, available at http://www.colorado.edu/studentgroups/libertarians/issues/fried man-soc-resp-business.html.
2. T. Roosevelt, Speech at Osawatomie, August 31, 1910.
3. See especially A. Chandler, *The Visible Hand* (Cambridge, MA: Belknap Press, 1977).
4. J. Madison, *The Federalist Papers,* 1982, No. 10, p. 44.
5. *Head v. Providence Insurance Co.,* quoted in Charles W. McCurdy, "The Knight Sugar Decision of 1895 and the Modernization of American Corporation Law, 1869–1903," *Harvard History Review* (1979).
6. See especially on the subject of government corruption C. Perrow, *Organizing America: Wealth, Power, and the Origins of Corporate Capitalism* (Princeton, NJ: Princeton University Press, 2002).
7. H. Brands, *Traitor to His Class* (New York: Doubleday, 2008), p. 298.
8. Perrow, *Organizing America,* p. 145.
9. Perrow, *Organizing America,* p. 145.
10. Henry Demarest Lloyd, "The Lords of Industry," *North American Review* 331 (June 1884), available at http://www.fordham.edu/halsall/mod/1884hdlloyd.html.
11. McCurdy, "The Knight Sugar Decision."
12. E. Rauchway, *Murdering McKinley: The Making of Theodore Roosevelt's America* (New York: Hill and Wang, 2003). Roosevelt is quoted from Rauchway, p. 93.
13. Rauchway, *Murdering McKinley,* p. 42.
14. Rauchway, *Murdering McKinley,* pp. 17–18.
15. T. Roosevelt, speech to New York State Agricultural Association, September 7, 1903.
16. Roosevelt, speech, 1903.
17. McCurdy, "The Knight Sugar Decision," p. 331
18. R. Chernow, *Titan: The Life of John D. Rockefeller, Sr.* (New York: Random House, 1997), p. 554.
19. T. Roosevelt, *An Autobiography* (New York: Charles Scribner Sons, 1920 [1916]), Chapter 12.

20. Brands, *Traitor to His Class,* p. 336.
21. See especially T. McCraw, *Prophets of Regulation* (Cambridge, MA: Harvard University Press, 1984).

CHAPTER SEVEN

1. C. Darwin, *The Descent of Man* (Amherst, MA: Prometheus Books, 1998 [1871]), p. 97.
2. E. Pagels, *The Gnostic Gospels* (New York: Viking Press, 1989).
3. Pagels, *The Gnostic Gospels,* pp. xviii–xix.
4. Pagels, *The Gnostic Gospels,* p. xxxv.
5. Pagels, *The Gnostic Gospels,* p. 41.
6. Pagels, *The Gnostic Gospels,* pp. 128–129.
7. Pagels, *The Gnostic Gospels,* pp. 104–105.
8. L. Machan, "On Loan, Sublime Awe: A Jewel of the MFA Staggers Crowds in Japan," *Boston Globe,* May 7, 2009, p. 1.
9. E. O. Wilson, *Consilience: The Unity of Knowledge* (New York: Alfred A. Knopf, 1998).
10. K. Miller, *Finding Darwin's God: A Scientist's Search for Common Ground Between God and Evolution* (New York: HarperCollins, 1999).
11. The "intelligent design" argument has relied heavily on the work of Michael Bethe. See *Darwin's Black Box: The Biochemical Challenge to Evolution* (New York: Simon and Schuster, 1996), which argues that genetic mutation could not have generated enough variety for the selection process to create complex organisms such as humans. The most recent and convincing rebuttal of Bethe's claim is presented in M. Kirschner and J. Gerhart, *The Plausibility of Life: Resolving Darwin's Dilemma* (New York: Yale University Press, 2005).
12. From the preface of *Teaching About Evolution and the Nature of Science* (Washington, DC: National Academies Press, 1998), p. 16.
13. As quoted in L. Eiseley, *Darwin's Century* (Garden City, NY: Doubleday, 1958), p. 346.
14. D. Hull, "The God of the Galapagos," *Nature* 352 (1991): 485–486.
15. R. Dawkins, *River Out of Eden* (New York: HarperCollins, 1995), pp. 132–133.
16. Quoted from Kurt P. Wise, "Truly a Wonderful Life," review of Stephen J. Gould *Wonderful Life: The Burgess Shale and the Nature of History,* Origins Research Archive, Access Research Network, vol. 13, no. 1, 1997; available at http://www.arn.org/docs/orpages/or131/wise.htm.
17. Miller, *Finding Darwin's God,* p. 227.

18. S. Hawking, *A Brief History of Time* (New York: Bantam Books, 1988), p. 121, quoted in Miller, *Finding Darwin's God.*

19. Miller, *Finding Darwin's God,* p. 228.

20. J. Boslough, *Stephen Hawking's Universe* (New York: William Morrow, 1985), p. 121, quoted in Miller, *Finding Darwin's God.*

21. Hawking, p. 127, quoted in Miller, *Finding Darwin's God.*

22. While the Big Bang theory about the start of our universe is the currently well-established explanation supported by the evidence from numerous astronomical findings, there are still a few dissenting physicists. For example one proposed alternative theory known as the Quasi Steady State Universe was summarized in F. Hoyle, G. Burbridge, and J. V. Narlikar, *A Different Approach to Cosmology: From a Static Universe Through the Big Bang Towards Reality* (New York: Cambridge University Press, 2000).

23. R. Jastrow, *God and the Astronomers* (New York: W.W. Norton, 1978), p. 116.

24. I. G. Barbour, *Religion and Science* (San Francisco: HarperCollins, 1997), p. 216, quoted in Miller, *Finding Darwin's God.*

25. Miller, *Finding Darwin's God,* pp. 238–239.

26. G. Schroeder, *The Science of God: The Convergence of Scientific and Biblical Wisdom* (New York: The Free Press, 1997).

27. D. Goleman, *Destructive Emotions: How Can We Overcome Them?* (New York: Bantam Dell, 2003), p. xiv.

28. R. Dawkins, *The God Delusion* (New York: Houghton Mifflin, 2006), p. 13.

CHAPTER EIGHT

1. F. D. Roosevelt, Second Inaugural Address, January 20, 1937.

2. B. George, *Authentic Leadership* (San Francisco: Jossey-Bass, 2003).

3. George, *Authentic Leadership,* pp. 1–2.

4. George, *Authentic Leadership,* p. 62.

5. George, *Authentic Leadership,* p. 66.

6. George, *Authentic Leadership,* pp. 66–67.

7. George, *Authentic Leadership,* pp. 72–73.

8. George, *Authentic Leadership,* p. 71.

9. George, *Authentic Leadership,* pp. 128–129.

10. George, *Authentic Leadership,* p. 77.

11. O. Williamson, *Markets and Hierarchies* (New York: The Free Press, 1975).

12. George, *Authentic Leadership*, p. 71.
13. N. Byrnes, "The Art of Motivation," *Business Week*, May 1, 2006, pp. 57–62.
14. M. Salter, *Innovation Corrupted: The Origins and Legacy of Enron's Collapse* (Cambridge, MA: Harvard University Press, 2007), pp. 3-1, 3-2, 3-7, 3-8, 3-9.
15. See especially M. Jensen and W. Meckling, "Theory of the Firm: Managerial Behavior, Agency Costs and Ownership Structure," *Journal of Financial Economics* 3, no. 4 (October 1976): 305–360; and also M. Jensen and W. Meckling, "The Nature of Man," *Journal of Applied Corporate Finance* 7, no. 2 (Summer 1994): 4–19.
16. The Press Trust of India, Limited, *Financial Times*, March 13, 2009.
17. R. Simons, *Levers of Organization Design: How Managers Use Accountability Systems for Greater Performance and Commitment* (Boston: Harvard Business School Press, 2005).
18. Simons, *Levers of Organizational Design*, p. 252.
19. J. C. Baker, *Directors and Their Functions* (Boston: Graduate School of Business Administration, Harvard University, 1945), pp. xiii, 145.
20. D. McGregor, *The Human Side of Enterprise* (New York: McGraw-Hill, 1960). McGregor's Theory Y was a direct precursor to the RD four-drive model of human motivation.
21. T. Wilson, "Regulate Me, Please," *New York Times*, April 16, 2009: A23.
22. C. Lewis, *The Buying of the President 2004* (New York; Harper Paperback, 2004), p. 479.
23. Lewis, *The Buying of the President 2004*, p. 34.
24. Lewis, *The Buying of the President 2004*, p. 104.
25. Lewis, *The Buying of the President 2004*, p. 87.
26. Lewis, *The Buying of the President 2004*, p. 83.
27. Lewis, *The Buying of the President 2004*, p. 472.
28. I am a member of ARCs National Advisory Broad.
29. Lewis, *The Buying of the President 2004*, p. 473.
30. J. Lorsch, *Back to the Drawing Board* (Boston: Harvard Business School Press, 2004).

CHAPTER NINE

1. A. Efrati and P. Lattman, "U.S. Loses Bear Fraud Case: Fund Managers Acquitted in First Big Trial of Financial Crisis; Blow to Prosecutors," *The Wall Street Journal*, November 11, 2009, pp. A1 and A6.

2. W. Cohan, *House of Cards: A Tale of Hubris and Wretched Excess on Wall Street* (New York: Doubleday, 2009), p. 450.

3. M. Hovanesian, "Sex, Lies, and Mortgage Deals," *Business Week,* November 24, 2008, p. 71.

4. P. S. Goodman and G. Morgenson, "A Relentless Push to Approve Loans at Washington Mutual, the Policy Seemed to Be: Don't Ask, Just Sell," *International Herald Tribune,* December 29, 2008, pp. 1 and 14.

5. Goodman and Morgenson, "A Relentless Push."

6. Hovanesian, "Sex, Lies, and Mortgage Deals."

7. Bloomberg.com, "Bring Down Wall Street as Ratings Let Loose Subprime Scourge," September 24, 2008.

8. J. Becker, S. G. Stolberg, and S. Labaton, "Bubble Fed on Bush's Vision—and His Ambition. As Lenders Eased Credit, U.S. Regulators Fell Behind the Housing Crash," *International Herald Tribune,* December 22, 2008, pp. 1 and 14.

9. Eric Lichtblan, "Policing of Stock Fraud Falls in the U.S.," *International Herald Tribune,* December 26, 2008, p. 12.

10. J Becker, S. G. Stolberg, and S. Labaton, "The Housing Crash: 'How Did We Get Here?'" *New York Times Media Group,* December 22, 2008.

11. Becker, Stolberg, and Labaton, "The Housing Crash."

12. Becker, Stolberg, and Labaton, "The Housing Crash." Contribution amounts attributed to the nonpartisan Center for Responsive Politics.

13. Becker, Stolberg, and Labaton, "The Housing Crash." Readers interested in learning more about Karl Rove in this regard can turn to the book by James Moore and Wayne Slater, *Bush's Brain: How Karl Rove Made George W. Bush Presidential* (Hoboken, NJ: John Wiley & Sons, 2003).

14. Hovanesian, "Sex, Lies, and Mortgage Deals," p. 71.

15. G. Morgenson, "Merrill Danced, Stumbled and Fell," *International Herald Tribune,* November 10, 2008, p. 10.

16. J. Nocera, "Tough Rules Kept Indian Banks Sound: Regulator Saved India from U.S.-Style Bubble," *International Herald Tribune,* December 20–21, 2008, p. 12.

17. G. Morgenson and D. Van Natta Jr., "Bank Lobby Resists Regulation," *International Herald Tribune,* June 2, 2009, p. 15.

18. Cohan, *House of Cards.*

19. K. Phillips, *Bad Money: Reckless Finance, Failed Politics, and the Global Crisis of American Capitalism* (New York: Viking, 2008), p. 31.

CHAPTER TEN

1. R. Cockburn, "Death by Dilution," *The American Prospect*, December 2005, pp. 35–41.
2. R. W. Baker, *Capitalism's Achilles Heel: Dirty Money and How to Renew the Free-Market System* (Hoboken, NJ: John Wiley & Sons, 2005).
3. B. Friedman, *The Moral Consequences of Economic Growth* (New York: Knopf, 2005), p. 435.
4. L. Browning, "U.S. Rich Get Richer and the Poor Poorer, Data Shows," *The New York Times*, September 25, 2003.
5. S. Rattner, "The Rich Get (Much) Richer," *Business Week*, August 8, 2005.
6. N. Kristof, "Under Hu, China's Malaise Just Grows," *International Herald Tribune*, June 19, 2006, p. 19.
7. A. Chua, *A World on Fire* (New York: Anchor Books, 2004).
8. A recent book by Moises Naim, the editor of *Foreign Policy*, titled *Illicit: How Smugglers, Traffickers, and Copycats Are Hijacking the Global Economy (New York: Doubleday, 2005)*, offers strong support for Baker's conclusions about the nature and scope of dirty money flows.
9. Cockburn, "Death by Dilution."
10. Tom Friedman has brilliantly heralded this potential in his book, *The World Is Flat* (New York: Farrar, Straus & Giroux, 2006).
11. C. K. Prahalad and Allen Hammond, "Serving the World's Poor, Profitably," *Harvard Business Review* 80, no. 9 (September 2002): pp. 48–58.
12. G. Zaccai, "Design Research and Co-creation for Socioeconomic Innovation: Applying Design Research and Design Thinking to Problems of Pure Water and Sanitation in a Rural South African Village," *Asia Design Journal* (forthcoming).
13. N. Davies, *Europe: A History* (New York: Oxford University Press, 1996), pp. 897–899.
14. A. Hochschild, *King Leopold's Ghost: A Story of Greed, Terror, and Heroism in Colonial Africa* (Boston: Houghton Mifflin Harcourt, 1998).
15. Hochschild, *King Leopold's Ghost.*
16. G. Sharp, *Waging Nonviolent Struggle* (Boston: Porter Sargent, 2005).
17. A tragedy of the commons is a situation in which individuals who are each acting according to their own rational self-interest will ultimately use up or destroy something necessary or valuable to all of them, such as a local forest or a grazing area (the "common"). The phrase comes from Garrett Hardin's article, "The Tragedy of the Commons," *Science* 162, no. 3859 (December 13, 1968): pp. 1243–1248.

18. Graham Allison, an expert on this issue, after citing some positive steps taken by the Bush administration, concludes, "Despite these praiseworthy successes, if we jump to the bottom-line question of whether we are safer from a nuclear terrorist attack today than we were on September 11, 2001, the answer is no. . . . The brute fact is that in Russia, fewer potential nuclear bombs were secured in the two years after 9-11 than in the two years before. . . . Developments in Russia, Iran, and North Korea leave Americans more vulnerable to a nuclear 9-11 today than we were four years ago" (G. Allison, "The Gravest Danger," *The American Prospect,* March 2005, pp. 48–49).
19. J. Diamond, *Collapse* (New York: Viking, 2005).
20. A. Hamilton, *The Federalist Papers,* 1982, No. 6.
21. J. Carroll, *The House of War* (New York: Houghton Mifflin, 2006), pp. 221–222.
22. Carroll, *The House of War,* p. 351.
23. J. Madison, *The Federalist Papers,* 1982, No. 51.
24. C. Darwin, *The Descent of Man* (Amherst, MA: Prometheus Books, 1998 [1871]), pp. 126–127.

CHAPTER ELEVEN

1. C. Darwin, *The Descent of Man* (Amherst, MA: Prometheus Books, 1998 [1871]), p. 116.
2. J. Groopman, *The Measure of Our Days: New Beginnings at Life's End* (New York: Viking Adult, 1997).
3. Groopman, *Measure of Our Days,* pp. 7–38.
4. W. Shakespeare, *Twelfth Night,* Act II, Scene V.
5. See especially P. Lawrence and J. Lorsch, *Organization and Environment: Managing Differentiation and Integration* (Boston: Division of Research, Harvard Business School, 1967).
6. For an excellent summary article see R. Kim, K. Dirks, and C. Cooper, "The Repair of Trust: A Dynamic Bilateral Perspective and Multilevel Conceptualization," *Academy of Management Review* 34, no. 3 (July 2009): 401.
7. P. Herr, *Primal Management; Unraveling the Secrets of Human Nature to Drive High Performance* (New York: Amacom, 2009).
8. "Dilbert Is Right, Says Gallup Survey: A National Employee Survey Confirms That Uncomfortable Work Environments Do Make for Disgruntled Employees," *Gallup Management Journal,* April 13, 2006.
9. T. Rath and D. Clifton, *How Full Is Your Bucket?* (Omaha, NE: Gallup Press, 2004), p. 33.

10. M. Gladwell, *The Outliers: The Story of Success* (New York: Little Brown, 2008).

11. R. Kaiser, *So Damn Much Money: The Triumph of Lobbying and the Corrosion of American Government* (New York: Alfred A. Knopf, 2009).

12. S. Greenhouse, *The Big Squeeze: Tough Times for the American Worker* (New York: Anchor Books, 2009).

13. E. Moskowitz, "Dalai Lama Inspires Reverent Silence, Cheers at Stadium," *Boston Globe,* May, 3, 2009, p. B3.

14. Economic expert.com, "Ismail of Morocco," n.d., http://www.economicexpert.com/a/Ismail:of:Morocco.html.

15. R. Harris, "The 'War on Terror' That Ruined Rome," *International Herald Tribune,* October 2, 2006.

16. B. Oakley, *Evil Genes: Why Rome Fell, Hitler Rose, Enron Failed, and My Sister Stole My Mother's Boyfriend* (Amherst, NY: Prometheus Books, 2008).

17. J. Seabrook, "Suffering Souls," *The New Yorker,* November 10, 2008, p. 72.

18. T. Hesman Saey, "Male Monkeys See in Red, Green with Added Gene: Creating Color Vision May Not Require Rewiring of the Brain," *ScienceNews,* October 10, 2009, p. 14.

19. T. R. Insel and L. E. Shapiro, "Oxytocin Receptor Distribution Reflects Social Organization in Monogamous and Polygamous Voles," *Proceedings of the National Academy of Sciences, USA* 89 (July 1992): 5981–5985.

CHAPTER TWELVE

1. C. Darwin, *The Descent of Man* (Amherst, MA: Prometheus Books, 1998 [1871]), p. 100.

2. N. Wade, "Darwin's Evolving Genius: Even Biologists Now Agree He Was Right," *International Herald Tribune,* February 10, 2009, p. 1.

3. "Unfinished Business," *The Economist,* February, 7, 2009.

4. C. Darwin, *On the Origin of Species,* 6th ed. (London: Oxford University Press, 1956 [Originally published 1872]), p. 560.

APPENDIX

1. E. Mayr, *One Long Argument: Charles Darwin and the Genesis of Modern Evolutionary Thought* (Cambridge, MA: Harvard University Press, 1991).

2. R. Dawkins, *The Selfish Gene,* new ed. (New York: Oxford University Press, 1976), p. ix.

3. S. Pinker, *The Blank Slate: The Modern Denial of Human Nature* (New York: Viking, 2002).

4. E. Durkheim, *Suicide* (J. A. Spalding and G. Simpson, trans.) (New York: The Free Press, 1951/1897).

5. E. Mayr, *What Makes Biology Unique?* (New York: Cambridge University Press, 2004), p. 26.

6. Mayr, *What Makes Biology Unique?* p. 28.

7. Mayr, *What Makes Biology Unique?* p. 29.

8. Mayr, *What Makes Biology Unique?* p. 30.

9. Mayr, *What Makes Biology Unique?* p 32.

10. Mayr, *What Makes Biology Unique?* p. 34.

11. Mayr, *What Makes Biology Unique?* pp. 34–35.

12. Mayr, *What Makes Biology Unique?* p. 35.

13. S. Pinker, *How the Mind Works* (New York: Norton, 1997).

INDEX

Page references followed by *e* indicate an exhibit; followed by *fig* indicate an illustrated figure.

Byzantine Empire, 105, 148, 230
Byzantium (Constantinople, Istanbul), 106

C

Campaign financing: Americans for Campaign
Reform (ACR) of the, 189–191; corporate
corruption of, 185–186; corporate
donations to, 187; good/moral leadership
promoted by reforming, 255–256; lobbying
role in, 188–189; rising cost of election
campaigns and, 187
Capitalism, 221, 222, 260
*Capitalism's Achilles Heel: Dirty Money and How to
Renew the Free-Market System* (Baker), 215
Carter, Rita, 41
CDO (collateralized debt obligation) bonds,
196–197, 199, 206
CEO/board model, 181–182
Changing environments: ability to adapt to, 54;
human brain's ability to adapt to, 54
Charisma, 81
Chatman, A., 81
Chernow, Ron, 138
Chimp dA experiments, 43, 76–77
China: increasing income gap in, 221;
mercantilist model used in, 219–220
Christianity: conducting historic study to help
refine and enhance, 258; Constantine the
Great's role in legitimizing, 105–107, 121,
148, 260, 264; early history of, 105–106;
good/moral leadership and Gnostic
challenge to orthodox, 144–149; Holy
Crusades in name of, 107; Nicene Creed of
early, 148, 163; Protestant Reformation of,
149; Spanish Inquisition in name of, 225;
warfare in the name of, 106–107. *See also*
Religion; Roman Catholic Church
Christoff, Kalina, 41, 42
Civilization: leaders-w/o-conscience rise during
cultural shift to, 103–104; as opening power
to people-w/o-conscience, 102–103
Cleveland, President, 135
CMO (collateralized mortgage obligation)
bonds, 196–197
Cohan, William, 194, 210–211
Cold War, 225, 230
Coleridge, Samuel Taylor, 247
Colonial system: description of, 217; Leopold
II's established, 226–227, 260; South
African diamond industry example of,
218
Common Cause, 189
Communal sharing skill set: checks and
balances function of, 45–46*fig*; description
of, 45
Conant, James, 211
Conflicting motivations: good leadership
decision making and, 2–4; Helen's
dilemma over, 1–2; leadership as means of
dealing with, 4

Congressional Budget Office report (2003),
220
"Consilience," 154
"Constant of nature," 156
Constantine the Great, 84*e*, 105–107, 121, 148,
260, 264
Constantius Chlorus, 105
Conway-Morris, Simon, 269
Cooking utility, 55–56
Copernicus, 84*e*, 152, 154
Corporate structure: CEO/board model of,
181–182; RD Theory for designing
balanced, 180–181; RD Theory suggestions
for designing, 191–192; reform in the
corporate charters, 256–257; stakeholder
model of, 182
Corporations: agency theory and misguide
leadership of, 177–180; benefits versus
harms perpetuated by, 126–131; *corpus* (or
body) Latin root of, 142; early European,
131; electoral process corruption by,
185–189; empowered to fulfill drive to
acquire (dA), 126–138; Enron scandal, 141,
170, 176–177, 265; failure to establish
impulse/check/balance system for, 142;
Framer's unable to anticipate structure of,
130–131; good/moral leadership of,
169–176, 180–183; governmental
regulation role in keeping on track,
183–185; imbalance between dA and dB by,
129, 130, 141; Interstate Commerce
Commission (ICC) regulating, 134; legal
definition of, 128; legislator manipulation
by lobbyists of, 188–189; Medtronic,
169–175, 192, 257; "mission-driven,"
170–172; Nucor, 175–176, 182, 257;
off-track leadership of, 176–177;
people-w/o-conscience's role in harm done
by, 128–131; potential role of science in
keeping on track, 191–192; reforming
chartering of, 256–257; reforming
regulation of, 257–258; transnational
outsourcing by, 218; Wagner Act allowing
collective bargaining by labor with, 140. *See
also* Global economy
Costa Rica, 232–233
Creation: Big Bang Theory of, 157, 158, 159,
161, 164; convergence of science and
religion to explain, 155–160; leadership
challenges related to convergent
understanding of, 160–165*fig*; *The Science of
God* reinterpreting symbolism of, 161–162.
See also Evolutionary theory
Creator's hope, 159–160
Cripus, 105
Cultural information: decision-making process
role of, 36–38; universal traits of, 38, 39*e*.
See also Organizational culture
"Culture of deceit," 176–177
Czolgosz, Leon, 135–136

People-w/o-conscience: (continued)
perpetuated by, 128–131; Darwin's
"unnatural monsters" as, 241, 260, 265;
description of, 72–73, 261–262; drive to
bond (dB) missing from, 102–103;
economic conditions allowing power by,
124–125; economic meltdown and bankers
as, 203–205, 209; establishing
check-and-balance structures for, 235;
genetic defect of psychopathy by, 73–77;
importance of understanding nature of,
259–264; Ken Lay as, 177; misguided
leadership allowing damage by, 89–90;
reviewing historic impact of, 83, 84e, 264;
Rex and Comus leadership study on
controlling, 94; RT Theory on
war/genocide role of, 225–228; war and
genocide and the role played by, 225–228;
willing to instigate global chaos, 233. See
also Leaders-w/o-conscience; Power;
Psychopathy
Performance-driven company, 173–175
Peterson, Jordan, 44
Pharmaceutical Research and Manufacturers
of America, 187
Phillips, Kevin, 211
Pilgrims of Plymouth, 65
Pinker, Steven, 38–39, 60–61, 62, 66
Plutarch, 263
Pol Pot, 120, 225
"Policing of Stock Fraud Falls in the U.S."
(*International Herald Tribune*), 202
Political institutions: cultural shift of civilization
and rise of, 103–104; during Dark Ages,
105–107; federal electoral system, 185–191,
255–256; Framers' checks and balances to,
113–115, 130, 175, 184, 195, 236; Framers'
design to control pillars of oppression,
111–113; Framers' fear of factions among,
112–113, 130–131; Machiavelli's treatise
on, 101, 107–109, 179; progress and regress
in the 20th/21st centuries, 119–121. See also
Government; State/states
Political leaders: cultural shift of civilization
and leaders-w/o-conscience, 103–104; fall
and rise of leaders-w/o-conscience as,
101–103; Framers' checks and balances to,
113–115, 130, 175, 184, 195, 236; historic
and impactful, 84e; ideologies and causes
of, 260–264; leaders-w/o-conscience during
the Dark Ages, 105–107; Lincoln's
good/moral leadership as, 84e, 115–119,
213, 246; Machiavelli's view of
leaders-w/o-conscience, 101, 107–109, 179;
solution to problem of
leaders-w/o-conscience as, 109–113. See also
Bush administration
Pompey the Great, 263–264
Ponzi scheme, 196
Positive psychology, 96–97

Power: civilization allowing
people-w/o-conscience access to, 102–103;
definition of despotic, 104; economic
conditions allowing people-w/o-conscience,
124–125; good leadership as preventing
people-w/o-conscience access to, 94;
ideologies to rationalize seizing of, 221,
222, 260–264; "pack of lions" approach to,
89–90; people-w/o-conscience's natural
pull toward, 228; psychopaths drawn to
positions of, 265. See also
Leaders-w/o-conscience;
People-w/o-conscience
Prahalad, C. K., 222
Prefrontal cortex: conflict detection function
of the, 34–35; decision proposal sent to
neural connections from, 41;
decision-making process and the, 32–34;
evolutionary leadership capabilities of the,
72; impulse/check/balance system and the,
41–43; information accessed through
neocortex of the, 35–36, 37; U.S.
Constitution function as, 184. See also
Human brain
*Primal Management: Unraveling the Secrets of
Human Nature to Drive High Performance*
(Herr), 252
Prince, Charles, 204–205
The Prince (Machiavelli), 108
Private property rights: establishment of,
125–126; expending state's role in
protecting, 229
Problem solving capability, 11–12
Proceedings of the National Academy of Sciences, 269
Proposer (ultimatum game), 47–49*fig*
Protestant Reformation, 149
Psychopathy: characteristics of, 73–76;
demographics on, 77; genetic defects
leading to, 72–77; Napoleon's, 86–87;
people-w/o-conscience as form of, 72–73;
power positions sought by, 265; twin studies
on, 76. See also Leaders-w/o-conscience;
People-w/o-conscience
Psychotherapy, 75–76
Pullman strike (1894), 135
Punishment, 81

Q

Al Qaeda, 262–263

R

Railroad industry: rise and abuse of the,
132–133; *Wabash* decision granting federal
regulating of, 133, 134
Rape, 57
Rational self-interest, 178
Reciprocity skill set, 45
Reddy, Yaga Venugopal, 208
"Regulate Me, Please" (Wilson), 184–185

Regulations. *See* Government regulations
Reid, Thomas, 153
Religion: art created using themes of, 150;
    constitutional checks on, 115; dC
    dedication by science and, 164;
    good/moral leadership for reconciling
    science and, 164–165; human meaning in
    institution of, 143–144, 258–259;
    leadership challenge of convergence of
    science and, 160–165*fig*; meaning of
    human existence and convergence of
    science and, 155–160. *See also* Christianity
Religious leaders: convergence of
    religion/science challenges for,
    160–165*fig*; Gnostic challenge to orthodox
    Christianity and, 144–149; historic and
    impactful, 84*e*
Renaissance, 125
Renewed Darwinian (RD) Theory: on agency
    theory impact on misguided leadership,
    179–180; based on Darwin's insights, 254,
    265–266; Dalai Lama's comments and
    similarity to, 259; electoral system reform
    using, 190–191, 255–256; Ely and Meyerson
    study findings supporting, 94–96; on
    evolution of political leadership, 101–103;
    evolutionary development of human brain
    and, 54–68; Framers' arguments in terms of
    the, 112–115; good/moral leadership
    applications using, 180–183, 245, 247–248,
    255–259, 270; harms perpetuated by
    corporations, 127–131; internalizing
    good/moral leadership concept of, 245;
    keeping global economy on track using,
    216; leadership definition in context of,
    81–83; leadership distinctions within the,
    82; Lincoln's good/moral leadership in
    terms of, 115–119; Machiavelli's treatise in
    terms of the, 108–109; microcredit
    movement as application of, 222–223;
    Nucor's "best practices" reflecting the,
    175–176; on organizational culture
    balancing four drives, 174–175; on
    people-w/o-conscience bankers controlled
    by regulations, 209; on
    people-w/o-conscience role in war and
    genocide, 225–228; on pre-wired
    requirement to make moral choices,
    159–160; predicting conditions leading to
    slavery, 124–125; reclassifying
    "inexplicable" people using the, 121;
    schematic of the, 51*fig*; on using science to
    keep corporations on track, 191–192; sizing
    up the leadership role by using, 247–248;
    suggestions for keeping global community
    on track using, 229–233; on trusting moral
    skill set moral choices, 160, 250–252;
    understanding globalization in context of,
    217–221; on whole drive being more than

sum of its parts, 96. *See also* Four drivers;
    Leadership; Social behavior
Representative Men (Emerson), 85
Republican Convention (1860), 117
Republican National Committee, 188
Republican Party, 203
Reserve Bank of India, 208
Responder (ultimatum game), 47–49*fig*
Reward, 81
Rex and Comus leadership study, 90–96, 97
Rhodes, Cecil, 218
Ricardo, David, 217
Ricardo's classic trade system, 217, 224
Rift Valley (Africa), 66
Rockefeller, John D., 137
Roman Catholic Church: Constantine the
    Great's impact on rise of, 105–107, 121,
    148, 260, 264; rivalry between Gnostic
    Christianity and, 144–149. *See also*
    Christianity
Roman Empire: Constantine's promotion of
    Christianity in the, 105–107, 121, 148, 260,
    264; Gnostic and Orthodox rivalry in the,
    144–149; the "war on terror" that ruined,
    262–264
Roosevelt, Franklin D., 84*e*, 140, 169, 207, 238,
    265
Roosevelt, Theodore, 123, 135, 136–138
Rove, Karl, 203

S

Salter, Malcolm, 176–177
Sans people, 66–67
Schom, Alan, 85, 86
Schroeder, Gerald, 161–162
Schultz, E., 65
The Science of God (Schroeder), 161–162
Science institution: "consilience" unification
    of the, 154; dC dedication by religion and,
    164; good/moral leadership for reconciling
    religion and, 164–165*fig*; human meaning
    of the, 151–154; leadership challenge of
    convergence of religion and, 160–165*fig*;
    meaning of human existence and
    convergence of religion and, 155–160;
    potential role for keeping corporations on
    track, 191–192; society role of, 153–154. *See
    also* Evolutionary theory
Science leaders: chronological list of, 152–153;
    convergence of religion and science
    challenges for, 160–165*fig*; historic and
    impactful, 84*e*
Securities and Exchange Commission (SEC):
    Bush administration elimination of
    regulations by, 202; establishment of the,
    140
Self-interest: agency theory on, 178–180;
    definition of, 178. *See also* Drive to acquire
    (dA)
Serbian genocide, 225